THE CHINA CAMBODIA VIETNAM TRIANGLE

ALSO BY WILFRED BURCHETT

Pacific Treasure Island
1941

Bombs over Burma
1944

Wingate Adventure
1944

Democracy with a Tommy-Gun
1946

Cold War in Germany
1950

Peoples Democracies
1951

The Changing Tide (play)
1951

China's Feet Unbound
1952

This Monstrous War
1953

Koje Unscreened (with Alan Winnington)
1953

Plain Perfidy (with Alan Winnington)
1954

North of the 17th Parallel
1955

Mekong Upstream
1959

Gargarin — 1st Man Into Space
1961

Titov — Flight Into Outer Space
1962

Come East Young Man
1962

The Furtive War: The United States in Viet Nam and Laos
1963

My Visit to the Liberated Zones of South Viet Nam
1964

Viet Nam: Inside Story of the Guerilla War
1965

Viet Nam North
1966

Viet Nam Will Win
1968

Again Korea
1968

Passport
1969

The Second Indochina War
1970

My War With the CIA (with Prince Norodom Sihanouk)
1973

Portugal After the Captains' Coup
1975

China: The Quality of Life (with Rewi Alley)
1976

The Whores of War: Mercenaries Today (with Derek Roebuck)
1977

Grasshoppers & Elephants: Why Viet Nam Fell
1977

Southern Africa Stands Up
1978

At the Barricades: Forty Years on the Cutting Edge of History
1981

WILFRED BURCHETT

THE CHINA CAMBODIA VIETNAM TRIANGLE

Vanguard Books, P.O. Box 3566, Chicago, IL 60654, USA
and
Zed Press, 57 Caledonian Road, London N1 9DN, Britain

The **China-Cambodia-Vietnam Triangle** was first published jointly by Vanguard Books, P.O. Box 3566, Chicago, IL 60654, USA and Zed Press, 57 Caledonian Road, London N1 9DN, Britain.

Vanguard Books — ISBN 0-917702-13-1

Zed Press — ISBN 0-86232-085-2

Printed in the USA

Library of Congress Cataloging in Publication Data

Burchett, Wilfred G., 1911-
  The China-Cambodia-Vietnam Triangle.

  Includes bibliographical references.
  1. Cambodia — History — 1953-1975.
2. Cambodia — History — 1975-   . 3. Cambodia — Foreign relations — Vietnam. 4. Vietnam — Foreign relations — Cambodia.
5. China — Foreign relations — Indochina. 6. Indochina — Foreign relations — China. I. Title.
DS554.8.B87   959.6'04   81-13087
                            AACR2
ISBN 0-917702-13-1

British Library Cataloguing in Publication Data

Burchett, Wilfred
    The China, Cambodia, Vietnam triangle.
    1. Cambodia—History
    I. Title
    959.6'04   DS554.8

    ISBN   0-86232-085-2

THE
CHINA
CAMBODIA
VIETNAM
TRIANGLE

CONTENTS

Author's Note

Khmer Rouge (Red Khmer or Red Cambodians) was the name given by Prince Norodom Sihanouk to an ultra-leftist faction of the Khmer Communist Party after it launched armed struggle to overthrow his neutralist regime. The Khmer Rouge renamed their country Kampuchea, one of the historic names for what used to be known as Cambodia. Today the country is known as the People's Republic of Kampuchea. The terms Kampuchea and Cambodia are used interchangeably in this book.

PREFACE

In the spring of 1975 the overthrow of the U.S.-supported governments in Saigon and Phnom Penh deprived the United States of any direct influence over Vietnam and Cambodia. Thus ended an era in which the people of both countries, alongside the people of Laos, waged a struggle for independence lasting more than fifty years. In fact, independence had to be won twice. After the people of Indochina defeated France, direct colonial rule was replaced by indirect, neocolonial forms of control. The United States became the strongest power in the region, willing and able to topple governments and to commit arms, ammunition, military advisers, and even the lives of hundreds of thousands of its finest young people to the struggle to ensure that the natural, human, and strategic resources of the region remained under its control.

Since its ignominious retreat from Indochina, the United States has done everything it could to de-stabilize the area and to exacerbate any and all factors that could lead to the downfall of the present government of Vietnam. During this period the United States and China finally found the basis for cooperation in foreign affairs. China's interest in keeping her southern neighbors weakened and embattled has led her directly into collusion with her former archenemy, the United States. As a consequence, these two great powers — one socialist, one capitalist — have joined forces to support and defend the Khmer Rouge, a gang of terrorists whose crimes are at least as great as those of Hitler's Nazis.

It is now almost two years since the Khmer Rouge were driven from power. Still the United States and China continue to defend their right to Cambodia's seat at the United Nations and plot to set the conditions for their return to power in Phnom Penh. In championing their cause, the United States and China have distorted the true nature of the Khmer Rouge regime and hidden the fact that the threat to peace and progress in Indochina today comes not from the governments presently in power there but rather from exactly the forces which the United States and China endorse and actively support.

In the work which follows, Wilfred Burchett presents a picture of life under the Khmer Rouge as it was described to him by those who endured and survived. Recognizing that it is impossible to understand events in Cambodia apart from the world process with which they are intertwined, he has focused especially on the consequences of the relationships among the countries of "The China-Cambodia-Vietnam Triangle."

This is not a book specifically about the role of the United States in Southeast Asia. It is a book which shows that the isolation of Cambodia and Vietnam and the defeat of their revolutions — goals being actively pursued by the U.S. government today — are not in the interest of the peoples of the world. And, most importantly, "The China-Cambodia-Vietnam Triangle" provides its readers with the understanding necessary to determine what they must demand of their own governments in the interest of peace and progress in Southeast Asia and throughout the world.

Arlee Frantz
Chicago
September 1981

INTRODUCTION

The full dimensions of the horrors inflicted on the people of Cambodia by the Khmer Rouge will never be known. In the mass graves and death pits there are millions of anonymous skulls and skeletons that can never be counted or classified. Enough documentation does exist to confirm that crimes almost without parallel in history were committed against their own people by the Khmer Rouge leadership between 17 April 1975, when the Lon Nol forces capitulated and the Khmer Rouge took over, and 7 January 1979 when they in turn were overthrown, mainly by Vietnamese forces.

During the 1960's my family and I resided in Cambodia for four years. My wife taught history of art at Phnom Penh's University of Fine Arts and our three children studied at the Lycée Descartes. It was natural that our friends were intellectuals, writers, journalists, teachers, university professors, diplomats, and political personalities. Such were among the earliest targets of the torture and extermination squads. The first victims were those who had studied abroad or spoke foreign languages; gradually the criteria for extermination were broadened to include anyone who wore spectacles or could read and write. With the exception of the half-a-dozen who threw their lot in with the Khmer Rouge leaders, all the people I had known during a quarter of a century of regular contact with Cambodia have been killed. Many died only after barbarous torture.

All of the crimes committed by the Nazis have been committed by the Khmer Rouge, who also invented many more. Hitler, Goering, Goebbels, and the rest of the Nazi gang were monsters, the incarnation of what has been considered the ultimate in evil in our times. Yet even their crimes pale by comparison with those of the

Khmer Rouge under the leadership of Pol Pot, Ieng Sary, and Khieu Samphan. Hitler tried to exterminate Jews, Slavs, Gypsies, and other "non-Aryan" groups. Pol Pot set about exterminating not only Vietnamese, Chinese, Islamic Chams, and other ethnic groups but also those of his own Khmer race. Hitler brought in slave labor from France, Poland, and other countries and worked them to death in labor camps. The Khmer Rouge leadership transformed their entire country into one great concentration camp. Hitler burned and desecrated the synagogues and persecuted various religious groups. The Khmer Rouge suppressed every form of religious worship. They turned Buddhist pagodas, Muslim mosques, and Catholic churches into torture centers, pigsties, and warehouses, or else simply destroyed them. Hitler burned books by anti-fascist writers. Pol Pot and his gang destroyed all books and libraries, trampling on every vestige of Cambodian culture and tradition. Hitler tried to relegate German women to the notorious "kitchen, church and children" role; the Khmer Rouge separated wives from their husbands and parents from their children and totally suppressed family life.

Some leftist, armchair intellectuals in the West prefer not to believe all of this. They defend the Khmer Rouge regime as a justifiable "social experiment." Their disclaimers are nullified by the overwhelming testimony of those who have actually been to Cambodia, including representatives of international relief agencies who have to deal with that part of Cambodian society which has survived.

The horrors of what happened in Cambodia are becoming better known. The facts are clear, brought into sharper focus by the very magnitude of the international effort required to repair the damage to every facet of Cambodian society. Virtually every Khmer citizen is both victim and witness. No on-the-spot investigator can have any doubts as to what occurred. But how and why it happened are far from clear. The importance of finding out is obviously crucial. Scholars, writers, journalists, and filmmakers are at work. Between us we might be able to shed some light on how and why one of the darkest events of our age could have happened. The chapters which follow represent my contribution to this light-shedding process.

Wilfred Burchett
Paris
July 1981

THE REVOLUTIONARY STRUGGLE FOR NATIONAL LIBERATION

1.
THE INDOCHINA COMMUNIST PARTY

During her relatively leisurely digestion of the components of what later became known as the Associated States of Indochina, France first acquired the three eastern provinces of Cochin-Chine in 1862. Five years later she also acquired the three western provinces, thus securing her sovereignty over the rich rice-growing areas of the Mekong Delta. On 18 February 1859 a French-Spanish expedition had occupied Saigon and thus had given France her first toehold in that area. It was just thirty years later that she put the three territories of Vietnam — Cochin-Chine in the south, Annam in the center, Tonkin in the north — together with the separate entities of Cambodia and Laos to the west to form a single administrative unit of Indochina. That the cultures, languages, and nuances of religion in Cambodia and Laos were different from each other, and those of both even more distinct from those of Vietnam, was the least of French worries in those days. The worries didn't really start until 1930 when Ho Chi Minh, then known as Nguyen Ai Quoc (Nguyen the Patriot), threw down the gauntlet. He challenged the single French administrative unit of Indochina by forming a single Indochina Communist Party. From that moment on, French colonial rule was doomed.

Ho Chi Minh was a man of many parts and of great — mainly self-acquired — culture. On the question of ending colonial rule in Indochina, he was absolutely single-minded.

He fired his first shots from afar. In June 1919 he brashly presented a petition to the victorious powers at the Versailles Conference. It was a document simple and to the point — all eight of them set out on a single piece of paper — as was the testament he

7

wrote just half a century later when he knew his days were numbered. The essence of the eight points was his demand for basic human rights for the peoples of Indochina, including the substitution "of the rule of law instead of government by decree." Predictably, his petition made no impression on the French or any of the other Versailles delegations. But it created a sensation within the large Vietnamese community in France — mainly "coolies" conscripted to dig trenches on the French battlefields — and moderate interest in left-wing political circles.

As a result Nguyen Ai Quoc found himself a full-fledged delegate to the famous Tours Congress (25-30 December 1920) at which the French Socialist Party split over whether it should adhere to the Second (Social Democrat) or Third (Communist) International. When the crucial vote came, Nguyen Ai Quoc voted for the Third International because the delegates favoring it were more inclined to support independence for France's colonies. After the split Leon Blum and Paul Faure continued to lead the minority French Socialist Party. Marcel Cachin and Paul Vaillant-Couturier became leaders of the newborn Communist Party, the creation of which was supported by the majority of delegates.

Thus Nguyen Ai Quoc became — to his great astonishment — a founder-member of the French Communist Party and consequently the first Vietnamese communist. He was not the only one to be astonished. After his first speech in favor of independence for Indochina — as the lone delegate from the French colonies — his photograph appeared in the press. The police came to arrest him the next day. But the tough delegates fought them off and Nguyen the Patriot continued to take part in the debate, stubbornly supporting his favorite theme!

Nguyen Ai Quoc's intention was to return home and form a party, similar to the new French Communist Party, which would have at least some international backing. After extensive travel in Europe (mostly by hitch-hiking, although that name for it did not yet exist), he set out for the Soviet Union, hoping to gain the ear — and support — of Lenin. He arrived in Leningrad toward the end of January 1924, shivering from the cold of a Russian winter despite the fur-lined clothes pressed on him by sailors of the Soviet ship on which he travelled. Two days before he arrived unknown and unannounced, Lenin had died. But Cachin and Vaillant-Couturier were in Moscow for Lenin's funeral and Nguyen the Patriot managed to contact them. They were able to introduce him to those who could be of the most help. The result was a brief period of study in revolutionary strategies and tactics. He then turned up — a little more than a year after his arrival in Leningrad — in China's Canton. Officially he was adviser on Asian problems to Mikhail Borodin, the Soviet Comintern envoy to the revolutionary government of Sun Yat-sen, founder-leader of the Kuomintang (National People's Party).[1]

Within a few months after "setting up shop" in Canton, Nguyen Ai Quoc had teleguided the formation of a Vietnamese Revolutionary Youth League. This in turn gave birth to the country's first trade unions. In Paris he not only had agitated for the right to freedom of his own people but also had organized the "League of Colonial Countries," which brought together nationals of all other colonies living in France. And he edited his paper "La Paria," secretly distributed throughout the French Empire. So too in Canton. Here the future Ho Chi Minh, internationalist *par excellence*, founded the "League of Oppressed Peoples of Asia." Its members were not only Vietnamese but also Koreans, Indonesians, Burmese, Thais, and other Asiatics. After Chiang Kai-shek broke the Kuomintang alliance with the Chinese Communists and Borodin and the other Comintern advisers managed to escape Chiang's assassination squads and make their way back to the Soviet Union, Nguyen Ai Quoc moved his base into Siam (now known as Thailand) where there was a large Vietnamese minority.

Always with agents of the French police at his heels, he moved from place to place in different disguises, organizing, awakening the consciousness of his compatriots, training them, and always maintaining contact with the revolutionary groups and independence movement inside his homeland. He earned his living as well as he could, his varied professions being his best disguises. At times he was an agricultural laborer; thanks to his peasant background he could plough and do general agricultural work. Sometimes he was a Buddhist monk with a shaven head and begging bowl or a street-corner merchant selling cigarettes. But wherever he was and however he was earning a living, he organized, agitated, and taught. In Siam he founded the "Vietnam Association for Mutual Assistance" and put out a weekly paper, "L'Humanité," which was infiltrated across the frontier into Cambodia and from there to Vietnam.

Did Nguyen the Patriot occasionally slip across the frontier himself to check on how the seeds he had planted were germinating? There is a fascinating reference in the book by Ben Kiernan and Chanthou Boua[2] on Cambodia's first known communist agitators — a certain Ben Krahom, who worked as a "coolie" at the Phnom Penh electricity works, and his wife. Arrested for distributing Vietnamese-language leaflets advocating "proletarian struggle against imperialism" and for hanging "red banners with Soviet emblems" from trees, the couple said they had been given some of the leaflets by a fellow-worker at the electricity plant and the others "by a travelling hairdresser." This was one of Nguyen Ai Quoc's favorite disguises. If it were not the itinerant revolutionary leader himself, it was certainly a proselyte trained in his image!

That Nguyen Ai Quoc's seeds were falling on fertile soil is clear from the fact that in June 1929 an "Indochina Communist Party" was set up in the northern-most Vietnamese province of Tonkin. A few months later "Red Trade Unions" were activated in the same area. And by late 1929 there were three Communist parties in Vietnam, bearing different names according to the whims of their leadership.

Near the end of 1929 Nguyen Ai Quoc returned to China from Siam for a conference in Kweilin — then capital of China's Kwangsi province which bordered northern Vietnam — with delegates from the three revolutionary parties. Each wanted to be recognized as the sole Communist Party. As usual, Nguyen Ai Quoc's words were few but to the point.

> In the Soviet Union, England, France and China, and in colonial countries such as India, Indonesia and others, there is only one Communist Party. Vietnam cannot afford three. We must unite the entire people to fight for national independence and to achieve this there must be unity of organization. This organization could keep its old name of "Revolutionary Youth League" or adopt that of "Communist Party," but its political programme must be: National Independence, Freedom to the People, Forward to Socialism.[3]

After a short discussion those present agreed to form a single Communist Party. The delegates then left to report back to their respective organizations, having agreed to meet a few months later in Hongkong to formalize their decision.

Despite the fact that the working class in Vietnam totalled only 220,000 — less than 1 percent of the population — Nguyen Ai Quoc insisted that the Party must be formed under working class leadership. One of his arguments was that it was only after the founding of the Revolutionary Youth League that the first trade unions were formed and that they looked to the Youth League for guidance.

The significance of all this was explained to me half a century later at the Historical Institute of the Vietnamese Communist Party by Nguyen Can, founder-member of the trade union movement.

A special characteristic of our Vietnamese Party was that the workers originated from the peasantry and retained family-type relations with the villages. This is what Lenin once described as a highly desirable "miracle" greatly facilitating the link between economic and political problems. The peasantry for centuries had always loyally fought under feudal leadership to repel foreign invaders, without ever being rewarded by satisfaction of their own interests. After the invader was repelled, the feudalists reverted to their traditional role as the oppressors and exploiters of the peasantry.

When the French colonialist invaders arrived with their more modern military techniques, the peasants saw that the feudal leadership was no longer valid. Indeed, rival feudal clans competed for having the colonialists, with their modern weapons, on their side! When one clan put down its rival, it could better exploit the peasantry under its control. The working class, through its party, could immediately attract mass peasant support for its honest slogan: Independence for the Nation. Land to the Peasants! But there was a great problem.

The Youth League from which the Communist Party would emerge, although convinced of the need for working class leadership, was ninety percent composed of petit-bourgeois intellectuals.

What followed was, I believe, possible only in a Vietnam already almost spellbound by the clarity and compelling idealist-realist amalgam of the line spelt out by Nguyen Ai Quoc in his short articles, which were passed from hand to hand among Vietnamese militants. Nguyen Can continued his account of how the "petit-bourgeois intellectual" leadership tempered itself to the realities of proletarian work and life styles.

> On the eve of the formation of the Party, they started to go into the factories and workshops, to acquire working class ideology. Thus Nguyen Chi Thanh (later *General* Nguyen Chi Thanh, chief political commissar to the Vietnamese People's Army, second only to Vo Nguyen Giap in military prestige) went to the Hongay coalfields to work as a miner; Nguyen Luong Bang (vice-president of the Democratic Republic after Ho Chi Minh's death in September 1969) went to Haiphong as a rickshaw puller; Le Thanh Nghi, later to become head of Economic Planning, also went to work in the Hongay coal mines. Most of our leaders took part in this movement.

As with everything that Nguyen Ai Quoc undertook, meticulous attention was paid to the long-range strategic effects of each move to be made. The Vietnamese Communist Party was formed in Hongkong on 3 February 1930. Soon afterward, on 1 May 1930, there was a worker-peasant uprising in the two neighboring provinces of Nghe An (Ho Chi Minh's home province) and Ha Tinh, in which the rebels seized administrative power, carried out land reform, abolished or reduced taxes, and defeated for over one year French attempts to crush the uprising. Known as the "Nghe-Tinh Soviet" rebellion, it was one of the significant landmarks of the Vietnamese national liberation movement. Although the French seemed to have ignored this at the time, it was an ominous warning that they were no longer dealing with feudal dynastic rulers, temporarily backed by their duty-bound peasant subjects, or with the heroic scholar-patriots who had taken over defense of national sovereignty from the effete feudalists. This uprising was carried out by a tough new alignment of forces composed of worker and peasant allies whose material interests could be identified with those of the nation. The struggle for national liberation would never be the same after the Nghe-Tinh uprising!

One of the important by-products of this — and something specific to the Vietnamese national liberation struggle — was that the working class had an important influence over those intellectuals who quickly recognized the new, patriotic element which they represented. Nguyen Can and the Institute's head of research, Le

Thanh Can, were specific about this.

> Because intellectuals grasp new phenomena easily, they could quickly understand why the previous movements of the bourgeois scholars, Buddhist bonzes and others, despite great heroism and readiness for self-sacrifice, had been defeated. In feudal and, later, colonized Vietnam, the intellectuals had suffered from domination and lack of independence to pursue their creative activities. In the working class, they saw the emergence of a virile, patriotic leadership right away.

Warming to this theme, Le Thanh Can stressed that although the image of the great feudal patriots — from the Trung sisters who briefly threw out the Chinese occupiers in 43 AD to Tran Hung Dao who thrice defeated the Mongol invaders in the thirteenth century and others like the Tay Son brothers who repelled the Manchu occupiers in the eighteenth century — would never be tarnished or forgotten, an entirely new force appropriate to the challenge of the colonialist era had emerged with the formation of the Communist Party.

> After it was formed, neither the bourgeoisie, which emerged late on the scene in Vietnam, nor the peasantry in separate, organized political forms were decisive in the struggle for national salvation. The feudal class, which had played an important patriotic role in the past, abandoned the field with the arrival of the French. Rival feudal rulers competed for French patronage.[4]

On 30 April 1930, shortly after the Vietnamese party was formed, Communist Party cells were set up in the Laotian administrative capital, Vientiane, and in the nearby Bo Nen tin mine. Others were set up at about the same time in Phnom Penh and in Cambodia's rubber-producing province of Kompong Cham. It was the formation of these cells which paved the way for transforming the Vietnamese Communist Party into the Communist Party of Indochina at a founding congress in Portugal's Chinese colony of Macao in October 1930. The congress was presided over by Nguyen Ai Quoc, in his capacity as representative of the Moscow-based Communist International. Significantly, the new party's constitution included the statement that the party was to lead all the Indochinese nations in the struggle "for the complete independence of Indochina and for land to the peasants."

The Chinese and the Khmer Rouge leadership charge that Vietnam has always advocated an "Indochina Federation" under its leadership. It is worth noting that it would have been incongruous at the founding congress to set the task as that of struggling for the separate independence of Vietnam, Cambodia, and Laos when the French exercised administrative and military control over Indochina as one single unit. However, an ICP resolution on the nationalities question, adopted at Nguyen Ai Quoc's initiative in March 1935, stated that:

> After driving the French imperialists out of Indochina, each nation will have the right to self-determination; it may join the Indochinese Federation or set up a separate state; it is free to join or leave the Federation; it may follow whichever system it likes. The fraternal alliance must be based on the principles of revolutionary sincerity, freedom and equality.

This was the guideline on the question, consistently adhered to at every stage of the anti-French (and later the anti-U.S.) struggle. It coincided with Ho Chi Minh's internationalist principles on the self-determination of peoples, which were later expressed by his advocacy of maximum autonomy for the ethnic minorities in Vietnam itself.[5]

On the question of freedom for the Cambodian and Laotian peoples to choose their own road, there was another specific decision of the 8th Plenum of the Central Committee of the Indochina Communist Party in June 1941, by which time the Japanese had moved into Indochina and were sharing power with the Vichy French administration. It stated:

> After driving out the French and Japanese, we must correctly carry out the policy of national self-determination with regard to the Indochinese peoples. It is up to the people living in Indochina to either organize themselves into a Federation of Democratic Republics or to remain separate states.

Shortly after the seizure of power from the Japanese and the French in August 1945 and the establishment of the Democratic Republic of Vietnam in September of that year, the Indochina Communist Party was formally dissolved for tactical reasons. In fact, it went underground with clandestine branches active in three countries (Vietnam, Cambodia, and Laos). Because Vietnam was far more advanced economically and socially, the Communist Party there was proportionately much stronger and the rate of growth much faster. In the first year of clandestinity, the membership of the Vietnamese section of the underground Indochina Communist Party increased from 5,000 to 20,000. This was the period of armed struggle against the French colonialists, who were seeking to reimpose their rule in all three countries. The three branches of the underground party functioned through front organizations: the Vietminh (Vietnamese Independence League), the Lao Itsala (Free Lao), and the Nekhum Issarak Khmer (Khmer Freedom Front).

In February 1951 the formation of a separate Vietnamese Lao Dong (Workers) Party was announced at a special congress of the Indochina Communist Party also attended by delegates of embryonic Cambodian and Laotian parties. A resolution adopted at this congress stated that the Lao Dong Party, which was in effect the Vietnamese Communist Party, had the duty of helping communists in Laos and Cambodia to set up revolutionary organizations suited to the specific conditions in each country. Boards, or embryonic central committees, were set up in both Laos and Cambodia to organize the founding of separate Communist parties. From that time on, the Indochina Communist Party was really dissolved. The Lao Dong Party had 76,000 members, Cambodia about 300, and Laos 170, which corresponded partly to differences in population but mainly to the great disparity in the levels of socioeconomic development and political consciousness.

The front organizations continued to function. On 3 March 1951 there was a conference of the three national front organizations at which it was decided to set up a Vietnamese-Khmer-Lao alliance to coordinate the struggle against the French colonialists. It was on the basis of this decision (published 11 March 1954) that Vietnamese troops later entered Cambodia and Laos to fight side-by-side with what were by then the Khmer National Liberation Army and the Pathet Lao, the armed forces of the Lao Itsala.

"From the beginning," continued Le Thanh Can:

> Ho Chi Minh stressed the close relationships of the three peoples of Indochina; related by geography, nationalities (especially the ethnic minorities of the border areas), economics, and above all by political relationships. Our common enemy was French colonialism and in

order to win victory, unity of the three peoples was essential.

There is no question that it was the degree of unity that was achieved which led to the French defeat in Indochina, symbolized by the historic victory of the Vietnamese People's Army at Dien Bien Phu. That victory was a product of unified and coordinated military effort. While the major role was played by the forces of Vo Nguyen Giap at Dien Bien Phu, vital subsidiary roles were played by the Pathet Lao, which blocked French attempts to send reinforcements from Laos to relieve the beleaguered garrison, and by the Khmer Issarak forces, which had by then liberated one-third of Cambodia and played havoc with French communication lines.

Those who try to explain the degeneration of relations between Cambodia and Vietnam after the Khmer Rouge came to power as due to "traditional hostility" between the two peoples ignore the important battlefield solidarity and coordination of effort which occurred from the earliest days of French occupation. Even before there was any organization to coordinate the struggle for the liberation of Indochina, French officers were complaining of constantly being attacked on two fronts simultaneously along the Vietnam-Cambodia border. The Vietnamese attacked when they saw the French in difficulty on the Cambodian side and the Cambodians did likewise. It was, however, the formation of the Indochina Communist Party which provided the essential ingredient for victory. With the liberation of the peoples of Indochina as its principal aim, it mobilized and organized the solidarity among the three peoples and coordinated their armed national liberation struggle. Any objective study of the role of the Khmer Rouge under the leadership of Pol Pot and Ieng Sary must conclude that its leaders' aims were to destroy this solidarity and set the Cambodian, Laotian, and Vietnamese peoples at each other's throats!

1. Formed in 1905 by Sun Yat-sen, the Kuomintang overthrew the ruling Manchu dynasty in 1911 and established a republic. However, power soon passed into the hands of traditional warlords. Sun Yat-sen, in an alliance with the Chinese Communist Party, built up a modern military organization in Canton — with the help of Soviet advisors — for a "march North" to reunify the country under Kuomintang rule. He died in March 1925, shortly before the "march North" was due to start. Leadership of the Kuomintang passed into the hands of his brother-in-law Chiang Kai-shek, who soon broke with the Communists and precipitated what was to become a long and bloody civil war from which the Communist leader Mao Tse-tung was to emerge the prestigious victor.

2. Kiernan, Ben, and Boua, Chanthou, *Peasants and Politics in Kampuchea, 1942-79*. London: Zed Press, in press.

3. Burchett, Wilfred, *North of the 17th Parallel*, pp. 20-21. Hanoi: Published by the author, 1955. Based on a conversation with Ho Chi Minh in 1955 and on documents in his possession.

4. For the previous two thousand years, the confrontation between the Vietnamese and the "invaders from the North" had been expressed in a rather qualitative equality in weapons: archery including fire-arrows, thrusting and chopping hand-wielded arms, and ballistics including locally made explosives. Even if quantitatively the invaders were vastly more powerful, the Vietnamese were more experienced in the effective and economic use of the arms and men at their disposal. The arrival of the French, with rapid-firing machine guns and relatively long-range artillery, upset the old military equations and the Vietnamese feudalists bowed out of the struggle to preserve national sovereignty. Thus the stage was set for new forces to pick up the banner which the feudalists had abandoned!

5. This was given practical effect as soon as the northern half of Vietnam had thrown off the French yoke. In March 1955 — two months before the French troops left North Vietnam — the Vietminh set up the Thai-Meo autonomous region. There the Thai and Meo minorities accounted for 75 percent of the total population; another fifteen ethnic minorities made up most of the rest.

2.
THE KHMER ISSARAK

Within a year after the Indochina Communist Party went underground and began functioning through front organizations in Vietnam, Laos, and Cambodia, the Cambodian organization — the Khmer Issarak — struck its first real blow. In August 1946 Khmer Issarak guerrillas wiped out the entire French garrison at Siem Reap and captured its stock of arms intact. They gradually began to set up guerrilla bases extending over large areas in northwest, southwest, and southeast Cambodia. "Capture enemy arms to kill the enemy" was the slogan, the "enemy" clearly being the French occupation forces. After they had gotten off to a good start, the Khmer Issarak set up jungle arsenals for the manufacture of hand grenades, mines, light bazookas, and other weapons suitable for partisan warfare. Between 1946 and 1949 People's Committees were formed at district and even village levels in many provinces, as were self-defense units to protect the villagers. As these organizations developed, resistance groups in isolated areas were linked up until a large, united military-political front was established.

There were no dramatic military developments in the Indochina war between 1947 and the end of 1949. The French concentrated on "pacification" and the resistance forces on building up their organizations and laying the foundation for protracted armed struggle in all three states of Indochina. The victory of the Chinese Communists and the establishment of the People's Republic of China on 10 October 1949 — with the prospect of a friendly frontier for the passage of arms between northern Vietnam and China — were obviously going to change the situation.

The French Government sent their War Minister, General

Revers, to look over the situation in Indochina. His assessment — like that of Malcolm MacDonald, the British High Commissioner in Southeast Asia who accompanied him on his tour — was that southern Vietnam, Cambodia, and Laos were already "pacified." The only remaining problem was to wipe out the Vietminh in northern Vietnam. The essential thing, as they saw it, was to hold on to the Red River Delta; from there the French could develop a campaign to mop up Giap's Vietnam People's Army. It was the kind of simplistic, colonialist, chauvinist analysis that the French (and the Americans after them) continually made, based on the implicit assumption of their own superiority.

Nevertheless, the decision to concentrate French forces in the north was something which Cambodia's King Sihanouk was quick to take advantage of. He used the inroads made by the Khmer Issarak, fighting under the banner of "national independence," as a key argument to convince the French that he should be the "crowned champion" of national independence. On 8 November 1949 France granted Cambodia some of the superficial trappings of independence. Sihanouk was even allowed to have his own armed forces.

The Khmer Issarak were careful not to attack Sihanouk's forces. But behind the scenes, as one leading Khmer Issarak survivor was to tell me later:

> We mobilized the people to put pressure on Sihanouk as the spiritual Father of the People in his dual role as King and head of the Buddhist clergy. He had to be brought to understand the sufferings of the people under colonialism and come down on the side of the people. He would be dishonored if he remained a valet of the French who had placed him in power. The line was while militarily attacking the French to place before Sihanouk his responsibilities. To a certain extent we succeeded.

On the political front the elections to the Legislative Assembly in December of 1947 had given fifty-four seats to the Democratic Party and twenty-one to the pro-monarchist Liberal Party. The increasing sympathy of the Democrats for the Khmer Issarak led Sihanouk, probably under French pressure, to dissolve the National Assembly in September 1949. He then appointed a right-wing government of conservative Democrats led by Yem Sambaur, one of a group of rightists who opposed the French presence in the hope of picking up some of the economic plums that would become available after their departure.

After installing the Yem Sambaur government, whose obedience he could count on, Sihanouk submitted a five-point demand to the French High Commissioner.

1. Genuine internal sovereignty for Cambodia.

2. Freedom to conduct foreign relations with the main world powers and representation at the United Nations.

3. A progressive and rapid reduction of French military zones in Cambodia and the replacement of French presence there by a Cambodian presence.

4. Pardon for all resistance fighters.

5. A generous attitude towards freeing and according complete amnesty to military and political prisoners and exiles — including Son Ngoc Thanh.[1]

All these demands were eventually met and Cambodia took its place as an independent and sovereign member of the United Nations.

The tempo and scale of armed struggle quickened. The transfer of French troops out of Cambodia to north Vietnam in 1950 facilitated the activities of the Khmer Issarak but did nothing to ease the overall French military situation. On the night of 16 September 1950 General Giap launched one of the decisive campaigns of the long resistance war, one which paved the way for Dien Bien Phu. Known as the "Frontier Campaign," it lasted six weeks. When it was over, the whole of the north Vietnam-China frontier area was securely in Vietminh hands in depth as well as in length. Cao Bang, Langson, and Lao Cai in the immediate frontier areas, as well as Thai Nguyen and Hoa Binh in the rear, were among the provincial capitals liberated.

The Vietminh had opened a frontier with the socialist world and, as historian Nguyen Khac Vien expressed it, had established a "vast rear extending from China to Czechoslovakia." It was by far the greatest French defeat until that time and was exceeded only by that at Dien Bien Phu three-and-a-half years later.

The French Commander-in-Chief, General Raoul Salan, was withdrawn and replaced by France's most illustrious soldier, Marshal Jean de Lattre de Tassigny, with another 20,000 troops at his disposal. De Lattre succeeded in losing key positions in the Red

River Delta. Within a couple of years he had been replaced by General Henri Navarre, who arrived in March 1953 with a famous plan, endorsed by Washington, "to end the war in eighteen months." Exactly one year later the battle of Dien Bien Phu started.

The internal political wrangling in Cambodia, the rise and fall of governments, and Sihanouk's trampling on democratic procedures when they did not produce the sort of results he wanted — matters to which some scholars have attached great importance — were largely irrelevant. The future of Cambodia, and especially the key question of her independence, was not going to be decided by the Democratic Party, headed by Prince Hay Kanthoul after the death of Prince Yutevong, or the Populist Party of Son Sann or the Khmer Renovation Party of Lon Nol or any of the other parties wrangling for power. It would be decided by the battlefield victories of the Vietminh, aided by the Vietminh-dominated Pathet Lao and Khmer Issarak national liberation movements.

That the Vietnamese resistance forces bore the brunt of the struggle is indisputable. The French (and later the Americans) treated Indochina as a single battlefield. Ho Chi Minh, Vo Nguyen Giap, and their co-leaders were obliged to do the same. But they did it in a way that respected the national feelings of their Cambodian and Laotian allies and aided them in achieving their own independence and sovereignty. While the main fighting forces in each of the three states were Vietnamese, in Cambodia and Laos they fought in the Khmer Issarak and Lao Itsala organizations. Within these organizations the Vietminh leadership did their best to develop genuinely national Khmer and Laotian political and military structures.

The main battlefield continued to be Vietnam until the end. By 1952 the French had 237 battalions in Indochina. Of fifty-four combat battalions, fifty were concentrated in Vietnam and all but ten of them were in the north. Of 179 "pacification" battalions, thirty were being used in Laos and Cambodia and 149 in Vietnam, sixty-one of which were in the north. Within a year the combat battalions had been increased to eighty, of which seventy-one were in Vietnam and the other nine in Laos. By March 1953 there were in Cambodia only two French "pacification" battalions and five battalions of the Royal Khmer Army under French command. It was the Vietminh victories on the battlefields of Vietnam and Laos that were the major factor in setting the conditions for achieving Cambodian independence under the monarchy by the end of 1953.

Sihanouk was one of the few to recognize this and he used every victory on any of the various fronts to clamber up one more rung of the independence ladder. He had acquired a taste for personal participation in politics, rare for someone of his status, which he has never lost. In June 1952 he dismissed the government and took over as Prime Minister and Foreign Minister. He then launched what he later called the Royal Crusade for Independence.

At that time France was refusing to grant Cambodia full independence on the grounds that Cambodian bases were necessary for the French to press their war against the Vietminh. Sihanouk explained his position:

> I made my position clear to the French. Although I did not want the Vietminh on Cambodian soil, what they did in their own country was not Cambodia's business, and I did not want Cambodia to be used as a base of operations against them. I continued to push for complete independence.[2]

To frighten Sihanouk into slowing up his campaign for independence, the French formed a false Khmer Issarak movement which carried out terrorist attacks aimed particularly at the monarchy. Sihanouk's typical riposte was to encourage some officers and men from the Royal Khmer Army to "desert" to the real Khmer Issarak and to make sure they did not lack arms. In a note to French president Auriol on 5 March 1953 Sihanouk made greater claims for the strength of the Khmer Issarak forces than they made for themselves. He also steadfastly rejected the French argument that they needed to retain their hold on Cambodia as a base from which to fight the Vietminh.

> The present policy of France in Indochina is based on the idea that the principal aim at the moment is success in the fight against the Vietminh. [He wrote.] But this had nothing in common with the interests of the Cambodian people, who above all desire peace and are sincerely attached to the ideas of liberty and independence.

He claimed that three-fifths of Cambodia's territory was occupied by the Khmer Issarak (who claimed only one-third). But instead of using this as an argument to ask the French to stay on,

Sihanouk used it to advance his claims for independence, pointing out that the Khmer Issarak had deep roots among the people and that their strength lay in the fact that they fought under the banner of national independence.

> Native sons, peasants and even townspeople. . .their patriotic proclamations find a favorable response among the population and also among the clergy, whose influence is enormous throughout the kingdom, and they are assured of faithful followers among the masses as well as amongst the elite of the nation. . .The Issarak danger is real in itself. . .These rebels frequently mount ambushes against our patrols of provincial guards, police and troops and recently — alone or together with the Vietminh — have obtained results which have greatly affected public opinion. . . .

> What can I reply when the Issarak propaganda proves to the people and the clergy that Cambodia is not really independent?

> The solution which I propose would be to transfer to the sovereign (Sihanouk) and his government the principal responsibilities for ruling the country. This could include the transfer of prerogatives till now withheld by France and which in consequence would make it incumbent on the king and the royal government to find themselves the means necessary to exercise their powers and responsibilities. . .Only by such a step could French policy be understood and accepted by our people, who, I must stress, have developed considerably and demand more than ever the real attributes of independence. . . .[3]

The response of the French government was certainly not what Sihanouk hoped for.

> My hopes were raised when I was invited to Paris to lunch with President Auriol on 25 March 1953. I had been assured that my communications to the French government had received the closest study. The luncheon discussion was sterile and President Auriol let it be known that the sooner I left French soil for Cambodia, the better pleased he would be. He went so far as to include in the official communiqué the offensive phrase that King Sihanouk "should return to Phnom Penh within a few days.". . .

> Why a France that had so recently emerged from its own struggle against the Nazi occupiers could not understand the aspirations of the Cambodian people — indeed the peoples of Indo-China as a whole — was more than I could fathom. That a socialist president could take such an attitude was even more perplexing. Hints that I

might "lose my crown" if I pushed things too far also rankled. Was the crown really theirs to give and theirs to take away?[4]

Defying the "Protector's" injunction, Sihanouk left for the United States via Canada on 13 April 1953, confident of finding support there for the urgency of granting "full independence" to the three states of Indochina.

That was the main theme of an hour-long discussion with John Foster Dulles. His reaction was sour, to say the least: "Defeat communism in your area! Then we will put pressure on France to do what is necessary," was the essence of his patronizing advice. His *idée fixe* was the urgency of destroying the Vietminh, and the importance of Cambodia's contribution to this.... "We are at the most crucial moment of the war. It has to be won. That is why more than ever we must unite our forces and our means and not quarrel and divide ourselves. Your dispute with France would only play into the hands of the common enemy.... Without the help of the French Army, your country would quickly be conquered by the Reds and your independence would disappear."[5]

Sihanouk was then a realist if ever there was one. His knowledge of his own country's history told him that if the French succeeded in defeating the Vietminh, whatever crumbs of independence he had secured would disappear overnight. The history of French colonization in the area had been one of repeated use of one country as a base to subdue its neighbor. The attainment of true Cambodian independence depended on an overall victory by the Vietminh.

Sihanouk drew shrewd conclusions from his contacts with western leaders. While on his return trip from the United States, he received a cable from Dulles. In it Dulles urged him once again to work together with France "at a moment when the threat of a Communist invasion from Laos is so apparent and the United States is applying itself to intensifying and speeding up their aid to save the Khmer people from Communist aggression." Commenting on this cable, he later remarked:

My detractors like to pretend that, somewhere in my development, I must have been brainwashed by Mao Tse-tung and Chou En-lai. But it was men like Vincent Auriol and John Foster Dulles — and later, Richard Nixon — who were responsible for my political education. Independence, in the eyes of these leaders, was a bargaining counter to be offered or withdrawn according to how it suited their interests, not those of the little country concerned.[6]

By a judicious combination of diplomacy, blackmail, and finally the use of his own armed forces to disarm some French units — with the timing of each step carefully synchronized with maximum French military embarrassment in north Vietnam and Laos — Sihanouk extracted the attributes of full independence from France on 9 November 1953. From there it was but a short step to the 1954 Geneva Conference and international recognition of Cambodia's full independence. The added bonus at Geneva was to be the withdrawal of his potentially most dangerous enemies — the battle-hardened Khmer Issarak guerrillas and their Vietminh allies, including political and military cadres who had fought together in the most difficult initial period.

1. Son Ngoc Thanh enjoyed considerable support from certain circles inside the Democratic Party. The fact that the French had arrested him as a traitor in the service of the Japanese and had taken him off to France gave him a sort of martyr-hero status.

2. Sihanouk, Norodom, and Burchett, Wilfred, *My War With the CIA*, p. 152. New York: Pantheon Books, 1972.

3. Sihanouk's mention of the patriotic role of the Buddhist clergy was significant. As in Vietnam and Laos, patriotic bonzes in Cambodia played important roles during various stages of the French occupation. For instance, in 1943 Achar Hem Chieu, a bonze-lecturer at the Buddhist seminary in Phnom Penh, was arrested because he had written a number of works denouncing French colonialism. He was suspected of heading an anti-colonialist movement. Two thousand bonzes (or *bhikkhus* as they are called in Khmer) were joined by tens of thousands of ordinary citizens in a mass demonstration demanding his release. The protest movement developed into an armed insurrection, which was put down by the French with their customary brutality. Achar Hem Chieu and hundreds of his followers, including many *bhikkhus*, were deported to the notorious prison island of Poulo Condor, from where many — including Hem Chieu — never returned.

In April 1950, at a Conference of People's Representatives to set up a Central Committee for Khmer liberation, 105 of the 200 delegates were Buddhist bonzes. Later this Central Committee was transformed into a Provisional Government and then into a Government of National Resistance to administer the Khmer Issarak Liberated Zones. A high-ranking Buddhist bonze of great prestige, Son Ngoc Minh, was chosen as president of the resistance government. He later became one of the founder-leaders of the Khmer Communist Party.

4. Sihanouk and Burchett, *My War with the CIA*, pp. 152-3.

5. *Ibid.*, p. 153-4.

6. *Ibid.*, p. 155.

3.
THE 1954
GENEVA CONFERENCE

When historians put their fingers on the major impediment to the Cambodian revolution, they must point to the consequences of the 1954 Geneva Conference on Indochina and, in particular, of the role played by China at that conference. Pol Pot and his faction have no cause to dispute this, having themselves played no role in defeating the French. But the Khmer resistance fighters who had participated in that struggle were robbed at Geneva of their share of the fruits of the common victory by the three peoples of Indochina over French colonialism.

The Indochina part of the Geneva Conference (which had started with abortive discussions on Korea) opened on 8 May 1954. Heading the Democratic Republic of Vietnam's delegation was its foreign minister, Pham Van Dong. On the previous day he had received a most fabulous negotiator's weapon in the form of the victory by General Vo Nguyen Giap, his close comrade-in-arms, over the cream of the French Expeditionary Corps in the historic battle of Dien Bien Phu.[1]

At the first session Pham Van Dong raised the question of representation of the Khmer Issarak and Lao Itsala. After all, it was a conference to end the war in Indochina! France was one of the belligerents; the resistance forces of Vietnam, Cambodia, and Laos represented the other. Already participating were delegates of the French protégés: "Emperor" Bao Dai of Vietnam, King Sihanouk of Cambodia, and King Savang Vatthana of Laos. French foreign minister Georges Bidault objected strongly to Khmer Issarak and Lao Itsala presence, sneering that they were "non-existent phantoms."

This was an unfortunate phrase which Bidault had used before, in reference to Pham Van Dong during a debate at the United Nations a few months earlier. The latter lost no time in reminding Bidault of this.

> But now I am here to discuss with you. The Pathet Lao² and the Khmer Issarak fight as the Vietnamese fight. They are not phantoms. There are those at this conference who perform and talk here and among them are the shades of real phantoms, who do not represent reality. They represent a past which has gone forever, but like you, they want to cling to their illusions. These are the real phantoms.

It was a telling point, the more so because the whole French delegation had turned up in black, mourning the Dien Bien Phu defeat. Bidault and his colleagues thus unwittingly emphasized to the world the dimensions of that defeat and the fact that it was a historic event, the importance of which would be felt far beyond the confines of Geneva or Indochina. The question of "phantoms" made headlines in the French press the following day.

At all the early sessions Pham Van Dong returned again and again to the question of Khmer Issarak and Pathet Lao representation. His was a lone voice. While Bidault could count on solid backing from the West (Britain and the United States), Pham Van Dong was isolated on the question of representation as on other crucial questions. The socialist camp was represented by Soviet foreign minister Vyacheslav Molotov and by Chinese premier and foreign minister Chou En-lai. Molotov was mainly occupied with his post as co-chairman of the Conference with his opposite number, Sir Anthony Eden. And Chou En-lai had made it clear, even during the Korean part of the Conference, that "Asian problems should be solved by Asians, just as European problems were by Europeans."³

The Khmer Issarak and Pathet Lao delegations were in Geneva but very much as "uninvited guests." Their presence was a well-guarded secret and the only delegation with whom they had contact was that of the Democratic Republic of Vietnam (DRV). Eventually Chou En-lai persuaded Pham Van Dong to take a "realistic" and "pragmatic" approach and drop the question of their representation at the Conference from the plenary sessions, thus allowing it to be buried in a commission.

The debate continued, tougher than ever, on the question of regroupment areas and the demarcation lines which would delimit them. The DRV delegation fought very hard for a regroupment area for the Khmer Issarak but got no support from Chou En-lai on this question for the very simple reason that China had no common frontier with Cambodia. Later it became clear that while the Vietnamese were fighting to save the revolutions in Cambodia and Laos and to secure for the revolutionary forces of each country the just rewards of their common victory, China was interested only in the establishment of buffer zones to guarantee security along her own frontiers.

Thus Chou En-lai supported setting up a regroupment zone for the Pathet Lao but it had to be shaped in a way that served China's security interests rather than the interests of the Laotian revolution. The big discussion was over whether Laos should be divided longitudinally or latitudinally. The strongest Pathet Lao resistance bases were in the center and the south, especially in the provinces of Attopeu, Saravane, and in the Bolovens Plateau. China's interest was served by creating a buffer zone which included Phong Saly, a sparsely populated province in the extreme north which had a common frontier with China. Again Pham Van Dong fought a lone battle with the West united against him and Chou En-lai siding with them. Isolated and forced to negotiate on behalf of the Cambodian and Laotian resistance movements, he had to make concessions not justified by either the relationship of forces or battlefield realities but motivated by Chinese interests and the general spirit of "detente" and "peaceful co-existence" which reigned in the European socialist camp at the time. Thus the Laotian revolutionary forces had to withdraw from their strong positions in ten of the Laotian provinces and regroup in the two northern-most provinces of Phong Saly and Sam Neua. Chou En-lai pointed out that this would give North Vietnam a common frontier with Laos and thus a "buffer zone." But it meant that the Pathet Lao would have to abandon its most important base areas and the people who had loyally supported its armed struggle for many years.

Years later, one of Pham Van Dong's senior aides at the Conference was to tell me:

For us it was not a question of buffer zones. It was the question of

Laos as a whole, the unity and independence of Laos, the preservation of bases to ensure final victory. Independence, unity, sovereignty, territorial integrity. These were our watchwords. We did everything possible to have these principles accepted and we never abandoned that stand.

The enemy position was: "Let's be realistic. To stick out for principles now is not realistic. Let's deal with concrete questions. Military affairs — get the fighting stopped, and deal with principles later." They didn't want to talk about the past: "It will only poison the atmosphere. Let's deal only with the present." Unfortunately we had allies who in the name of "realism" and "pragmatism" also advised us not to "poison the atmosphere" but to yield.

Covering the Geneva Conference from the first to the last day, I — and other journalists with close relations to the socialist delegations — had no suspicion that the Chinese and Soviet delegations were not solidly backing the Vietnamese. For many years after the Conference, Vietnamese leaders were still loyally saying: "The results were arrived at after discussions and mutual agreements." While literally true, this was not even half the real truth.

When the Conference came to the question of fixing a demarcation line behind which the French troops would withdraw to the south and the Vietminh troops would withdraw to the north, Pham Van Dong proposed a line along the 13th parallel. Given the disastrous situation of the French forces after the defeat at Dien Bien Phu and the fact that the rest of their elite forces were encircled in the Red River Delta and other sectors in the north, this was not an unreasonable proposal. It would have given the Vietminh a hundred kilometer-long frontier with Cambodia and compensated them for the failure to get a regroupment zone for the Khmer Issarak forces. But in the name of "realism" and "pragmatism," gradually Pham Van Dong was forced to move his line north past the 14th parallel (which still would have given the Vietminh a small frontier with Cambodia) and past the 15th to the 16th, where he made a strong stand.

Twice before in Vietnam's history, the 16th parallel had been a temporary dividing line. After World War II, when Kuomintang Chinese troops had entered from the north and British troops from the south (ostensibly to round up the rest of the Japanese occupation army and transport them back to Japan), the demarcation line between the two forces ran along the 16th parallel and through the southern outskirts of Danang. When the country was partitioned between the Trinh and the Nguyen dynasties in the 17th century, it was also divided along the 16th parallel. And there were geographical as well as historical reasons which made the 16th parallel the logical demarcation line — if one there had to be.

But the French demanded a line along the 17th parallel. Following a private meeting between the new French premier and foreign minister Pierre Mendès-France and Chou En-lai, the latter supported the French position.[4]

The question of the 17th or 16th parallel was of crucial strategic importance. Between those two parallels runs Highway 9, which links Laos to the Vietnamese coast. The French wanted to retain Highway 9 in order to maintain their control over Laos. Pham Van Dong wanted it in order to be able to continue Vietminh support for the Pathet Lao. Pham Van Dong's aide, who later briefed me on what really went on at Geneva, commented:

> The French did everything to have this road. It was at the Berne meeting between Chou and Mendès-France that the Chinese gave way. Before that meeting, and behind our backs, they had already drawn up a draft agreement, the final touches to which were given at Berne. We were faced with a *fait accompli*, but on one matter we dug in our heels and refused to yield. Chou En-lai advised us to place Hanoi and Haiphong, and Highway 5 which links them, under joint French-Vietnamese control! It suited the Chinese because the area north of the Hanoi-Haiphong line would still provide a substantial buffer zone to protect China's southern frontier. We rejected this as we did a later French attempt to push the demarcation line up to the 18th parallel.
>
> With hindsight, we saw that the Chinese did everything possible—at our expense—to win over the new French government. Their relations with the USA were still bad and they needed one western friend.

The other major question linked with that of fixing the demarcation line was the timing of the elections. All participants agreed in principle that elections would be held after the separation of combatant forces. Pham Van Dong wanted elections in Vietnam to be held as quickly as possible. The French wanted them to be postponed as long as possible, just as they wanted the demarcation line to be pushed as far north as possible. The Chinese supported the French in time as in space.

Chou En-lai made it quite clear to the French that China was above all at Geneva to protect her own interests and not those of revolutionary forces in Indochina. This becomes cruelly clear in a book on the Geneva Conference, based on hitherto unpublished documents of the Conference, by the French historian and Asian specialist François Joyaux. He refers to a meeting between Chou En-lai and Anthony Eden in Geneva on the day before the British Foreign Office announced that diplomatic relations between the two countries would be upgraded to the ambassadorial level.

> The head of the Chinese delegation had, in fact, come to inform Eden that he thought he "could persuade the Vietminh to withdraw from Laos and Cambodia." China had thus taken an enormous step forward toward the positions of the Cambodians, the Laotians, the British and the French. It was to implicitly admit, contrary to what had always been maintained by the Vietminh, that the latter really was an invader of these two states. It was also to admit that the cases of Laos and Cambodia were not identical with that of Vietnam. Further, Chou En-lai said he was prepared to recognize the legitimacy of the royal Laotian and Cambodian governments as soon as he was assured that no American bases would be established in these countries.[5]

China had indeed decided to turn its back on the national liberation struggles in Laos and Cambodia and instead to curry favor with the British and French governments. Obviously, Eden quickly passed the word around. On the afternoon of Chou En-lai's meeting with Anthony Eden (June 16), the delegations of the Kingdoms of Cambodia and Laos vigorously demanded the "total withdrawal" of Vietminh troops from their territories. Chou En-lai then made a six-point proposal which called for a cessation of hostilities in Laos and Cambodia at the same time as in Vietnam. It also proposed that the representatives of the "belligerent parties" (which meant the Vietminh and France and ignored the Khmer Issarak and Pathet Lao) should negotiate in Geneva the end of hostilities and that "separate negotiations would determine the categories and quantities of arms necessary for self-defence, which could be introduced into these countries." Joyaux notes that China had made considerable concessions since this meant:

> The arming of government troops which were already fighting against the Pathet Lao and Khmer Issarak guerillas and which in future might have to repulse any new Vietminh activities outside Vietnamese frontiers.[6]

In effect, it meant that Chou En-lai was conniving at breaking the revolutionary solidarity between the forces of the three peoples of Indochina and helping to create the conditions for the liquidation of the Pathet Lao and Khmer Issarak, as there was to be a total prohibition of new military personnel and arms of all kinds except for those necessary for the "self-defence" of France's client states. Joyaux remarks that Pham Van Dong "maintained with tenacity and rigidity" his position in defense of the Pathet Lao and Khmer Issarak.

> The logic of facts, he declared, demands that one recognizes the liberation movements in these two countries and refute the tendentious affirmations of those who would like to explain them by external influences. The Vietminh delegation hails with sympathy and respect these liberation movements, products of ferocious oppression, which have emerged from the depths of their peoples and which it is impossible to create artifically from abroad.[7]

Joyaux comments drily: "It was such a lively intervention that, in the context, one might well ask for whom it was really intended?"[8] Chou En-lai undoubtedly understood, but it did not inhibit him. The following day he told the discredited Bidault that:

> Vietnamese volunteers have indeed entered Laotian and Cambodian territory for military operations. For the most part they are no longer there but those who remain must withdraw.[9]

Concerning the famous Berne meeting, Joyaux relates that one of its surprises was that Chou En-lai, in his opening remarks, said he was "urging the Vietminh to become reconciled not only with France but also with the Vietnam of Bao Dai." Joyaux describes this as an "astonishingly new remark." He then gives a resumé of the reports on the meeting sent by Mendès-France the following day to the French embassies in London and Washington.

> He picked out five notable points. Firstly China had not sought the slightest compensation for the concessions which she had made regarding Laos and Cambodia. Secondly, Chou En-lai had not only

reaffirmed his agreement on the necessity for military discussions having precedence over those on political matters but still more — a point of capital importance — he declared for the first time that the political settlement could be stretched out over a relatively long period after the military settlement. Thirdly the head of the Chinese delegation agreed with the need to speed up the negotiations for the regroupment in Vietnam — Chou En-lai spoke of a period of about three weeks — indicating that the Vietminh also wanted to get rapid results. Fourthly, China had not raised either the question of recognition by France, or that of Taiwan or the United Nations. We [the French government–W.B.] hastened to inform Taipei of this. Finally, Chou En-lai had not sought to obtain any special favours from the new French government. In short, the head of Chinese diplomacy had in no way sought to exploit the political difficulties which France is going through.[10]

On the first three points the Chinese position was diametrically opposed to that of the Vietnamese and their Khmer and Laotian comrades-in-arms. They were being robbed of the possibility of exploiting their strong battlefield positions to get favorable political settlements. A speed-up of the regroupment procedures was to the benefit of the French because it enabled them to extricate their forces from untenable positions. Stretching out the political settlement — adjourning as long as possible the elections to reunify the country — was also in the French interest. So too was the insistence on cease-fire procedures, thus establishing a military settlement before the French were pinned down to specific political objectives without the means necessary to achieve them.

Mendès-France had pledged to resign if he did not obtain a cease-fire agreement by midnight on July 20. The closing session was fixed for 9:00 p.m. on the 20th. Journalists who waited in the Conference Press Center are not likely to forget that night. Nine p.m. approached; the hour sounded but there was no word from the conference hall. Minutes passed and turned into hours. Whiskey flowed in the bar and the clock hands advanced towards midnight. As the hour chimed out, several American journalists rushed to the phone booths to inform their papers and agencies that Mendès-France had lost his gamble and had no choice but to resign on the morrow. More hours passed. It was too late to catch the last editions of the London dailies. Most of the journalists left, many confident that an expanded war was on the immediate agenda for Indochina.

What was happening? Walter Bedell Smith, U.S. Under-Secretary of State for Foreign Affairs, had been left behind in Geneva by his immediate boss, John Foster Dulles, to do his best to prevent an agreement.[11] Bedell Smith had refused to take part in any of the final stages of the work, insisting however that all essential documents be brought to him at his hotel. He also intrigued with the delegates of the Kingdoms of Cambodia and Laos to create as many last-minute hitches as possible. Whatever the cost, prevent agreement by midnight of July 20! Perhaps in a fit of pique Mendès-France would throw in his hand and resign. It was a hope, reflected in the dispatches of many U.S. journalists and columnists (especially the Alsop brothers), which lingered in the minds of Bedell Smith and Dulles until the last moment.

Late on the afternoon of July 20 Sam Sary, "personal delegate of His Majesty King Norodom Sihanouk," hurled a potential wrecking device into the drafting machinery. Agreement had been reached between Eden, Molotov, Chou En-lai, and Mendès-France that the Associated States (Bao Dai-Vietnam and the Kingdoms of Cambodia and Laos) must not enter into any military alliances. Nor could any foreign military bases be established. The only exception to the latter provision was Laos, where France was allowed to retain two military training bases. Chou En-lai — with the experience of China's costly confrontation with the United States in Korea very fresh in his mind — was particularly insistent about blocking any loophole the United States might later be able to use to move into Indochina. Chou En-lai and Mendès-France had identical interests on this point, as did Pham Van Dong.

But France was caught in a trap of her own making. She had granted all the trappings of independence to Cambodia in November 1953. Sam Sary turned up at the 11th hour and 59th minute to assert that the Kingdom of Cambodia, an independent and sovereign state, could not accept any restrictions on her options regarding foreign alliances or on her right to permit even the United States to establish military bases on her territory.

It seems that this was an individual initiative by Sam Sary (who would later participate in a plot against Sihanouk and ally himself with the CIA-backed Son Ngoc Thanh, Sihanouk's bitterest enemy). The head of the Cambodian delegation, Tep Phan, had had a two-hour meeting with Chou En-lai earlier that day and had raised no such problem. As a device to beat the clock, the Sam Sary bombshell worked. But at a 2:00 a.m. meeting on July 21 Eden, Mendès-France, and Molotov — in the absence of Chou En-lai— agreed to include in the text a clause stating that "in the case of threats to its security" Cambodia would be authorized to establish foreign military bases on her territory. (This was something against which Sihanouk later fought with great tenacity.) In the interests of "symmetry," Mendès-France insisted that the same provision be made in respect to Laos. Pham Van Dong first learned of these two new measures to reinforce the potential encirclement of what had by then become North Vietnam at the closing session of the Conference at 3:30 p.m. on July 21.[12]

His brief speech at the closing session reflected his bitterness at having to accept decisions imposed by others, friends as well as adversaries. Journalists were not present at this (or any other) session but Joyaux summed up what occurred:

> Pham Van Dong contented himself with a phrase thanking the two co-presidents, but did not utter a single word of gratitude either toward the Soviet Union or toward China. Could this silence be interpreted otherwise than as a mark of Vietminh resentment toward its two allies, who although constituting solid supports during the negotiations, neverthless did not hesitate, when their national interests required it, to limit the ambitions of the Democratic Republic?[13]

On the evening of July 22 Pham Van Dong and other members of the DRV delegation went to a dinner hosted by Chou En-lai to "celebrate the success of the conference." They expected it to be a "celebration among comrades." To their astonishment the Soviet delegation had not been invited but the delegations from "Emperor" Bao Dai and the Kingdoms of Laos and Cambodia were there. Chou En-lai first toasted Emperor Bao Dai and then the monarchs of Laos and Cambodia. Pham Van Dong's senior aide (whom I have quoted earlier) told me:

> We could hardly believe our eyes and ears. Later we saw things more clearly. China wanted to have the countries of Indochina in her pocket and hoped that the three monarchies would be retained as

tributary states. The Emperor of Heaven reigning over the Middle Kingdom with his vassal states! China couldn't care less about the social content of those states or the fate of their revolutionary forces. With hindsight, what was to happen later with the Khmer Rouge in Cambodia and the Chinese invasion of Vietnam was clearly set forth by China's conduct at the Geneva Conference and especially the final dinner.

Chou En-lai had arranged things at the dinner so that the Cambodian and Laotian heads of delegations, Tep Phan and Phoui Sananikone respectively, were at one table with some of Chou En-lai's top aides. At the table presided over by Chou En-lai, Ngo Dinh Luyen (brother of Ngo Dinh Diem, whom the CIA had recently installed in power in Saigon) was seated between Pham Van Dong and Ta Quang Buu, the deputy defense minister of the DRV. Ngo Dinh Luyen and Ta Quang Buu had studied together in France and Chou En-lai did his best to get them to exchange reminiscences of their youth. At one point he suggested that Ngo Dinh Luyen should visit Peking. When the latter asked under what title, Chou En-lai replied: "Why don't you set up a Legation in Peking?" Noting Pham Van Dong's startled reaction, Chou En-lai remarked blandly that the fact that Pham Van Dong was closer to China ideologically did not preclude Saigon's diplomatic representation in Peking. "After all you're both Vietnamese and aren't we all Asiatics?" This was one more bitter pill that Pham Van Dong had to swallow at Geneva. The reason behind Chou En-lai's support for pushing the nationwide elections to unify the country back as far as possible became abundantly clear. China was more interested in extending her own influence in Saigon than in helping the Vietminh to achieve political victory and reunification of the country.[14]

Chester Ronning, who had been alternate head of the Canadian delegation to the Korean part of the Conference and had stayed on as an observer during the Indochina negotiations, noted that:

> It was the concessions Chou made and those he induced Ho Chi Minh to make that helped Mendès-France to reach agreements on Vietnam, Laos and Cambodia. Despite General Giap's victory over French military forces in Vietnam, Pham Van Dong made the most important concession when he accepted the temporary division of

Vietnam for a period of two years. That concession ultimately prevented reunification.[15]

The Canadian diplomat was almost right. In fact, the major concession made by Ho Chi Minh and Pham Van Dong was to agree to *attend* a Geneva Conference. Their forces were in a position of victory. Together with those of the Pathet Lao and Khmer Issarak, they could have ended the French military presence throughout the whole of Indochina. But this was not in line with what China perceived to be her interests in the area. As Joyaux expresses it, China had "a vision of a multiple Indochina in which Laos and Cambodia would counterbalance the weight of the Vietnamese world," a vision which "after the cease-fire became one of the constants of Chinese policy in Indochina."[16]

Joyaux, who has done a most impressive job of research not only into the day-by-day work of the Geneva Conference but also into its aftermath, finds the Chinese attitude at Geneva in keeping with traditional Chinese policy whether under imperial, republican, or socialist rule. It was totally divorced from any notions of proletarian internationalism or revolutionary solidarity. That these were simply non-factors cost the Vietnamese, Laotian, and Khmer peoples very dearly. Joyaux writes:

> Let us try to answer this question. Was Chinese policy towards Indochina in 1954 close to traditional Empire policy in the region?
>
> Among the most salient traits of the latter, one of the most striking was the permanent desire of China to preserve peace on its southern flank by striking a balance based on the multiple rivalries of the different states of the region. A *pax sinica* which would be a sort of cancelling out of the activities of the opposing forces. A policy very close to the old "divide and rule" which in its most elementary form was content to fight against any hegemony which would disturb the equilibrium and force direct intervention. To this end, the Empire paid continual attention to preserving harmony in its relations with the most powerful neighbor states and to maintaining direct relations, as many as possible, with the weaker ones....
>
> During the Geneva Conference, on at least three points, China checked Vietminh ambitions, in a way which clearly recalls classical policy. Firstly the June 16 proposal to disassociate the Laotian and Cambodian question from that of Vietnam which contributed, im-

mediately after the Dien Bien Phu victory, to reinforce the prestige of the royal governments of Vientiane and Phnom Penh and, at the same time, to ruin the hopes of the Vietminh to set up on the west and southwest flanks, revolutionary governments which would have been devoted to them. The same, on June 23 at Berne, in indicating to Mendès-France when he (Chou En-lai) said he would push the Democratic Republic of Vietnam to reconciliation with the Vietnam of Bao Dai and then on July 19, at Geneva, in proposing a delay of two years for Vietnamese nation-wide elections, Chou En-lai clearly indicated that China...saw no objection to the Vietminh being repressed in the south...Thus an Indochina unified by revolution as it had been by French colonialisation would give place to a multiple Indochina, symbolized by Chou En-lai's final dinner.[17]

On the day following the end of the Geneva Conference Pham Van Dong received a group of journalists in the garden of his villa headquarters at Versoix on the slopes leading down to Geneva's quietly beautiful Lake Leman. One of the questions we asked was whether the United States would succeed, as their spokesmen were already boasting, in turning Vietnam south of the 17th parallel into another Korea south of the 38th parallel and thus make the provisional military demarcation line one of permanent division. A smile lit up his somber, austere face.

The Americans came to Geneva with their plans and we with ours. They intended at first that there would be no Geneva Conference. Instead of a cease-fire they wanted an extended war with U.S. intervention as in Korea. But, as you witnessed, we have a cease-fire. And you will see, we will achieve the unity of our country.

As for reports that the United States was pouring in dollars to make the South a "paradise" so the people would not want unity, he replied proudly:

A people that had shed its blood so generously for unity and independence can not be bought with American dollars. No government can be maintained in the South — even with American aid — that stands openly against the unity of the country. The main tasks now are consolidation of the North to safeguard the peace and unification of Vietnam by free elections.[18]

His face grew somber again and with tears in his eyes he said slowly: "I don't know how we are going to explain all that has been decided here to our compatriots in the South." I reminded him of this twenty-six years later (in April 1980) and he replied:

> We could have obtained far, far more. We had reached agreement with the Chinese on everything beforehand. But Chou En-lai had his secret meeting with Mendès-France and it was all changed. If we had continued the war at that time, we would have won — there was everything to gain. One must say that the Chinese played an extremely dangerous role throughout the negotiations and betrayed us in a most ignoble manner.

It was a tribute to their discretion, responsibility, and sense of solidarity within the socialist camp — but also a criticism of their lack of public relations — that the Vietnamese leadership kept the secret of China's role at the Geneva Conference very much to themselves. Although I covered that conference, was based in Hanoi for several years to report on the implementation of the decisions reached, and had innumerable conversations with Ho Chi Minh, Pham Van Dong, Vo Nguyen Giap, and others, I had no inkling of what had been going on behind the scenes at Geneva until after China committed the ultimate betrayal by invading Vietnam!

That the Vietminh had made considerable sacrifices in accepting the Geneva Agreements was clear. But the impression conveyed by them was that the sacrifices were freely consented to in the interests of the general line of "peaceful co-existence" which prevailed in the socialist world at the time. Over a quarter of a century later Pham Van Dong's aide, in the course of briefing me on what really happened at Geneva, commented:

> We learned a great lesson through China's machinations. It is decisive in diplomatic negotiations to have things firmly in our own hands. Don't let others interfere! Negotiate only in our own interests. That is why at the Paris Conference — to the great indignation of the Chinese — we were firmly in control. We carried on the war and were capable of making the peace, or at least putting ourselves in a winning position in case there had to be another round on the battlefield.

> Everything that China and Nixon-Kissinger agreed in their Peking talks was aimed at dictating terms, to gain advantages from our battlefield victories. The Chinese people are our friends and always will

be. But their leaders exploited our blood for their own interests, using Vietnam-Chinese friendship for their own expansionist aims.

Because of the betrayals at Geneva, our struggle lasted another twenty years, but our military, political and diplomatic experiences proved one thing: One must be absolutely independent. This is a living reality touching our own flesh and blood.

Apart from other aspects of the Geneva Conference, it was a monumental exercise in hypocrisy. The French and their allies, who had never referred to the area as other than "Indochina," suddenly threw up their hands in horror when they discovered that the national liberation fighters also considered it as a single battlefield and that the single enemy against whom they were fighting were the French colonial masters of the "Associated States of Indochina." If this was not the reality, then why was there a Geneva Conference on Indochina?

One of the most sickening, hypocritical statements in this respect was made by Sir Anthony Eden, representing the power which had militarily and physically put the French back into Indochina after World War II. The following is an extract from Eden's Geneva Conference speech on 10 June 1954, in which he rejected both the right of the Khmer Issarak and Pathet Lao to take part in the Conference and that of Vietminh troops to be fighting on Laotian and Cambodian soil.

By race, religion, language and culture, the peoples of these two countries are essentially different to those of Vietnam. The Vietminh invaders have not only crossed a political frontier. They have crossed the frontier which separates the two great civilizations of Asia, that of India and that of China.[19]

Such an outstanding illustration of "one law for the rich, another for the poor" projected into international diplomacy would have attracted the attention of the press, except that Eden had taken measures in advance to cover up his tracks. He reveals that at the beginning of the Indochina part of the Conference, in a meeting with the acting head of the U.S. delegation, Walter Bedell Smith, and the French foreign minister, Georges Bidault, he had proposed:

that we should continue our talks in restricted sessions, consisting of the heads of all nine delegations with only two or three advisers apiece. *No account of the proceedings would be given to the press.* The proposal was agreed upon, and on the following day Molotov and Chou En-lai also accepted it. . . .The military situation might compel us to make concessions to the communists in Vietnam, and they wanted these to apply to Laos and Cambodia as well. We had at all costs to prevent this. The civil war in Vietnam on the one hand, and the direct invasion by the Vietminh of Laos and Cambodia on the other, could not be dealt with on the same basis.[20]

Thus the Western powers, with China's connivance, dismembered Indochina, abolished it even, at Geneva in the hope of exterminating the revolutionary forces in Laos and Cambodia and confining the Vietminh victory to the area north of the 17th parallel. This was a prefiguration of what China was to do in 1975, by trying to dissuade the Vietnamese from launching an offensive to unify their country. When the dissuasion failed and the offensive succeeded, China then backed the Khmer Rouge in their senseless military adventures against Vietnam and set up rival political organizations in Laos, muscled by Meo mercenaries inherited from the CIA, to try to overthrow the Pathet Lao government in order to "divide and rule" in the former states of Indochina.

The Geneva Agreement provided for the withdrawal of Vietminh forces from Cambodia. This inevitably meant that the main part of the Khmer Issarak forces, with which they were inextricably intertwined, had to leave also. Had they remained in Cambodia, they would have been impossibly vulnerable. During the 300 days in which the Vietminh forces and cadres withdrew to north of the 17th parallel and the French Expeditionary Force to south of the 17th parallel, the overwhelming majority of the Khmer Issarak forces and cadres also withdrew to North Vietnam.

---

1. The dimension and timing of the Dien Bien Phu victory, which sealed the fate of all French troops in the decisive northern part of Vietnam, was the supreme expression of Ho Chi Minh's doctrine that the only

criterion for measuring military activity is its political effect.

2. Lao Itsala and Pathet Lao are interchangeable terms.

3. Ronning, Chester, *A Memoir of Chinese Revolution*, p. 222. New York: Pantheon Books, 1974.

4. The government of Prime Minister Joseph Laniel and Foreign Minister Georges Bidault fell on 6 June 1954 following an adverse vote in the National Assembly over their handling of the Indochina question. A new government was formed on June 17, headed by Pierre Mendès-France. He promised to secure a cease-fire in Indochina by July 20 or resign. This fixing of a deadline by which a cease-fire should be achieved or the conference broken off was used as an added means of pressuring Pham Van Dong to make concessions in order to meet the deadline. The Chou En-lai-Mendès-France meeting took place at the French Embassy in Berne on the afternoon of June 23. It was there, according to the most highly placed Vietnamese sources, that the draft agreement was worked out without consultation with the Vietnamese delegation. Chou En-lai left Geneva the following day for New Delhi, Rangoon, and Peking, returning to Geneva on July 12. His tour included a meeting with Ho Chi Minh on the Chinese-Vietnamese frontier on July 5.

5. Joyaux, François, *La Chine et Le Règlement du premier Conflit d'Indochine, Genève* 1954, p. 227. Paris: Publication de la Sorbonne, 1979.

6. *Ibid.*, pp. 228-9.

7. *Ibid.*, p. 229.

8. *Ibid.*

9. *Ibid.*, p. 231.

10. *Ibid.*, pp. 240-1.

11. Secretary of State Dulles had angrily left the Conference one week after it started, having distinguished himself by refusing to shake the proffered hand of Chou En-lai. He was furious over his failure to transform the Korean part of the Conference into a recruiting ground for an internationalized war in Indochina.

12. Sihanouk fought hard against any attempt to partition his country by granting a separate regroupment zone for the Khmer Issarak, similar to that agreed upon for the Pathet Lao in Laos. It is virtually certain that Sam Sary acted not on instructions from Sihanouk but on an American (undoubtedly well-financed) initiative. Bedell Smith and his staff worked hard to buy up at least one each of the delegates from Laos and Cambodia. (For Vietnam this was not necessary because Prime Minister Ngo Dinh Diem was the United States' "own man" in Saigon, installed during the course of the Geneva Conference.) Phoui Sananikone, the Laotian Royal Government's Minister of Foreign Affairs allegedly was paid one million dollars

— into a Swiss account — not to sign the Geneva Agreement. The other delegate, Minister of Defense Kou Voravong, who *did* sign on behalf of Laos, was murdered in Phoui Sananikone's Vientiane home shortly after he charged this in the National Assembly. Kou Voravong also revealed that the Royal Government's army planned to attack the Pathet Lao forces from behind as they moved into their regroupment areas in Sam Neua and Phong Saly provinces!

13. Joyaux, *La Chine et Le Règlement du premier Conflit d'Indochine*, p. 295.

14. Joyaux reports (*Ibid.*, p. 297) that Ngo Dinh Luyen relayed the idea to his brother, but it was turned down.

15. Ronning, *A Memoir of Chinese Revolution*, pp. 240-1.

16. Joyaux, *La Chine et Le Règlement du premier Conflit d'Indochine*, p. 324.

17. *Ibid.*, pp. 357-8.

18. Burchett, Wilfred, *North of the 17th Parallel*, pp. 102-3. Hanoi: Published by the author, 1955.

19. *Ibid.*, pp. 215-6.

20. Eden, Anthony, *The Full Circle*, p. 118. London: Cassell, 1960 (emphasis added).

BACKGROUND TO THE TRAGEDY OF KAMPUCHEA

4.
THE RISE OF THE
KHMER ROUGE, PART I

The rise, rule, and fall of the Khmer Rouge is bound to be a subject of controversy among historians, political and social scientists, ideologists, Asia watchers, and others for decades to come. The question of questions is how such monstrous aberrations of human behavior and revolutionary morality as Pol Pot, Ieng Sary, and their handful of family members[1] and followers could have risen to the top and implemented their genocidal policies. The mountains of skulls and bones still being uncovered in all corners of Kampuchea silently scream for an answer. That answer is also demanded by millions of people throughout the world.

There is no simple explanation. Most of those who knew what went on in the inner circles of power and who disagreed were eliminated. Those who won out are loath to explain their indefensible methods and motives. Combined with the paucity of documents and the often contradictory nature of those that do exist, the lack of testimony from those who participated in the ruling elite of the Khmer Rouge makes it extremely difficult to piece together a complete explanation of what happened. However, the investigations that have occurred so far have clarified some of the points that are key to understanding the contradictions which led to the betrayal of the revolutionary movement in Kampuchea by a part of the leadership of that movement.

The Khmer Rouge never was a monolithic organization. In fact, the term "Khmer Rouge" was invented by Sihanouk to designate the extreme left-wing opposition in Cambodia. As distinct from the term "Vietminh" in the anti-French resistance war — an abbreviated form of Fatherland Front under whose banner the national liberation struggle was being waged — "Khmer Rouge" was a label stuck on by one outside the movement. It has been applied to the veterans of the Indochina Communist Party and to the students who came to be known as the "Paris Group," as well as to the followers of both groups. The differing experiences and perspectives of the veterans and the Paris Group resulted in ongoing and fundamental disagreements concerning the goals and tactics of the movement. This was true even within the Paris Group, but the differences there were fewer and mostly on the tactical level. As the struggle intensified, the Pol Pot faction of the Paris Group increasingly dealt with disagreements by simply murdering those who opposed it theoretically and organizationally.

One point on which most observers agree is that the revolutionary movement was born under very particular circumstances whose roots reached back to the Kingdom of Cambodia itself. When the French started their colonization of Cambodia by establishing a "protectorate" in 1863, they grafted a colonialist system onto an absolute monarchy. Democratic movements had little chance of birth and if they did see the light of day their "infant mortality rate" was almost total. If the monarchy did not strangle them, the new colonialist rulers certainly did. There was no intelligentsia of any importance, and Buddhist bonzes represented the only, very limited intellectual infrastructure.

Despite the passive, nonviolent Buddhist philosophy, the bonzes played a militant, vanguard role in opposing the colonialists, partly because the latter imported with them an alien — Catholic — religion. Although individual Buddhist leaders displayed great heroism and were supported sporadically by the lesser clergy and Buddhist masses, they could not supply the ideological base for protracted armed struggle against a modern colonial power. Nevertheless, historians would do well to note that the Buddhist clergy in Cambodia, as well as in Vietnam and Laos, played an important patriotic role — many making great sacrifices — in the struggle against both French and American invaders.[2]

When she gained her independence — whether one situates this in November 1953 when the French accorded at least nominal independence to Sihanouk or in July 1954 when Cambodian independence was written into international law at Geneva — Cambodia was a semi-feudal state. Although slavery had been officially abolished, vestiges of it remained.[3] And the situation of at least part of the Cambodian peasantry was much the same as it had been when a French bureaucrat described it in 1939.

> The blows of fate catch him disarmed; sickness, death and calamities make him prey to the Chinese usurers. From then on he struggles hard, working more and more land in the vain hope of wiping out a debt that usury is ceaselessly swelling. His harvests are automatically confiscated, his family goes into slavery, beginning with the youngest and the females, and the day comes when despite all his sacrifices, he is brutally dispossessed of his property by his creditors. There is nothing left for him to do but go and live off a relative whom luck has made better off, or enter religious life.[4]

How to carry on a revolutionary struggle in the absence of both a bourgeoisie and a working class was an obvious problem for the leadership of the Indochina Communist Party, which had assigned itself the task of helping the Cambodians to build up their own revolutionary organizations and their own Communist Party. In a conversation in Hanoi in May 1980 Vietnamese historian and publicist Nguyen Khac Vien summed up the situation for me.

> The national liberation struggle developed in an atmosphere of ideological confusion compounded of nationalist, traditionalist and some modern views. There was no clear, unified viewpoint. The only unambiguous element was that of solidarity with the Vietnamese in the anticolonial struggle. In so far as the cross-border solidarity developed, the situation was clarified. To the extent that struggle and solidarity weakened, the situation inside Cambodia slipped back into confusion. Sihanouk reflected that confusion. For a long period, he was ambivalent and vacillating, without a clear view of what he himself wanted.

> At times he was a paternalistic despot, at others a patriotic nationalist, and sometimes he combined both roles. His patriotic tendency pushed him into a pro-Vietnamese position in the struggle against the United States. His despotic side resulted in his stifling democratic elements, who could have been his allies. In this way the Khmer people were directed toward confusion again and the clarity gained during the anti-French struggle became clouded. In that anticolonialist struggle, the solidarity of the three countries of Indochina represented a rupture with the feudal-nationalist past, but the

momentum was later lost. This was a factor facilitating the rise of those who later became known as the Khmer Rouge, themselves a product of the ideological confusion noted earlier.

The role of the veteran Communists and of the Khmer Issarak guerrilla forces in Cambodia prior to the Geneva Conference has already been discussed. During the years that the anti-French national liberation struggle was being waged most intensely, most of the future Khmer Rouge leaders were students in Paris.

The first to arrive, in 1946, was Keng Vannsak, who was later to become the mentor of Ieng Sary and Pol Pot. The son "of a typical, servile mandarin in the pay of French colonialism," as he described himself to me over thirty years later, Keng Vannsak studied at the prestigious Saint Cloud "Ecole Normale Superieure" (Higher Teachers' Training College) in the outskirts of Paris and then went on as a Cambodian language expert to the even more prestigious School for African and Oriental Studies in London.[5] On returning to Paris Keng Vannsak became one of a three-member "political committee" of a Marxist study circle of Cambodian students who started arriving in Paris from 1949 onwards. They included Ros Samaoun, Thiounn Mumm, Hou Youn, Po-hung Pon, May Phath, Mey Nann, Sieng An, Ieng Sary, Toch Phoenn, and Saloth Sar. With Keng Vannsak in the "political committee" were Ieng Sary and Saloth Sar (who confided only to his French girlfriend that his real name was Pol Pot).

Many of these students started out as idealistic patriots, pledged to dedicating their talents and rare facilities of access to modern revolutionary theories — through their studies in Paris — to remolding Cambodian society to serve the interests of the under-privileged, especially the peasantry. With their abundant statistics and other documentation, the students were able to prove that although there were virtually no direct landlord-tenant relation-ships — as in Vietnam, China, and most other parts of Asia — the peasantry was nonetheless exploited and often driven into bank-ruptcy and off their land by merchants and moneylenders. In the process of winning masters' and doctors' degrees, some of the left-ist Cambodian students — especially Khieu Samphan, Hu Nim, and Hou Youn — produced the first in-depth studies of the Cambodian economic-social system and the prospects for change. But one cannot always be certain whether that which the future Khmer Rouge leaders wrote in their theses in Paris was based on their practical research or on their theoretical studies. The least one can say is that such postulations as the following, extracted from the thesis by Hou Youn, foreshadowed the policies they later applied.

> We can compare the establishment of commercial organizations in the colonial period to a large spider's web covering all of Kampuchea. If we consider the peasants and consumers as flies or mosquitoes which get trapped in the web, we can see that the peasants and consumers are prey to the merchants, the spider which spins the web. The commercial system, the selling and exchanging of agricultural production in our country, suppresses production and squeezes the rural areas dry and tasteless, permanently maintaining them in their poverty. What we habitually call "cities" or "market towns" are pumps which drain away the vitality of the rural areas. Any type of goods that the cities and market towns provide for the rural areas are just bait. The large rural areas feed the cities and market towns. The cities — the market towns with their fresh and up-to-date appearance — live at the expense of the rural areas — they ride on their shoulders....

> Those who work the land, ploughing, harvesting, enduring the entire burden of nature, under the sun and in the rain, getting gnarled fingers and cracked skin on their hands and feet, receive only 26 percent as their share...whereas the others, who work in the shade, using nothing but their money, receive a share of up to 74 per cent...The rural areas are poor, skinny and miserable because of the commercial system which oppresses them. The tree grows in the rural areas, but the fruit goes to the towns.[6]

The doctoral theses written at the Sorbonne in Paris by Hou Youn and Khieu Samphan both deal extensively with the direct and indirect exploitation of the Cambodian peasantry. Khieu Samphan insisted that the continuing backward state of Cambodian structures after independence was due to the conditions of Cambodia's "integration into the international economic systems" (essentially those of France and the United States) which inhibited — or even made impossible — any escape from the country's "semi-colonial and semi-feudal" socio-economic structures. In his argument for an autonomous, even autarchic, economic development one can see the seeds of the concepts which led the Khmer Rouge to isolate themselves almost completely from the rest of the world (except China) once they had seized state power.

> To accept international integration is to accept a mechanism by which the structural imbalance will be aggravated, an aggravation which could end in a violent explosion, seeing that it cannot fail to become insupportable for an ever greater part of the population. Indeed, the latter is already aware of the contradictions which lock up the integration of the economy within the international market of goods and capital.

> A conscious and autonomous development is thus objectively necessary.[7]

With hindsight, one can detect what Khieu Samphan felt should happen to Cambodia's feudal and nascent capitalist classes. What he wrote in his thesis turns out to be a fairly accurate, if understated, description of what did happen under Khmer Rouge rule.

> In our opinion, the essential measures to be taken more closely resemble a political and social programme proposing to destroy the former pre-capitalist economic relations and to set up a homogeneous national capitalist system, rather than a technical programme for mobilising financial means.

> Let our proposal be well understood....

> We do not propose to do away with the classes which possess the major part of the revenues. The structural reform which we propose does not intend to eliminate the contributive capacity of these groups. We consider that one can and should try instead to release their contributive potential in trying to transform these landlords, these middlemen traders, these moneylenders into a class of agricultural or industrial producers. We will thus try to divert them from unproductive activities and get them to participate in production. In the towns, we will try to promote a movement of reconversion of capital from the commercial sector, at present in a state of atrophy, towards directly productive sectors....

> But to carry out such a thorough-going transformation we must not be content with isolated measures. At least at the beginning, a complete set of very severe measures appears to us as absolutely essential. And among these measures, in first place, must be those which concern relations with the outside world. Without an adequate solution for relations from abroad, we do not believe that one can validly speak of structural reform and autonomous development....[8]

Among the first to return from Paris was Saloth Sar (who wasn't known by his real name, Pol Pot, until the 1960s). Returning with a small group of students in 1953, he linked up with the Democratic Party, a middle-of-the-road group of intellectuals headed by Prince Kanthoul, a progressive cousin of Sihanouk. With Saloth Sar was Khieu Ponnary, who became a member of the Democratic Party's Executive Committee and whom he later married. Not long after the group's return, Saloth Sar and a heterogeneous collection of opposition elements from right, left, and center were invited by Sihanouk to form a government. This was one of Sihanouk's moves to discredit the opposition before they could consolidate. It also foreshadowed his strategy of persuading all existing parties to dissolve and integrate with his own Sangkum (Popular Socialist Community), which was to gain 100 percent of the seats in the 1955 elections mandated by the Geneva Agreements. Saloth Sar interpreted the invitation as a first move to suppress the left and took off for the jungle.

There, in Kompong Cham province, was situated the headquarters of the embryo Khmer Communist Party, later known as the Pracheachon (People's Revolutionary) Party. Arriving in Kompong Cham, Saloth Sar and a few other returned students revealed that they had been members of the French Communist Party before leaving France and now wanted to join the Khmer Communist Party.

In accordance with the decisions of the February 1951 Congress of the Indochina Communist Party that three separate parties would be formed and that the Vietnamese party would help the comrades from Laos and Cambodia to form their own parties, Pham Van Ba, a Vietnamese, was in charge of organizational work in Kompong Cham. (Later Pham Van Ba was to become the representative of the Provisional Revolutionary Government of South Vietnam in Paris. And still later he was Vietnam's ambassador to Pol Pot's Khmer Rouge government in Phnom Penh!) Pham Van Ba later told me:

> In case of applications for membership in those days, we always had to check with the French Party when applicants claimed membership there. The risk of infiltration by French agents was very great. But confirmation from the French Party meant automatic membership in the Khmer Party without further formalities. In due course, word

came back that they had all been members of the Khmer language section of the Communist Party of France. In those days the French Party grouped foreign members, according to their native languages. Later we got further word from the CPF to the effect that the "Paris Group" were all influenced by Trotskyist and other ultra-leftist theories.' By that time Saloth Sar had been assigned to the Mass Propganda Section, under my leadership.

The formation of the Pracheachon Party was a long process because of the difficult wartime conditions. Separation from the Indochina Communist Party at the base was the first step, which often meant withdrawing local-born Vietnamese to make the new party really Cambodian. Next the separation was made at the district levels. But it was only after the battle of Dien Bien Phu that a provisional Central Committee at the national level could be formed.

Pol Pot's first task was to make a detailed study of conditions in the countryside to define different forms of exploitation, the state of mind of the peasantry, and relations between peasants and workers, all in order to develop a correct line in the future party program. Pham Van Ba described Pol Pot as a young man "of average ability but with a clear desire for power and short-cut means of getting to the top." He played no important part in the resistance struggle. After he completed his research and analysis, he was sent to study at a school for party cadres. "Later, he was clearly upset at not being among those named to the Central Committee."

After agreement was reached at Geneva to regroup the Vietminh and Khmer Issarak fighting forces to North Vietnam, a mixed commission of French and Vietnamese officers was set up to supervise the redeployment of these forces. A certain number of Khmer Issarak cadres and Communists were left behind to carry on clandestine work. Saloth Sar was thus assigned to the Phnom Penh area, as a member of the Pracheachon Party's municipal committee, to organize students for revolutionary activities. There is little doubt that he used this position to recruit a nucleus of students around which to build his own faction within the party.

More of the Paris Group returned to Cambodia. Basing themselves on the 1951 decision to form a separate Khmer Communist Party, they agitated for the formation of a party which would sever all ties with the former Khmer section of the Indochina

Communist Party and renounce further relations with the Vietnamese Lao Dong Party. Because most of the veteran Khmer revolutionary leaders — especially those who understood the need for rice-roots' democracy and the connection between national and international policies — had been regrouped to North Vietnam, the Paris Group was able to take over the leadership of the revolutionary movement. Had there been in Cambodia a revolutionary organization as strong as that left behind by the Vietminh in South Vietnam, the returnees from Paris would have been integrated into it and realistic policies based on the concrete objective situation would have emerged.

In fact, the Paris Group despised the veterans of the former Indochina Communist Party, considering them to be "country bumpkins" with little theoretical knowledge. The veterans believed the Paris Group to be totally ignorant of conditions inside Cambodia and equipped only with apt phrases from Marx and Lenin. Friction arose between the two groups from the first encounters.

One of the first and major differences between the Paris Group and the veterans was over whether Sihanouk or U.S. imperialism was the greatest danger. "Sihanouk," argued Pol Pot and Ieng Sary; "U.S. imperialism," said the veterans. This argument lasted until 18 March 1970!

Much later, historian Nguyen Khac Vien — today one of Vietnam's most esteemed scholars — said of the Khmer Rouge:

> Their greatest error was to regard Cambodia as if it was in a vacuum — isolated in its own territory. Had Ho Chi Minh thought like this, we would never have united with the Laotian and Kampuchean resistance forces in the struggle against the French colonialists and the Japanese militarists. The Paris Group did not see Kampuchea's struggle in relation to the major confrontation with U.S. imperialism, but rather in isolation from it....

> In true revolutions, either the notions of nationalism and internationalism are fused or the revolution turns into some mystical sort of nationalism, divorced from the true interests of the people.

While Pol Pot and Ieng Sary were consolidating their following in the clandestine section of the Pracheachon Party, Khieu Samphan, Hou Youn, and Hu Nim completed their studies in Paris and returned to Phnom Penh to pursue careers in teaching and government service. Upon returning from Paris, Khieu Samphan and Hou Youn were appointed to the Faculty of Law and Economic Sciences at Phnom Penh University. Among their pupils was Nguyen Huu Phuoc, a Cambodian-born Vietnamese, who later became tutor in mathematics to my son, Peter, and who managed to escape to Paris in time to avoid the anti-Vietnamese extermination campaigns. What were his impressions of the two future Khmer Rouge leaders?

> As professors they both taught from the prescribed textbooks. The two were always together. Khieu Samphan had a gentler aspect than Hou Youn, but in fact he was much tougher. In private conversations, they both insisted that the future society must be based on the peasant masses and that all other classes must be eliminated. I had many conversations with Khieu Samphan, apart from the faculty lectures. He was more adamant than Hou Youn about the need to start the new society from zero, basing it on the peasant masses. "They are the pure," he kept repeating. "Everything in the old society must go. We must return to nature, based on the peasantry." Such ideas were a constant in all conversations with Khieu Samphan. But he also believed in the role of selected intellectuals, saying that they were best qualified to rule the country and to charter a shortcut to social and economic progress. Pol Pot and Ieng Sary were against this and were afraid of capitalist contamination by the spreading of such ideas.

Between 1958 and 1963 Khieu Samphan, Hu Nim, and Hou Youn all served in Sihanouk's government. Hou Youn was in the Ministry of Commerce and Industry from April to July 1958, in the Budget Office from July 1958 to February 1959, in the Planning Ministry from February to June 1959, and in the Ministry of Public Health from June 1959 to April 1960. He was recalled to the Finance Ministry from August to October 1962 and from there was transferred to the Planning Ministry until February 1963. His active, professional life under Sihanouk lasted almost five years. In contrast, his professional and physical life, before he opened his veins with a broken metal spoon at the Tuol Sleng torture-extermination center, was less than two years! Khieu Samphan served Sihanouk as Secretary of State for Commerce in 1962-63 while Hu Nim, who was later tortured to death at Tuol Sleng by his Khmer Rouge colleagues, put his French legal training to use as the head of various departments and ministries.

In Phnom Penh Pol Pot's accession to a leadership post in the Pracheachon Party was facilitated by the disappearance of the secretary of the party's clandestine section, Tousameuth, in 1962 while on a visit to his family. At the time there was speculation over whether he had been killed by Sihanouk's secret police or in a "settlement of accounts" within the Pracheachon Party itself. According to Sihanouk, Tousameuth was murdered by the Pol Pot-Ieng Sary faction in order to ensure Pol Pot's rise to the party leadership.[10]

Pol Pot and his faction took advantage of Tousameuth's disappearance to call for an "extraordinary congress" to elect a new party secretary. Due to the clandestine conditions under which the party operated, it was extremely difficult to convoke a full congress and hold normal sessions. Thus, those taking part were mainly from the Phnom Penh area and Pol Pot was elected party secretary.

The year 1963 began with student unrest, the promotion of which was a specialty of Pol Pot and his fellow-teacher and brother-in-law, Ieng Sary. In Siem Reap demonstrations took a particularly violent form, Sihanouk overreacted and purged his administration of its left-wing, pro-Pracheachon elements. Thus, Khieu Samphan was dismissed from his post as Secretary of State for Commerce and Hou Youn from his post as Secretary of State for Economic Planning. Pol Pot and Ieng Sary interpreted this as an ominous form of "writing on the wall" and left, together with some other intellectuals, for the jungle. Of this period Sihanouk later wrote:

> It was at this time, in 1963, that Lon Nol began compiling dossiers with "proof" that the left was plotting my overthrow. I cannot say that I have proof that the CIA was directly or indirectly involved in this attempt of Lon Nol to mislead me. It is reasonable to assume, however, that having been so thoroughly exposed in 1963, the Agency would not be averse to rigging something up against the left.

> In any case, false accusations and fabricated evidence were the order of the day, and Lon Nol used this as a pretext for one of his periodic witch hunts against the left, which included the summary execution of suspects at the moment of arrest. The result was that the first wave of intellectuals and others, including several hundred from Phnom Penh, left the cities for the former resistance bases.[11]

By this time the national liberation struggle was being waged with great intensity across the border in South Vietnam. It was the stage of "special war" in which the United States supplied military "advisors," arms of all categories, transport, air support — everything short of actual troops. It was a period when Sihanouk, as Head of State, was taking a more and more openly hostile position towards U.S. intervention in the area. As a result he was the object of numerous attempted coups and assassinations which were part of a U.S. plan to replace him with a CIA-backed puppet. These attempts were a part of the process which led to Lon Nol's coup in 1970. Among Lon Nol's chief co-plotters in 1970 were Sirik Matak, Long Boret, and Yem Sambour, all of whom had been involved in anti-Sihanouk plots in 1963.

Pol Pot used his position as secretary of the underground Khmer Communist Party to step up his campaign for armed struggle against Sihanouk while Lon Nol and the CIA were intensifying their efforts to do exactly the same thing. The line of the Paris Group continued to provoke major dissension within the party and was a serious bone of contention between Pol Pot's faction, dominant within the party's leadership, and the Vietnamese Lao Dong Party.

It was no accident that Pol Pot and Lon Nol would pursue the same goal. After many months of investigations in the frontier areas and more than four months in Kampuchea in 1981 Ben Kiernan, an Australian Khmer-speaking specialist on Kampuchean affairs, and Chanthou Boua, his Khmer wife, concluded that:

> Pol Pot's nationalist perspective is also a traditionalist one, comparable to Lon Nol's...who spelled out his hopes of "reuniting" the Khmers in Kampuchea, Thailand and Vietnam, the Chams in Kampuchea and Vietnam, the hill tribes in Kampuchea and Southern Vietnam and even the Mons in Thailand and Burma.[12]

Pol Pot and Lon Nol both wanted to restore the ancient Angkor Empire, but in Pol Pot's empire only racially "pure" Khmers and those politically pure by his standards would survive.

> In 1963 [write Kiernan and Boua] Pol Pot and Ieng Sary had secretly fled Phnom Penh for the tribal northeast, and probably spent much of the next five years there. As well as being National Secretary of the CPK, Pol Pot was also Party Secretary of the Northeast Zone from 1968 to 1970, during a period when some of the Zone's tribes rose up

in rebellion against the Sihanouk regime. At least during May 1970, at a time when Pol Pot was abroad (in Peking) both Ieng Sary and Son Sen were "responsible for the Northeast Zone." In July 1975, Pol Pot said that his movement "came out of the jungle" and the "remote" rural areas. In 1978, he told Yugoslav journalists that he knew "perfectly well these national minorities" and regarded them as among his strongest supporters.[13]

Obviously, there was nothing wrong with organizing the hill tribes (or "Montagnards" as they were commonly called). Ho Chi Minh did the same thing. But he organized them primarily for their own self-emancipation and not to be used as shock troops conditioned and indoctrinated to exterminate city-dwellers. The Vietnamese revolutionaries had confidence in the people — whether hill tribes in the border areas, peasants in the Mekong Delta or on the coastal plains, or workers and other city-dwellers — and built their activities upon this base of support.[14] An important element of the Kampuchean tragedy was that those who won out in the murderous power struggle at the top not only had never sought to sink organizational roots among the people but also had a profound contempt for them.

1. As the purges within the Khmer Rouge leadership continued spiraling upwards and some of the most illustrious members of the Paris Group were exterminated, power became concentrated in the hands of seven people. In the first government formed after the spurious "elections" alleged to have been held on 30 March 1976, Khieu Samphan succeeded Norodom Sihanouk as Head of State. Pol Pot became Prime Minister, and Ieng Sary became Deputy Prime Minister and Minister of Foreign Affairs. Khieu Thirith, the wife of Ieng Sary, was named Minister of Social Affairs. She later succeeded Hu Nim — after his death by torture — as Minister of Information and Propaganda. Khieu Ponnary, Khieu Thirith's sister and Pol Pot's wife, was President of the Kampuchean Women's Association. The Khieu sisters were both Paris-educated, and Khieu Thirith held a degree in English literature. Son Sen, who became Minister of Defense, had trained as a teacher in Paris in the 1950s and for a brief period had been in a

leading position at the Phnom Penh Teachers' Training College. His wife, Yun Yat, became Minister of Education and Culture. Pol Pot was also Secretary of the Khmer Communist Party and Chairman of its Military Affairs Committee. Pol Pot, Ieng Sary, and Son Sen were the three most important members of the Paris Group to flee Phnom Penh in 1963.

2. See Chapter 2, footnote 3 for more information on the patriotic, progressive role of the bonzes.

3. Evidence of the survival of forms of slavery well into the 1950s, documented mainly from French sources, is presented in the book *Peasants and Politics in Kampuchea, 1942-1979* by Ben Kiernan and Chanthou Boua (London: Zed Press, in press).

4. Kiernan, Ben and Boua, Chanthou, *Peasants and Politics in Kampuchea, 1942-79.*

5. The background to Keng Vannsak's chance to study in Paris is so relevant to the whole history of Cambodia and even to the mental attitude of the Khmer Rouge leaders that it deserves a few lines. In 1900 Sihanouk's grandfather King Norodom had sent his son and heir Prince Yukanthor to Paris to plead for a little more respect for his own and his country's dignity. The result was a warrant issued for Yukanthor's arrest. He made a last-minute escape to England and eventually went to Siam, where he died thirty-four years later without ever again setting foot on his native soil. (It was because of Yukanthor's exile that his younger brother Sisowath "loyal to all things French" was placed on the throne.) Prince Yukanthor's elder sister Princess Yukanthor Ping Pos was appointed Minister of Education by the French. She arranged for her impeccably respectable nephew, Keng Vannsak, to go to Paris.

6. Hou Youn, "La Paysannerie du Cambodge" ("The Cambodian Peasantry"). Paris: The Sorbonne, 1955. Having grown up in an agricultural community in Australia, dependent on the seemingly upredictable whims of city markets and marketeers for what we received for our butter and potatoes and other produce while "they" fixed the prices that "we" had to pay for seed, fertilizers, ploughshares, and any other manufactured goods, I know how easy it is to whip up antagonisms between a rural community and urban dwellers. The "city slickers" were our natural enemies, if one judged from the conversation of the "cow cockies" — as dairy farmers were then called in Australia — around the cattle pens on market days. If there happened to be an industrial strike going on, there would be mutterings from the World War I veterans: "Give me my old machine gun company. We'd stick the ringleaders up against a wall and the strike would be over in thirty seconds flat!" But I never heard, even from the most reactionary of our farmer-neighbors, suggestions that Melbourne (our nearest big city and when I was a lad, before Canberra was built, the Australian

federal capital) should be abandoned and its citizens transformed into slaves!

7. Khieu Samphan, "L'Economie du Cambodge et les Problèmes de l'Industrialisation" ("Cambodia's Economy and Problems of Industrialisation"), p. 100. Paris: The Sorbonne, 1959.

8. *Ibid.*, pp. 113-4.

9. In Paris in 1980 Keng Vannsak told me that the members of the Paris Group were all strongly "Stalinist" in those days.

10. *Prince Sihanouk on Cambodia*. Interviews and Talks with Prince Norodom Sihanouk, Number 110, p. 7. Peter Schier and Manola Schier-Oum in collaboration with Waldraut Jarke. Hamburg: Mitteilungen des Instituts für Asienkunde, 1980.

11. Sihanouk, Norodom, and Burchett, Wilfred, *My War With the CIA*, pp. 117-8. New York: Pantheon Books, 1972.

12. Kiernan, Ben, and Boua, Chanthou, *Peasants and Politics in Kampuchea, 1942-79*. London: Zed Press, 1981 (in press).

13. *Ibid.*

14. Pol Pot, Ieng Sary, and Son Sen fled to the jungle of northeastern Kampuchea to save their skins. When pursuit by Sihanouk's security forces became "too hot," they had the possibility — of which they often took advantage — of seeking sanctuary with the NLF guerrillas of South Vietnam. In contrast, the NLF maintained its forward military base for the whole of South Vietnam and its military headquarters for the Saigon area on the east and west banks of the Saigon River respectively, less than twenty miles from the center of the South Vietnamese capital. Huynh Tan Phat, the NLF General Secretary and later the Prime Minister of the Provisional Revolutionary Government, maintained his base in and around Saigon throughout the war. And Huynh Van Tam, who headed the NLF's clandestine trade union movement, set up his headquarters — to direct the seizure of key public utilities and other enterprises on the eve of Saigon's liberation — in the basement of the headquarters of his arch enemy, Tran Quoc Buu, the gangster head of South Vietnam's official trade union movement.

5.
THE RISE OF THE
KHMER ROUGE, PART II

In 1967 Khieu Samphan, Hou Youn, and Hu Nim disappeared after being publicly accused by Sihanouk of having inspired a peasant rebellion in Battambang. At the time it was rumored that Sihanouk had had them all killed. Actually, they had fled to the jungle to join the anti-Sihanouk guerrilla forces. By the time the Khmer Rouge seized power in 1975 Khieu Samphan, in particular, had degenerated from one of Cambodia's outstanding progressive intellectuals into a fascist. In his doctoral thesis Khieu Samphan had favored the development of a national bourgeoisie and evolution to a more equitable society by the creation of Cambodia's own capitalist class to develop its resources as an interim stage preceding the creation of a socialist society. Why did he later champion the ultra-radical policies of leaping over any and all intermediate steps in an attempt to attain "instant communism"?

One theory is that Khieu Samphan's brief experience as Secretary for Commerce in 1962-63 convinced him that revolutionary methods — including armed struggle to overthrow the Sihanouk regime and the physical liquidation of the parasitical middle class — were the only way to save the country.

Another is that the seizure of power by Lon Nol and Sirik Matak — the latter Sihanouk's cousin and life-long dynastic rival as well as a champion of the most corrupt elements of the Cambodian comprador business community — greatly accelerated the nefarious consequences of "international integration," against which Khieu Samphan had so strenuously warned. This is a point to which William Shawcross draws attention in his important and wonderfully well-researched book "Sideshow: Kissinger, Nixon and the Destruction of Cambodia."

From the beginning of 1971 until April 1975 (and in some ways, beyond), United States aid was the dominant factor in almost every aspect of political, economic and military affairs in Cambodia. Since the Doctrine demanded a pretense that the United States was not involving itself in the affairs of this small country, economic aid, like military, was handed over with few strings attached. Embassy officials with "low profiles" watched as the money they provided destroyed the will of the recipients.

The initial grants were to help Cambodia import commodities that had previously been financed by its exports. Despite the stagnation of the economy under Sihanouk, in 1969 exports of rice, rubber, and corn had brought in $90 million; a sizable portion of the Gross National Product of $450 million. By the end of 1970, the government was spending five times its revenue and earning nothing abroad. . . .

As more economic aid was invested in Cambodia every year, the economy deteriorated. One can glance at the consumer price index for food; the figures are the government's and are perhaps slightly exaggerated, but not greatly. From the base of 100 representing 1949 prices, the index had risen to 348 in March 1970, the last month of Sihanouk's rule. By the end of 1970 the index was 523; by the end of 1971, 828; by the end of 1972, 1,095; by the end of 1973, 3,907; and by the end of 1974, 11,052.[1]

What greater confirmation could there be of Khieu Samphan's analysis of over a decade earlier? Events dramatically justified his prophecies and must have raised his standing in the eyes of the Paris Group, especially those of its most radical elements. Then there were the American B-52 bombings which destroyed much of Cambodia's existing social and economic structures. Shawcross carefully documents the frightful escalation of the bombings from the top-secret "Operation Breakfast"[2] on 18 March 1969, along the Cambodian side of the frontier with Vietnam, to the holocaust bombings in the first half of 1973.

Over the next fourteen months 3,630 B-52 raids were flown against suspected Communist bases along different areas of Cambodia's border. Breakfast was followed by "Lunch," Lunch by "Snack," Snack by "Dinner," Dinner by "Dessert," Dessert by "Supper," as the program expanded to cover one "sanctuary" after another. Collectively, the operation was known as "Menu."[3]

Most of these raids took place before Sihanouk was overthrown and the United States officially entered the war on the side of Lon Nol. After that the whole territory of Cambodia became the target of the giant U.S. bombers, not to mention the fast-expanding South Vietnamese Air Force. The raids increased in intensity after the January 1973 agreement to end the war in Vietnam had been signed in Paris and U.S. air operations over Vietnam were halted. They reached their paroxysm in the six months preceding the cut-off date of 15 August 1973 imposed on Nixon and Kissinger by the U.S. Congress.

> The White House ignored its agreement with Congress that the intensity of the bombing during the last forty-five days not be increased. In June, 5,064 tactical sorties were flown over Cambodia; in July this was raised to 5,818; and in the first half of August, 3,072 raids were flown. In those forty-five days, the tactical bombing increased by 21 percent. The B-52 bombings also increased, though those planes were already almost fully committed. By August 15, when the last American planes dropped their cargoes, the total tonnage dropped since Operation Breakfast was 539,129. Almost half of these bombs, 257,465 tons, had fallen in the last six months. (During the Second World War 160,000 tons were dropped on Japan.) On Air Force maps of Cambodia thousands of square miles of densely populated, fertile areas are marked black from the inundation.[4]

On top of all this was the obsession of the Khmer Rouge with the Chinese Cultural Revolution: having the peasants "re-educate" the intellectuals; putting the peasantry — theoretically at least — on the top rungs of Chinese society; hounding down and massacring veteran party cadres and even the formerly well-tolerated national bourgeoisie. Those like Pol Pot and Son Sen, who took study courses in Peking at the height of the Cultural Revolution, received a strong injection of anti-Vietnamese propaganda, which they passed on to their fellow leaders. It was Khieu Samphan, often described as a "moderate," who was the most bloodthirsty when it came to the question of relations with the Vietnamese or with the Khmer veterans "contaminated" by having fought side-by-side with the Vietnamese against the French. Vandy Kaonn, a Paris-educated doctor of sociology and professor of philosophy, now a member of the Central Committee of the Khmer United Front of National Salvation, gave me the following analysis of Khieu Samphan's degeneration:

When Khieu Samphan returned from Paris, the leftist movement — whose members believed that Cambodia had to change its structure to solve the country's problem — was greatly reinforced. But within the government, he tried to resolve economic problems by radical solutions which, given the realities of the situation, were "leftist utopian." So he soon found himself out of the government.

With the Lon Nol coup and U.S. intervention, the destruction of existing structures was accelerated and Khieu Samphan started to look around for new ideas, new solutions. He looked to China. He already had adopted the Maoist line that revolution had to be led by the peasantry. China took advantage of much confused thinking at that time among the Khmer Rouge leadership to impose its own line on the revolutionary movement, which included destroying the plans of veteran revolutionaries who wanted to take the path of scientific socialism. This was a determinant factor in the later policy of genocide. You don't argue with the opposition; you exterminate it, down to its deepest roots!

When Sihanouk set up the resistance government in Peking, Khieu Samphan was named Minister of Defence and Commander-In-Chief of the Armed Forces. In fact he was a figurehead. It was Pol Pot who was in charge of military affairs from the beginning. But Khieu Samphan remained supreme as the ideologist. Ieng Sary was the executant and chief liaison officer with Peking and Hanoi. There are plenty of documents now available to prove without any doubt that Pol Pot and the Khmer Rouge leadership were under Peking's tutelage.

If the Chinese had wanted a more prestigious leader they would have chosen Khieu Samphan rather than Pol Pot, but Pol Pot was a Chinese robot, never a Cambodian patriot.

As the anti-Lon Nol struggle went on Khieu Samphan began to integrate new notions into his philosophy. To his basic idea that man is good but has been corrupted by civilization, that the more "civilization" is expressed by an industrialized society, the more man is corrupted, he acquired another much more dangerous one, that of dictatorship by a small, intellectual elite. Education he also considered to be a source of corruption for the masses. Only a very simple social system was necessary in order to remain "pure" and preserve one's sanity. "The more man is educated the more deceitful he becomes" became one of his favorite sayings.

An elite will do the thinking, the masses will do the work — the more they work, the less time they will have for futile thinking. It is quite clear that Khieu Samphan inherited such ideas from the old emperors and the doctrine of the supreme authority of leaders. The Emperor is closest to heaven and thus knows all! The people only need to work — and obey! People and soil, sun and water, that is all that is necessary for a pure tranquil existence. In a sense Khieu Samphan practised what he preached. He led a very simple life and worked in the fields in the days when he was a deputy to the National Assembly. After the Khmer Rouge took over, he rode a bicycle while Pol Pot, Ieng Sary and other leaders had chauffeur-driven Mercedes.

By 1970, when Khieu Samphan, Hou Youn, and Hu Nim resurfaced in response to Sihanouk's call to join his anti-Lon Nol National United Front of Kampuchea (FUNK), there were three distinct factions within the Khmer Rouge.

1) The chauvinistic, ultra-nationalist, and racist group headed by Pol Pot, Ieng Sary, Son Sen, their wives, and Khieu Samphan wanted to carve out Kampuchea's own original "communist" society, not patterned on Soviet, Chinese, Vietnamese, or any other models. They were inspired and strongly influenced by "Maoism" and by the Chinese Cultural Revolution. However, there is evidence that, while fawning on Chinese leaders and depending heavily on their material support, Pol Pot secretly despised them.

2) A group headed by Hu Nim, Hou Youn, Phouk Chhay, and Til Ov fought for applying the model of the Chinese Cultural Revolution to Kampuchean conditions.

3) A group headed by So Phim, Pen Sovan, Keo Moni, Chou Chet, and others favored building a socialist Kampuchea by following the Vietnamese model. This group was comprised mainly of veterans of the Khmer faction of the former Indochina Communist Party and those who supported their internationalist positions.

Each of the three groups had its own bases and power centers: Pol Pot initially in the northeast among the "Montagnard" tribespeople; Hu Nim in the south and southwest in the Elephant and Cardamom Mountains; and So Phim in the densely populated eastern provinces between the Mekong River and the frontier with Vietnam. Only the third group kept to the agreement reached with Sihanouk in Peking to unite in a common armed struggle against the Lon Nol regime. The first two groups set about destroying Sihanouk's nationalist forces and those of the third group.

The groups led by Pol Pot and Hu Nim still considered Sihanouk — and not U.S. imperialism — to be the main enemy of the Kampuchean revolution. They believed that the struggle in their country must be perceived in isolation from the overall conflict in Indochina and the world struggle against U.S. imperialism. But Pol Pot could not tolerate even the degree of deviation which the Hu Nim-Hou Youn enthusiasm for the Chinese Cultural Revolution implied. Perhaps he feared that the Hu Nim group would win out in the battle for Chinese favors.[5]

Most of the leaders of So Phim's "Eastern Zone" group were later killed, mainly after abortive military uprisings against Pol Pot. The few that survived include Heng Samrin who, although not one of the veterans of the Indochina Communist Party, was an enthusiastic militant in the anti-Pol Pot "Eastern Zone" group. Another of the group's members, Pen Sovan, was one of the few original veterans to survive the reign of the Khmer Rouge. Following the elections to a National Assembly on 1 May 1981, Heng Samrin became Chairman of the State Council and Pen Sovan became Prime Minister. Pen Sovan has also emerged as the General Secretary of the revived Pracheachon (People's Revolutionary or Communist) Party.

Among the most difficult knots to unravel in the Kampuchean tragedy are the contradictions between the various factions of the Khmer Rouge. Some of the basic documents (of which there are very few) relevant to the unraveling process are: (a) a history of the Khmer Communist Party published in the Eastern Zone in 1973, (b) a long report given by Pol Pot on 22 July 1975 when the armed forces of the various resistance zones were handed over to the Central Committee of the Khmer Communist Party, and (c) the "Black Paper," published in September 1978, which set forth Pol Pot's version of the history of the KCP and its relations with Vietnam.

From a comparison of the Eastern Zone party history with the other two documents emerges a fact of enormous significance. A careful study of these documents reveals a fundamental conflict between internationalism and nationalism. However, this conflict is often obscured because Pol Pot and his champions abroad con-

The "Black Paper" is the Khmer Rouge's most thorough attempt to prove this "Vietnamese domination." It is also the most complete synthesis of the ideology of the Khmer Rouge leadership available to the outside world. The form and content of the "Black Paper" explain the savagery with which they liquidated the veteran Khmer members of the former Indochina Communist Party and then those within the Khmer Rouge leadership itself who questioned the wisdom and expediency — and perhaps even the morality — of this.

Under the heading "The use of the banner of revolution to take possession of territories," one finds the Khmer Rouge version of the Vietminh contribution to the defeat of French colonialism. As "Vietnamese — Enemy Number One" it lumps together Vietnamese feudal rulers, the Vietminh and "Vietcong," Kampuchea's comrades-in-arms against French colonialism and American imperialism, and the various Saigon puppet regimes against which both Vietminh and "Vietcong" valiantly battled.

From 1946 to 1954, under the cover of "revolutionary solidarity" against French colonialism, the Vietnamese sought for taking possession of the Kampuchea's territory. Under the banner of revolution, the Vietnamese came in Kampuchea and settled up cells of the Indochinese Communist Party in order to grasp the Kampuchea's people. They organized a party, an army and a State power. They used this expedient in order to try to take possession of Kampuchea....

At that time, the Khmers who waged the struggle in Kampuchea had not an independent position. They were totally relying on the Vietnamese. They did not well understand for whom and for what they were making revolution. That is why the Vietnamese could easily enter into Kampuchea. They divided Kampuchea into zones: East zone, Southwest zone and Northwest zone. They could install there whoever they wanted to. They did everything at their place and acted at their will....

The Kampuchea's people, being victims of the acts of aggression and annexation of the Vietnamese and having successively lost an important part of their Kampuchea Krom's territory, foster a deep national hatred against the Vietnamese aggressors, annexationists and swallowers of Kampuchea's territory. The Kampuchea's people are perfectly aware of the Vietnamese treacherous acts, subterfuges and hypocrisy. They have always seethed with a deep rancour.[6]

In this passage the Vietnamese are referred to as "Youns" and a footnote explains that "Youn is a name given by the Kampuchea's people to the Vietnamese since the epoch of Angkor and it means 'savage.' The words 'Vietnam' and 'Vietnamese' are very recent and not often used by the Kampuchea's people."[7]

In May 1980 I asked Nguyen Khac Vien for his views about "traditional hostility" as an explanation for the Khmer Rouge aggressiveness toward Vietnam. He replied:

Among all peoples who have fought wars with each other, there are vestiges of "traditional hostility." Reactionary elements today lay emphasis on cultural differences and historical, feudal quarrels. Progressives stress traditions of solidarity in anti-colonialist struggles. The test as to who is reactionary and who progressive is the attitude they take on this question.

Our problem with the Kampuchea of the Khmer Rouge was not one between two socialist countries, as it is usually presented in the West, but one with forces which had turned into false revolutionaries, false Communists.

Behind the madness of Pol Pot was the deliberate policy of Peking to use him as an instrument first to outflank, then to conquer Vietnam. Without Pol Pot's madness and megalomania, Peking could not have created an anti-Vietnamese Kampuchea! There are historical precedents for the exploitation of such madmen. Hitler was a lunatic, but the Ruhr industrial magnates made good use of his madness to further their own schemes of world domination!

This image of "traditional hostility" which the Khmer Rouge have so assiduously propagated was very different from the impressions I gathered — and published at the time — in my meetings with veteran Khmer revolutionaries during my first visit to Cambodia in 1956. One of the main centers of resistance activity against the French had been in Kompong Cham province among the workers at the Chup rubber plantation, the second largest in the world. As I wrote at that time:

In Phnom Penh, I was fortunate enough to find an old Khmer Issarak cadre who had helped organize at Chup and we had a talk together with some more old plantation hands: "They (the French) counted on dividing us from the Vietnamese," one old worker chuckled as we discussed the resistance days. "But they didn't realize that when men work together and suffer together and die together, race doesn't count. They called the Vietnamese (who worked on the plantations as indentured laborers) the Vietminh and used to watch them closely. But as for us Cambodians, they didn't bother us so much. So we used to do the contact work. We formed a secret trade union and branches of Khmer Issarak all over the plantations....[8]

He went on to talk about the first strike that had ever taken place on the plantation and how the French management was forced to capitulate after three days, despite their efforts to split the office and factory workers from the plantation hands.

"It was a great moment for us," the old worker continued. "It was something new. Nothing of the kind had ever been known before, not even by the oldest worker. Those who had given their rice to the Issarak cadres were especially happy. We saw how right they had been when they stressed the importance of unity and not letting the French divide Cambodians and Vietnamese, and that if we were united we would surely win."[9]

The authors of the "Black Paper" and their immediate chief, Ieng Sary, could perhaps be pardoned for being personally ignorant of what transpired during the anti-French war. At that time they were busy studying Marxist, Maoist, Trotskyist, Titoist, anarchist, and other theories in Paris. But later, in the late 1950s and early 1960s, they had every facility to discover that the close unity which had developed among the revolutionary forces of the three peoples of Indochina was the decisive factor in their common victory.

In their work "Peasants and Politics in Kampuchea, 1942-79" Ben Kiernan and Chanthou Boua compare the Eastern Zone party history with the boastful claims of Pol Pot. First, from the party history:

The conditions for the formation of the Party in our country were not different in principle from those of the revolutions which formed the world's Marxist-Leninist parties. To the best of our knowledge of France, England, the USSR, China, Vietnam et cetera, all followed the same principle of revolution, that is the people's revolutionary movement; and the people are the workers (in the industrial countries) or farmers (in the underdeveloped agricultural countries).

The formation of the Party was certainly according to Marx and Engels' "Declaration of the Communist Party," Lenin's disciples'

Party, the Great October Socialist Revolution, China's People's Democratic Revolution, and revolution throughout the world.[10]

In his marathon speech before some 3,000 revolutionary army delegates on 22 July 1975 Pol Pot claimed:

> We have won a total, definitive and clear victory, meaning that we have won it without any foreign connection or involvement.

> We dared to wage a struggle on a stand completely different from that of world revolution. The world revolution carried out the struggle with all kinds of massive support, material, economic and financial, from outside world forces. As for us, we have waged our revolutionary struggle basically on the principles of independence, sovereignty and self-reliance... In the entire world, ever since the advent of revolutionary war and the birth of U.S. imperialism, no country, no people and no army has been able to drive the imperialists out to the last man and score total victory over them in the way we have.[11]

This was, of course, nonsense. The decisive battles against the Lon Nol regime were won by Vietnamese forces whose intervention was expressly requested by the Khmer Rouge.[12] The most that Pol Pot could legitimately claim was that he had crushed his rivals, starting with the Sihanoukist and Vietnamese-trained forces and ending with those of his own Khmer Rouge comrades who turned from allies into enemies, without the use of outside forces. In blunter terms, while the Eastern and to a certain extent the Southwestern commands cooperated in defeating the Lon Nol and U.S.-Saigon forces, the Pol Pot faction within the Khmer Rouge concentrated its military and political efforts on eliminating its perceived and potential rivals.

Kiernan and Boua also point out the differing assessments of the 1954 Geneva Conference by Pol Pot, the Eastern Zone group, and even Hou Youn of the pro-Cultural Revolution group. Pol Pot and his faction characterized the Geneva Conference as a "sell-out by the Vietnamese" wherein Communist gains — to which the Pol Pot faction had not made the slightest contribution — "vanished into thin air." Pol Pot regarded this as typical Vietnamese "treachery." In the Eastern Zone's party history the results of the Conference were described quite differently.

A victory over the French imperialists and their lackeys...(won) with the Party and people of Vietnam, Laos and those of the entire world, as a result of which the Kampuchean Party was able "to force the feudal, bourgeois and reactionary class, the landowners, to follow a policy of neutrality."[13]

At a meeting in May 1972 Hou Youn, who perhaps felt it necessary to justify the Chinese role at the Geneva Conference, is quoted as stating:

The socialist powers of Europe, bloodied by the Second World War, and the Asian socialists, much weakened by the Chinese and Korean wars, overestimated the strength of the imperialists at that moment and pressured the all-consuming (sic!) Indochinese revolutionary forces to end the fighting and accept the peace treaty with the imperialist forces.[14]

This was a much more perceptive evaluation of the Geneva Conference than the crude Pol Pot allegation of a deliberate Vietnamese "sell-out" of Kampuchea. Kiernan and Boua quote an ear-witness of the Hou Youn statement as saying that he "clearly recognized that the Vietnamese revolutionaries suffered as much from it (the Geneva Agreement) as the Kampucheans." The "sufferings" of the Vietnamese were aggravated because of their vigorous defense of Kampuchean and Laotian interests. While it can be reasonably argued that the Vietnamese knew that in defending Kampuchean and Laotian interests they were also defending their own, the interrelation of such interests is something which was totally ignored by Pol Pot and his accomplices. In essence, it was this difference between a national and an international outlook which later led Pol Pot step-by-step along the road to racism and genocide.

In a paragraph dealing with the start of armed struggle in South Vietnam against the Ngo Dinh Diem regime in 1959-60, the authors of the "Black Paper" note that revolutionary cadres from South Vietnam infiltrated into Kampuchea in search of support. This was quite correct, but the support was sought essentially from among the 600,000 or so ethnic Vietnamese living in Kampuchea. According to the "Black Paper,"

Their slogans were "solidarity among the three countries! Kampuchea, Laos and Vietnam are inseparable sworn friends fighting against the common enemy.'' The Kampuchea's people and revolution believed that they were sincere. Actually, the Vietnamese used these slogans in order to cover their activities of division and sabotage and to infiltrate in the Kampuchea's revolutionary movement. They worked up the friendship of the Kampuchea's cadres and population to afterwards introduce them in their organizations. They organized those who had carried out the struggle against the French colonialists and reinstate them in the Indochinese Communist Party.[15]

Then follows a footnote, remarkable for the brevity with which it dismisses an event of capital importance in Indochina's revolutionary history.

The Indochinese Communist Party was dissolved in 1951, but only in a formal way. In fact, this party continues to exist. At the moment of official dissolution of the Indochinese Communist Party, the Vietnamese have created one party for each country. But in Kampuchea, the ''Revolutionary People's Party (Pracheachon) existed only by name.[16]

This is a monumental piece of nonsense! The Indochina Communist Party was indeed dissolved at Ho Chi Minh's initiative after it had become clear that French colonialism would be defeated and its concept of a single administrative unit of ''Indochina'' was doomed to collapse. As had been provided for at the founding of the Indochina Communist Party twenty years earlier, at the appropriate moment that party was replaced by separate parties for Vietnam, Cambodia, and Laos. Any independent researcher into the political developments in those three countries during that period would agree that separate parties — camouflaged as ''fronts'' for very legitimate revolutionary reasons — were indeed formed with Vietnamese help. And who was better qualified than the Vietnamese to help in the struggle against a common enemy, a struggle bound to endure for years and perhaps decades. Kampuchean and Laotian revolutionaries certainly recognized that, confronted with a common enemy — at that time French colonialism — they needed common and coordinated strategies.

The ''Black Paper'' account of Vietnamese help, at the critical period when U.S. imperialism was trying to take over from the

French colonialists in the former states of Indochina, is qualified as follows:

> Through their contacts, the Vietnamese tried to see whether there was unity or not with the armed struggle policy of the Communist Party of Kampuchea. They dragged towards them all those who had no firm position. They secretly organized and set up a parallel State power. They attacked and ran down the Communist Party of Kampuchea by saying that its policy was wrong, leftist, adventurous etc. To the Kampuchean nationals who studied in North Vietnam, they handed out: "Leftism, infantile disease of Communism" (sic!) by Lenin. They intensified their attacks against the Communist Party of Kampuchea when the armed struggle in Kampuchea was broken out in 1968. At the same time, they established contacts at the administrative zones' level in order to spread discord and division within the Communist Party of Kampuchea. At the same time, they sabotaged the Kampuchea's economy. On the one hand, they took to smuggling through black market and on the other hand, they stole food from the population: farm products, pigs, poultry, etc.

> All these experiences were very bitter to the Kampuchea's people and revolution. From 1965, the struggle between the Kampuchea's revolutionaries and the Vietcongs became very arduous and keen. The Vietnamese came to Kampuchea not only to seek refuges, but also to work for annexing and swallowing her. Although they were in the most difficult situation, the Vietnamese continued to everywhere prepare their strategic forces to overthrow the Kampuchea's revolutionary power at the prospicious (sic!) moment.

> In the Northeastern part of Kampuchea, the Vietnamese had difficulties in carrying on their strategy because of the presence of the leadership of the Communist Party of Kampuchea.[17]

Based on my own experiences between 1965 and 1968 — deep inside the NFL's Liberated Zones, in areas of battle with the U.S.-Saigon forces, and while residing inside Kampuchea during those years — I can expose this "Black Paper" account as total rubbish. It was the year 1965 in which (in February) the United States started its systematic bombing of North Vietnam and (in March) started committing its combat troops to the war in South Vietnam. To believe that, at this climactic moment of confrontation with the mightiest of the imperialist powers, Vietnamese energies would have been diverted to overthrow some non-existent "revolutionary power" in Kampuchea is to stretch the imagination to its absurdist limits. The idea would not even be worthy of mention had it not been swallowed and regurgitated by some prestigious champions of the "left" in the Western world.

Furthermore, the reference to Vietnam's difficulties in the Northeastern part of Kampuchea, "because of the presence of the leadership of the Communist Party of Kampuchea" is a lie, apparently intended to place on the record that it was in the Northeast that Pol Pot had regrouped the survivors of his abortive insurrection against Sihanouk. Based on their very extensive research on the subject Kiernan and Boua conclude:

> The elimination of key party leaders at various points in the 1960s and 1970s, in circumstances for which the victims appear to have been totally unprepared, also was a means of advancing the position of the Pol Pot group. The secrecy of the group's operations is illustrated by the fact that Ieng Sary, in a private 1973 discussion with Kampuchean cadres and representatives of the revolution based in Europe said that there was no Communist Party active in Kampuchea. (This may also be related to the group's failure, up to that point, to win full control of the Party, which undoubtedly existed.)

> On a much wider scale, it is difficult to make sense of the ruthless brutality of the Pol Pot armed forces without supposing that this is how they have been trained to establish their authority and that it was the only way to implement their programs.

> It is clear that there were significant strains within the Communist Party of Kampuchea as early as the mid-1960s, and that vast gulfs of ideology and tactics separated many of its leaders. But then, how did they manage to work together for so long, as part of the same movement?

> Part of the answer is that to a large extent they did not. The Party was small (particularly in the 1960s) and many of its members were in North Vietnam or China, while others were members of autonomous guerilla groups, scattered throughout the countryside.[18]

In conversations with Ok Sakun and Dr. In Sakon, the chief and deputy-chief respectively of the GRUNK (Royal Government of National Union of Kampuchea) Information Bureau in Paris (1970-75), I was assured that no Communist Party existed inside Kampuchea and that — as I published at the time — attempts to establish a Soviet-oriented party had failed. I and other enquirers were assured that the Khmer Rouge had identified themselves entirely with the FUNK-GRUNK resistance movement. This was also stressed repeatedly at meetings in Peking with personalities such as the brothers Thiounn Prasith and Thiounn Mumm — later to appear as pillars of the Khmer Rouge regime — and at various encounters I had with Ieng Sary in Peking and at several international conferences.

The last of these encounters was a meeting over the breakfast table at a Non-Aligned summit meeting in Algiers in September 1973. "We will always keep Sihanouk as Head of State," said Ieng Sary on that occasion, leaving me to ponder over who constituted the "we" empowered to make such decisions. To my circumspect enquiry about this, he smiled blandly and said: "The true revolutionary forces and the Kampuchean people." Fair enough! (The inability to perform as a lie detector is one of the occupational hazards of a journalist.)

With top secrecy the order of the day in the conspiratorial business of party-building in Kampuchea, it was very difficult to know what was going on, even from a grandstand seat in Phnom Penh in the 1960s. And with the world's greatest drama working up to a climax on the other side of the frontier, factional strife among fledgling Kampuchean revolutionaries hardly seemed important.

Kiernan and Boua refer to the factional struggles, which were certainly ominous shadows of things to come.

> Some (of the leaders) were prepared to compromise more than others for the sake of internal unity, probably to their own eventual detriment. The following sad passage is one of the great ironies in the Party history, written in 1973, the year in which the internal purges by the Pol Pot group began in earnest, directed against the tendency which included the document's authors. (They were all subsequently executed.)

> "Disunity on the political point of view, with the personnel divided into partisan groups, should be a cause for alarm, and is a danger for the Party. These problems cause anxiety and suffering because instead of attacking the enemy outside, we are offering our own flesh as prey for the enemy....

> "During the period from 1960 to 1967 in its history, the Party

successfully confronted numerous and serious obstacles to building internal unity in all areas. Doing so is the Party's principal achievement."[19]

Kiernan and Boua comment: "This is the period in which Pol Pot achieved the position of Party leader." There is little further documentation on this. Of those able — and willing — to relate what happened, only a very few survived the terror and genocide which Pol Pot and his faction of the Khmer Rouge then proceeded to inflict upon the people of Kampuchea.

---

1. Shawcross, William, *Sideshow: Kissinger, Nixon and the Destruction of Cambodia*, pp. 220-1. New York: Simon & Schuster, 1979.

2. The first sixty B-52 strikes were given the code name "Breakfast" because the decision to carry them out — kept secret from the U.S. Congress and even key administration officials for months — was made at a cloak-and-dagger breakfast meeting at the Pentagon a few days before the first strike took place.

3. Shawcross, *Sideshow: Kissinger, Nixon and the Destruction of Cambodia*, p. 28.

4. *Ibid.*, pp. 296-7.

5. The fortunes of the first two groups closely followed the ups and downs of Teng Hsiao-ping in his wrangle with the "Gang of Four." The fall of the latter inevitably led to the execution of Hu Nim and his closest associates.

6. *Black Paper: Facts & Evidences of the Acts of Aggression and Annexation of Vietnam Against Kampuchea*. Phnom Penh: Department of Press and Information of the Ministry of Foreign Affairs of Democratic Kampuchea, September 1978 (quoted in English from the original version released by the Khmer Rouge).

7. *Ibid.*, pp. 12-13.

8. Burchett, Wilfred, *Mekong Upstream*, pp. 107-8. Berlin: Seven Seas Books, 1959.

9. *Ibid.*

10. *Summary of Annotated Party History*, edited in 1973 by the military and political service of the Eastern Military Zone of the Khmer Rouge.

Quoted in: Kiernan, Ben, and Boua, Chanthou, *Peasants and Politics in Kampuchea, 1942-79*. London: Zed Press, in press.

11. Kiernan and Boua, *Peasants and Politics in Kampuchea, 1942-79.*

12. See Chapter 10 for details of Vietnamese military assistance to the Khmer Rouge.

13. Kiernan and Boua, *Peasants and Politics in Kampuchea, 1942-79.*

14. *Ibid.*

15. *Black Paper*, p. 25.

16. *Ibid.*

17. *Ibid.*, pp. 25-26.

18. Kiernan and Boua, *Peasants and Politics in Kampuchea, 1942-79.*

19. *Ibid.*

INSIDE KAMPUCHEA, 1975-1979

6.
THE TESTIMONY
OF THE SURVIVORS

Ask any Kampuchean child to draw a sketch of life as he or she remembered it under the Khmer Rouge. More likely than not, the sketch will be dominated by a black-clad young man whipping someone at a work site or clubbing someone to death on the edge of a mass grave. Such were the most frequent images portrayed by the many people I interviewed in the refugee camps on the Vietnamese side of the Kampuchean frontier in December 1978 and during my five visits to Kampuchea between May 1979 and March 1981. It was also the image evoked by the scores of witnesses at the genocide trial held in Phnom Penh in August 1979.[1]

The testimony of a former state pharmacist, Pen Boun Piv, was typical. He had to abandon his home and belongings in Phnom Penh immediately after the Khmer Rouge takeover.

> My wife, with our ten-months-old baby in her arms, and my parents despite their advanced age set out with considerable sadness and trepidation, heading toward an unknown destination, an unknowable future. Altogether we were eight family members.

He enumerated the various places they were ordered to settle in for a few weeks or months and take up whatever work was allocated to them. In general, they worked ten to thirteen hours daily for less than four ounces of rice per day per person. "We tried to supplement the ration with edible leaves, snails and crabs." Within four months after leaving Phnom Penh, his parents-in-law and his younger sister had died of starvation, all in August 1975. The following month the remaining family members were transported to a remote village in Battambang province.

> The work was insupportable. I was forced to produce natural manure — a mixture of human and animal excreta. My wife had to work on building dykes, my smaller brothers and sisters on building dams.

> Then I was yoked to a cart for transporting paddy. Later, with five other companions, under the whips, threats and strict surveillance of the Angkar guards, I was yoked to a plough to till the soil in the rainy season of June, 1976. This was despite the abundance of domestic animals — oxen and buffalo — in the village. Despite the heavy nature of the work, all we got was a bowl of soup in which swam a few grains of rice — a ration of one kilogram for a hundred persons.

Pen Boun Piv named the other five members of his ploughing team. He was the only one to survive. Three, including two young women, died in October 1976; the other two, a schoolteacher and a male nurse, died the following month. The reasons? "Extreme physical exhaustion, starvation and lack of medical treatment." In the case of the schoolteacher and the male nurse, the cause of death was "physical extermination because they complained that to continue hauling the ploughs had become impossible." Pen Boun Piv attributed his own survival to the fact that he was "docile and did not complain" even when he had to do supplementary work of "burying the village dead by day and night." After the ploughing season was over, he was set to work as a carpenter, a lumberjack, a boatman, and a fieldhand.

> Despite my physical weakness, the Polpotists forced me to work until one day I collapsed in the field.

> To survive we were obliged to eat rats, grasshoppers, lizards, toads, centipedes, earth worms... The population of the village of Ta Amp was about 4,000 when we arrived, but by the time we were liberated, it was reduced to about 1,000 — by starvation and overwork — and the survivors were in an atrocious condition.

Among those attending the genocide trial at which Pen Boun Piv testified was a first cousin of Prince Norodom Sihanouk, Princess Savethong Sisowath Monipong. With twenty-four members of her family she, like all Phnom Penh residents, was forced to abandon her home on 17 April 1975. She too related the horror and brutality of the evacuation.

Family members who happened to be separated were given no chance to join up. Instead, they were ordered to go their separate ways from wherever they happened to be when the loudspeaker vans came by. The sick and those who could not keep up had to be abandoned by the roadside with whatever food or water could be spared. They were propped up under trees for a last few hours of shade, and the lucky ones got a mosquito net or a coat to cover them as family members were urged on by blows from rifle butts.

After weeks of trudging by foot, Princess Lola (as she was popularly known to my family when we resided in Phnom Penh) and her family group were assigned to a malarious area between Battambang — Kampuchea's second largest city, north of Phnom Penh — and the frontier with Thailand. By the time they arrived at their assigned village, the hunt was on for former members of the royal family as well as for anyone who had served the Lon Nol and Sihanouk regimes. All were to be exterminated together with their families from the youngest babe to the oldest grandparents. "Some villagers recognized me but they didn't betray me," said Princess Lola.

> My husband was a doctor and with malaria soon raging among the evacuees, he started giving what relief he could. The local Khmer Rouge noticed his skills; at first they were pleased and took him to treat their own sick and wounded. Then the campaign started to exterminate intellectuals and the local Khmer Rouge knew he must be a doctor. One night they came and said the Angkar Leu (Higher Organization)[2] needed him. They led him off. I followed from a distance with our baby in my arms and my elder daughter holding my hand. They took him to a small clearing where a hole had been dug, and started to tie a cloth over his eyes. He shouted that this was "not necessary." My daughter rushed towards him shouting: "Papa, papa." A soldier hit her over the head with the butt of his rifle, then shot my husband. He fell but was still moving so they shot him again in the head. My daughter died a few days later.

Of the twenty-four members of her family who quit Phnom Penh on 17 April 1975 Princess Lola returned nearly four years later with just her youngest son. Her three other children and the rest of the family had all been killed or had died of illness and starvation.

In May 1980 I met her again in Phnom Penh. The tragedy had disappeared from her face. She had remarried — again a doctor — and had adopted three orphan victims of the Khmer Rouge terror. She had an important post at the Ministry of Foreign Affairs. "Don't address me as Princess," she said. "Those of us who survived have been made equal and united by our suffering. Just Lola in the future."

Among those who gave eloquent testimony at the genocide trial was a Frenchwoman, Denise Affonço, who was born in Phnom Penh and had married a Vietnamese of Chinese origin. At the time the Khmer Rouge entered Phnom Penh, she was working in the Cultural Section of the French Embassy. Extracts of her testimony were as follows:

> On Monday, 17 April 1975, I started off for the Embassy to check up on the situation. But I'd just got into the car when I heard firing from all sides. It was the Khmer Rouge entering the city and announcing their arrival by shooting off their guns. My idiot of a husband, always an enthusiast, went to welcome and applaud them in the streets. Everybody went crazy with joy, yelling: *"Cheyo Yotheas! Cheyo Yotheas!"* (Long Live the Troops of Liberation!) I'll never forget that word *"Cheyo,"* because after we'd been liberated from the so-called slavery of Lon Nol, we were again imprisoned and suffered for three years a more atrocious slavery.
>
> A few hours after their arrival, the *Yotheas* went from house to house demanding that the Phnom Penh population evacuate the city. *Angkar* (the Organization) begged us to leave our "home" for a few days, just time enough to restore order. Several times I tried to get through to the French Embassy, but it was impossible. All roads to the north were blocked, nobody was authorised to pass and the population was ordered to head south. I was thus obliged to do the same. We — that means my husband, my two children, myself, my sister-in-law and her four children — took our baggage full of clothing, and everything we had in the way of foodstuffs (rice, saumur, dried fish, milk, cans of sardines, coffee, tea, sugar, etc.) in the car and left the house on April 18, heading south.
>
> I was scared the moment we got into the streets and, seeing the spectacle offered to my eyes, I cried like a child. Everything was deserted; pharmacies, grocery shops, second-hand shops, the cold-drinks factory, all were systematically pillaged. These places had been well

locked up by their owners before leaving. It was the *Yotheas* who were the first to break in to take whatever they fancied. After they had finished it was a free-for-all. Streets were blocked off; people walked with difficulty due to the heat, bowed down under the weight of their baggage. Who had ever seen anything like that? To empty an entire city of two or three million people — allegedly to put things in order.

The testimony of Denise Affonço is a rare one because she and her family did not leave on the 17th as was ordered. Certainly, with her husband's confidence in the Khmer Rouge, they had no idea they were risking their lives by not leaving on the day the orders were given. She explained that the attitude of the Khmer Rouge soldiers varied greatly: some shared their food and perhaps even a bottle of alcohol while others were cold and brutal.

Several times during the first days on the road they were stopped and searched. At one such halt:

They confiscated everything printed in foreign languages, school books, magazines, identity cards, birth certificates, radios, recorder tapes and wrist watches. I showed my passport and made them understand that I was French. Nothing to be done, they confiscated my passport and said that there were no more French, Chinese or Vietnamese — only Khmers. Once the confiscations were over, they ordered us to continue further south where the Angkar expected us.

Later, as they continued south, they were stopped and given some instructions for their future behavior. Only the Khmer language must be spoken and if anyone was not fluent, he or she must immediately set about learning the language. When they arrived at their first destination — a village on an island called Koh Tukveal in one of the tributaries of the Lower Mekong — they were given further instructions.

Women and girls must no longer wear their hair long but have it clipped very short. There will be a haircutter in the village for everyone. Men, women and children will have free service. If you want to be kind to him — give him a bit of fish or some old bit of clothing. You must dress only in black. If you don't have black clothes you must dye them — you can use a fruit called *Makhoeur*. When night falls, you must not talk. There are spies everywhere. They make their rounds and even listen under the houses.

Denise Affonç ɔ was put to work on the various cycles of growing corn (maize), while her husband was sent some distance from the maize fields to clear a submerged forest for cultivation.

> If he had been less talkative, he wouldn't have been taken off to a re-education camp, my poor husband. Alas. He had a blind confidence in the Khmer Rouge. Thien — the local Angkar chief — showed himself as very friendly — every night he came to chat with my husband and the latter told him his life story. When Thien was sick, my husband brought him medicine (at that time we still had reserves for three months). The second mistake of my husband was to ask for a friend of his to be permitted to come to the island. . . . He had been the owner of our Phnom Penh apartment and was a fellow who boasted a lot and often spoke English or French. Two months after his arrival, he was the first to be "admitted" to a re-education camp. They took him off one evening after dinner, saying that *Angkar* needed his services. Two weeks later it was the the turn of twenty other people — among whom, obviously, was my husband. They left after lunch. I couldn't be present at their departure because on that day I was harvesting maize. When I returned in the evening, Thien said: "Don't worry, he'll be back in two days. Angkar simply needed some information because your husband was denounced by his friend." Days, months, years passed. I have never seen my husband again. Those who were taken off with him have also never returned.[3]

In one of the regular "brainwashing" sessions, the evacuees were informed that they were considered as "prisoners-of-war." "Before our Khmer Rouge entered Phnom Penh, you were asked to leave the city. Why didn't you leave?" At the end of February 1975, the Khmer Rouge had radio-broadcast an order to all those in Phnom Penh and other "non-liberated areas" to leave and reach the "liberated areas." Physically this was impossible. But when the Khmer Rouge arrived in the "non-liberated areas" they considered the inhabitants as "captives," as "prisoners-of-war."[4]

There were three categories of citizens in the Kampuchea of the Khmer Rouge. Category A had supported the resistance and were in the "liberated areas" on 17 April 1975. Category B were caught in the "non-liberated areas." These became the "old" and "new" residents. Category C consisted of anyone who had served in the armed forces or administrations of the Lon Nol and Sihanouk regimes. They were to be hunted down and exterminated together with all members of their families.

In mid-September 1975 Denise Affonço and the other ·"new" residents of Koh Tukveal were told to prepare to move elsewhere. An Angkar circular announced that they would be returning to the provinces in which they had been born. They packed whatever was left of their belongings and were ferried across the river. There lines of military trucks were waiting to take them — so they hoped — back to their home provinces. Denise even dreamed she was returning to Phnom Penh.

> After having noted the names and numbers of people per family — another baggage control. Bags were emptied in great disorder and we lost another large part of our belongings. They confiscated our big family photo album which I greatly prized, saying: "No souvenirs. Everything related to the former regime should be wiped out, forgotten. It was a regime of the rotten, the corrupt."

The announcement that they were being taken back to their home provinces was a bit of typical Khmer Rouge trickery. In fact, they travelled by truck, train, and oxcart for about ten days before they started to be distributed to various villages at the foot of a mountain chain in Battambang province. Denise Affonço was assigned to the village of Ta Chen, which comprised five *krum* or hamlets.

> The village people immediately made a clear distinction between the refugees and themselves. We, the refugees, formed a colony of the "new residents." They called us the "new" whereas they were the "old". . . . Hardly had we arrived than the following bans went into force:
>
> Only speak Khmer.
>
> Don't speak to each other in the evenings for the *chlops* make their rounds and listen at the doors.
>
> Don't eat more than two meals per day.
>
> Don't cook your rice. Eat rice soup for this region is still poor in rice.

In the second half of 1976, famine conditions forced people to try to steal from the fields and seek food in the forests just to keep alive. The reaction of the local Angkar leaders was to strike terror into the hearts of the people with the most barbarous types of executions. To be taken to the "western forest" was synonymous with death by torture.

People, old and young, took anything which fell into their hands: manioc, vegetables, sugar cane, etc.... But if you were caught, you might as well say your prayers and consign your soul to the Good Lord! One day a lad called Touch was arrested for having pulled up a few manioc roots. Ta Ling (the hamlet Angkar chief) informed of this simply said: "Take him to the western forest."

Denise Affonço described how he was led off by "three butchers" and how she followed at a respectable distance to see what happened, hiding herself in a thicket where she "could see but not be seen."

The condemned lad was attached, nude from the waist up, to a tree, his eyes bandaged. Butcher Ta Sok, a big knife in his hand, made a long incision in the abdomen of the miserable victim, who screamed with pain like a wild beast. (I can still hear his cries today.) Blood gushed out from all sides and from his intestines also while Ta Sok groped for his liver which he cut out and started to cook in a frying pan already heated by Ta Chea... They shared the cooked liver with a hearty appetite. After having buried the body they left with a satisfied air. I didn't dare leave my hiding place until they were far away....

Another Dantesque scene witnessed by Denise Affonço occurred when she was hospitalized during a serious illness at a place called Phnom (Mount) Leap, not far from Ta Chen village. "I knew there were no medicines or treatment," she explained, "but at least I thought I could rest." She was mistaken.

After night fell, no one could sleep. We awaited the arrival of the usual truck. Towards nine o'clock it stopped not far from the hospital at the foot of Phnom Trayono; male voices shouted orders, then complete silence. After a moment cries of pain could be heard: "Ah...Oh..." They were quickly stifled. Then silence. After an hour the truck left. One could again hear stifled cries. They were from people who had become unconscious, then buried alive. The next day, to satisfy my curiosity, I took a walk to the place. What I saw rooted me to the spot. There were giant trenches, big enough to receive forty or fifty corpses; some had been badly covered up in the darkness and there were arms and legs sticking out. The following night, shortly before the time of the truck's arrival, I went and hid behind a big bamboo thicket to get a detailed picture.

At nine o'clock sharp, a military truck loaded with people drew up at the edge of the trenches. One, two, three men got down and ordered everyone else to do the same, one by one, and to march in line behind the driver to a freshly-dug trench. There were 40 — I counted. Men, women, children of all ages. The two other men followed, axes and short spades in their hands. Once at the trench, those with the axe and spade stood face to face — the driver pushed the victims toward them, two at a time. With a blow of axe or spade, they lost consciousness and were kicked into the trench, dead or alive. Some, seeing what was happening, tried to flee. It was useless. They were quickly caught. Once all of them were in the trenches, the whole place was covered with earth and the truck left.... A month later a tractor came and levelled the whole area and orders were given to the chief of a nearby village to plant it all with manioc. Till my dying day I will never forget these horrors, of which only wild beasts such as the Pol Pot-Ieng Sary gang are capable.

The testimony of Denise Affonço was long and full of incredible detail. In an interview after the trial was over, she told me that she had doubted she would survive the concentration camp existence, surrounded as she was by executions, torture, deaths from starvation, and unbearable working and living conditions. But she was also determined that if she did survive she would be well-fitted to denounce the regime with exact facts of what she herself had seen. This is why she risked her life time and again to witness such horrors as that behind the Phnom Leap hospital and the calvary of the lad Touch.

Equally graphic are her descriptions of daily life: the slave work in the fields twelve to fourteen hours a day, seven days a week on a starvation diet. Time and again, her legs gave way under her after days of intolerable hunger. Twice she almost drowned when through weakness she fell into irrigation canals. Once she was bitten by a dog when she fought him — and lost — for a bit of skin from a freshly slaughtered ox. On one occasion she fought with her fourteen-year-old son over a handful of grilled rice they had managed to steal. By early January 1979 she was near death from hunger and even the local Angkar chief conceded that she could no longer go to the fields. One morning she staggered out of her hut to try to beg a little palm sugar in the hope that it might restore her energy. She managed to make it to the house of the district chairman, whose wife had shown her an occasional kindness.

As soon as I arrived I saw the situation was bad. All the *Nearaday* (village chiefs) armed to the teeth, were gathered there.... Four or five tailors were busy — at full speed — sewing haversacks and others in the shape of ox-bladders for carrying rice. For the previous two days, I learned, the rice mill had been husking about 40 bags of paddy daily. Towards evening they piled everything helter-skelter into ox-carts, their wives and children also. They left the *Sahakar* (cooperative), heading north without deigning even to notice us — which didn't surprise us as they were always rude. The evening of their departure, everything was pillaged: the sugar-cane field behind Ta Sok's home, the rice and salt depots; all the pigs were stolen as well as the paddy in the rice-husking mill. No one could arrest pillagers who had been suppressed for so long.

I learned then that the liberation forces had already arrived at Phnom Leap. The population had been asked to leave the area and head east. Everybody packed their bags without asking anyone's permission. Supporters of the *Nearaday* who had still not left, tried to hold us back. "Where are you going? Who asked you to leave? Do you know that death awaits you on the road? No rice, no medicine, no transport — it's certain you'll die because Siem Reap is 60 kilometres from here." Nobody heeded them, some even said: "If we must die better do it further away than leave our bones in this cursed forest."

Denise Affonço doubted she would make it. She was suffering from hunger edema, with badly swollen legs, so she stayed on to build up her strength with the sudden plenitude of food. Oxen were slaughtered on the basis of one per twenty people: "I ate so much during those three days that I got diarrhea — there were rice and vegetables in profusion." After three days of solid food, she and her son set out with as much food as they could carry on their backs. At first they could walk only a hundred yards at a time. By easy stages, staying a few nights in every village, they made it to Siem Reap. It took them two weeks to cover thirty miles. "Even those who had ox-carts or hand-carts went in short stages and took seven to eight days."

She related her first impressions of the liberating Vietnamese troops.

For several days I lived due to the good nature of the liberating troops. Without even knowing you, if they saw you were hungry, they gave you something to eat — rice, dried fish, pork soup, noodles etc.

These liberators had nothing in common with the picture given by the Pol Pot-Ieng Sary gang (the *Nearaday*); according to them, they were throat-cutters, baby-killers, blood-suckers. They were skeletons who, having nothing else to eat, lived off rice-husks. I couldn't refrain from relating all this to the liberating troops, who listened with amusement. We, who had lived with the partisans of Pol Pot-Ieng Sary, we can testify that the real killers and cutthroats were the Pol Pot-Ieng Sary gang. For example, at Phnom Srok, those who had no time to flee had their throats cut, or at least their eyes gouged out. [Apparently so they could not identify their torturers and butchers — W.B.]

The liberating troops are very correct towards girls and young women and, incidentally, it was absolutely forbidden for them to take any local fruit or vegetables. They had to rely simply on what their government sent them by plane... They took nothing from the country; they only brought more to distribute in the form of aid.[5]

The testimony of Denise Affonço — who later came to Paris where she works in the French Foreign Ministry — is extremely valuable. Her descriptions and experiences constitute ample evidence of the primitive, piratical nature of the Khmer Rouge forces. Revolutionary forces do not plunder people's personal possessions. That the Khmer Rouge did proves only their contempt for their own people, their culture, and their traditions. The reaction when Denise Affonço begged to keep her family album was typical. "Forget the past."[6] In the eyes of the Khmer Rouge leaders, the history of Kampuchea started on 17 April 1975. Everything before that had to be forgotten, erased.

---

1. The "Trial for Genocide of the Pol Pot-Ieng Sary Clique" was held before a People's Revolutionary Tribunal in Phnom Penh from 17 August through 19 August 1979. The author, together with a number of other Western journalists and television teams, was present and had access to

witnesses and to facilities for visits to places where the crimes charged in the indictment were committed.

2. See Chapter 7 for a full discussion of the role of the Angkar Leu.

3. The fact that the friend of Denise Affonço's husband was arrested less than three months after the Khmer Rouge takeover because he was overheard speaking a foreign language suggests that a policy of exterminating intellectuals had been decided upon in advance and was not linked — as many had thought — to opposition by the intellectuals to the new regime.

4. According to feudal custom, which was far from being abolished in Cambodia, prisoners-of-war could automatically be treated as slaves. Slaves could be used for whatever work their owners required. Whether they lived or died was of no consequence! So the Khmer Rouge quite literally did introduce a modern slave society.

5. In Siem Reap more than a year later the manageress of the Siem Reap Grand Hotel, Mrs. Long Savann, said the same of the Vietnamese troops there: "They treat us as if they were indulgent parents. Even though we have plenty of fruit and fish now, they refuse to accept any. They eat only their own meager rations."

6. This attitude was to provide the title for a book by the Catholic priest François Ponchaud, *Cambodia: Year Zero* (New York: Holt, Rinehart and Winston, 1978), and the title for a film by British filmmakers John Pilger and David Munro, *Year Zero: The Silent Death of a Nation.*

7.
A TWENTIETH CENTURY
SLAVE SOCIETY

In the Kampuchea of the Khmer Rouge, everything was done in the name of Angkar. "Angkar Leu needs you" would say the head of the execution squad when he came at night to lead away his victim. "Angkar proposes to borrow your watch." "Angkar will provide." "Angkar wants to make true revolutionaries of you." Under the cover of revolutionary-sounding rhetoric, the Pol Pot-Ieng Sary clique imposed upon the people of Kampuchea a system which reduced them to slaves and which exercised its power over them by relying on terror, brutality, and genocide.

Although no ideological label for this society has yet been agreed upon, it is clear that the classical dictionary definitions of slavery describe perfectly the status of ordinary Kampuchean citizens under the Khmer Rouge. While it is true that they were not bought and sold — there were neither currency nor established exchange values — under the Khmer Rouge the Kampuchean people had no choice of employment, no possibility of changing their place of work, no freedom of movement whatsoever. They had no life except that of working twelve to fourteen hours a day, seven days a week, without wages, for a starvation food ration over which they had no control. Any citizen could be taken out and knocked on the head until he or she was dead, without any charges being made or any defense given. There could be no protest or claim for compensation by relatives, for these resulted in certain death for anyone who protested or even criticized the regime by weeping over an assassinated husband, wife, or child.

Whereas in the past it had been foreign captives — Thais, Laotians, Chams, and others — who had been pressed into slavery in

Cambodia, one of the original features of Khmer Rouge society was that Pol Pot enslaved his own people. At first the slave status was reserved for those who were not in the Khmer Rouge-controlled zones at the moment of "liberation" on 17 April 1975. But soon it included the whole population except for the privileged leadership. Officially, and much more explicitly unofficially (in the twice- or thrice-weekly political [sic!] courses which members of every organization were forced to endure), it was a war to the death between rural dwellers and urban dwellers, with the arms of repression exclusively in the hands of the former and their Khmer Rouge "protectors." While "class vengeance" was a favorite slogan of the Khmer Rouge leadership in exhorting their members at all levels to exert ever-greater "revolutionary vigilance and severity" in dealing with their "class enemies," in fact class stratifications had nothing to do with who did the dealing and who got dealt with. The Khmer Rouge leadership came exclusively from the property-owning petit-bourgeoisie and bourgeoisie, in some cases with feudal connections. The vast majority of those who were executed or deliberately forced to die of starvation or disease were small peasants, fishermen, workers, and educated persons of varied, though mostly humble, origin. How could it be otherwise when the death toll was between two and three million in less than four years?

The official policy directive handed down after "liberation" by the Angkar Leu to local executants for the deportees — who amounted to about two-thirds of the population — was expressed in a slogan: "Preserve Them — No Profit! Exterminate Them — No Loss!" Professor Keng Vannsak — former Dean of the Faculté des Lettres at Phnom Penh University, one of Cambodia's outstanding Marxists, and mentor (in Paris) of several of the future Khmer Rouge leaders — explained to me that the Khmer terms *Camnenh*, used for "profit," and *Khat*, used for "loss," in the slogan-directive were not abstract or philosophical terms; they indicated material and commercial values as used in standard accounting.

> Man was reduced to an object of profit or loss. Those who could survive the execution squads, the forced labour, lack of medical care, disease and famine could become objects of profit. If not they were

exterminated — their deaths not causing any loss!

Keng Vannsak also pointed out that Angkar was in fact "an immense apparatus of repression and terror as an amalgam of Party, Government and State not in the usual sense of these institutions, but with particular stress on its mysterious, terrible and pitiless character. It was, in a way, political-metaphysical power, anonymous, omnipresent, omniscient, occult, sowing death and terror in its name." As every Khmer Rouge cadre could automatically act in the name of Angkar, he — or she — was absolved of any sense of personal responsibility for the murder and torture committed in Angkar's name.

At the genocide trial held in Phnom Penh in August 1979 Dith Munty, a secondary school teacher who had survived by successfully concealing the fact that he was an "intellectual," gave one of the most thorough and interesting descriptions of how Angkar enslaved the Kampuchean people.

Angkar is the incarnation of an absolute militarist and arbitrary power which the Khmer Rouge had at their disposal. It had the power of life and death over the people. To sow discord between the urban and rural populations, Angkar divided people into three categories. The old, the new, the enemies. The first were those who resided in the liberated areas or in zones which had rallied to the Khmer Rouge prior to the collapse of the Lon Nol regime; the second were those deported from Phnom Penh and other areas. These were considered slaves. They were subjected to all sorts of humiliations by the "old" residents. The "old" had more rights and privileges than the "new." It was the "new" who carried out all the heavy work. For six months of the year Angkar allotted them work on building dykes and digging canals. They had to work 13 hours per day, from 3:00 a.m. to 10:30, from 13:30 to 17:30 and from 19:00 to 21:00, in exchange for 150 grams of rice per head, daily.[1] For them, there were no days off, even if they were sick they had no right to rest. Under pain of death, they had to continue working the whole day, the night as well, in sunshine and in rain. The third category included military and civil servants of the former regime, all intellectuals, pupils and students from the 7th class onwards. These were all to be killed because they were enemies.

The soil was arid, living conditions very difficult, there was a lack of medicines. Many died of starvation. In Sangkat Samorich commune, four to six people died every day. The inhabitants were so weak that the time arrived when they no longer had strength to bury the corpses so they loaded them onto ox-carts and abandoned them in the jungle.

Among the victims was Dith Munty's mother. In describing her death he provides an eloquent account of what was certainly the fate of hundreds of thousands of her compatriots: dead of hunger in a land which used to be one of Asia's leading rice exporters.

My mother also died of starvation. She was a gentle, modest, lovable woman. She was only 45, but worn out by grief, by forced labor, malnutrition and lack of any medicine, she looked like an old grandmother of 80. I had been sent off to build dykes for five months and when I returned she was already dying. She cried out: "Give me something to eat. I'm starving." At the risk of my life I rushed out and somehow got a bowl of rice. Unfortunately, she could no longer swallow. Her voice got weaker and weaker until it was inaudible. Weeping, I shook her gently and asked if she recognized me. She opened her eyes, looked at me, blinked at me in sign of recognition — and died.

The factual, moving, and analytical testimony of Dith Munty was among the most important presented at the genocide trial. For me it represented a synthesis of all that I had been able to discover from literally hundreds of interviews conducted first among the refugees and later among the "road people"[2] and among those who had finally made it back to their villages or to their homes in Phnom Penh. Obviously a keen observer with a retentive memory and a balanced sense of human values, Dith Munty gave an account of life under the Khmer Rouge which was one of the most effective indictments of the regime and, implicitly, of those — especially among Western intellectuals — who have become its apologists. There was not a word or phrase in his evidence which would not be endorsed by those who lived under Angkar, in the society which Ieng Sary had boasted was "something that never was before in history." To which one can most devoutly add: "and may never be again."

We were ill-fed, clad in rags and reduced to slavery. Human rights were trampled underfoot, the right to eat with one's family and free marriage were replaced by "eat in common" and forced marriage by groups of 30 to 50 or 60 couples each time. We, the "undesirables," had no right to return to our homes and reconstitute our family life and happiness. The right of residence, of free movement in the country, the right to freedom of opinion, of association, of belief, the right to work or rest or study, were totally suppressed. All citizens were not "free and equal" when most of the inhabitants were imprisoned in cooperatives by force and died of hunger, while the Khmer Rouge, representing Angkar, could circulate freely and live off the fat of the land. They had destroyed virtually all educational establishments, forcing children to abandon their studies. Children of 13 to 14 years were conscripted into the army, those of 6 to 12 years worked as cattle herders or collected excrement to make manure.

The Khmer Rouge despised all the traditions, the morals and customs of our people. They destroyed pagodas and temples or transformed them into prisons, forcing the bonzes to discard their robes.

The Angkar wanted to develop agriculture, but they killed all the technicians and agronomists, while closing factories one after another because of lack of raw materials and workers.

There was no money nor were there markets. Angkar practiced a "closed economy." Trade was carried on with a single country — China — which disregarded the interests of the Khmer people, recognizing only those of Peking.

If there was famine and starvation in Kampuchea, it was not due to crop failures. Rice was produced in substantial quantities, but it was either stored away for the army or exported to China. Documents were produced at the trial which showed that China pressed for ever-greater shipments of rice from Kampuchea. Some apologists for the regime in the West have used the fact that Kampuchea "even had rice for export" to prove that the Angkar agricultural system was working well! Rice, together with timber, crocodile skins, dried and smoked fish, rubies, zircons, other precious stones, and some rubber, represented Kampuchea's main exports to China. They paid for the Chinese arms imported by the Pol Pot-Ieng Sary clique.

Dith Munty's account continues:

Executions were frequent. Every night two or three "new" inhabitants were convoked for a "meeting" and disappeared without a trace. Nobody dared to enquire as to the fate of the unfortunates;

97

family members could not even weep, for fear of being accused of "complicity." If one was called for at an unusual time — above all at night — it was inevitably to be killed. We lived in perpetual fear, like fish in a trap, never knowing when our turn would come to be exterminated. To survive one had to be very prudent. Everybody distrusted everybody else, because spies were planted amongst us. The Khmer Rouge had set up a very efficient espionage system — children of 6 to 8 years had to spy on their parents.

The village chiefs, who constituted the cadres, had been chosen from amongst the most ignorant and to maintain their authority they displayed an excess of zeal. Justice was swift. Anyone who broke a plate by mischance could be accused of being an agent of the CIA and KGB or of Vietnam.

The greatest massacre started in June 1977. My friend Seng Meng Tech was the first victim. He had just started lunch with his family when two members of the local militia walked in. They took him off and clubbed him to death under a palm tree a kilometre away. His only "crime" was that he wore thick-lensed glasses!

June 1977 marked the beginning of a tidal wave of executions in every province. The oxcart convoys, reminiscent of the tumbrils of the French Revolution, rumbled towards the execution sites, crammed with innocent victims.

During this period, verbal instruction were passed around that "due to lack of cultivable land" Angkar was building hundreds of model homes elsewhere for the "new residents" in another region where there was plenty of land to cultivate. Every evening families were assembled to go to the new areas. Convoys of oxen and buffalo-drawn carts and a boat transported these unfortunate families to the "new villages," from which no one ever returned. From my hamlet alone, 36 families comprising 202 persons, men, women, old people, children and babies, were taken off in such convoys and have never been heard of since. I was certain that our turn would also come — to be sent off by Angkar to there from where none returned. Every night we watched out for the boat and the carts and we could never sleep until their sinister noise drew away from the village. "That's it! One more stay of execution" would murmur my wife.

We lived in a state of constant fear. My wife and I procured a score of poisonous nuts containing strychnine which we always kept in our pockets. If we had been convoked we would have poisoned ourselves. It was the only way to avoid further suffering. All the "new" residents taken away by the carts and boat were taken to the Staung college, transformed into a prison and torture centre. From there all trace of these unfortunates was lost. The killings followed a set pattern. At first the military and police, then the civil servants, intellectuals, technicians, doctors, school teachers and professors, then students and pupils.

Dith Munty, who had managed to conceal his class and intellectual status, was sent off to do all sorts of manual labor: "lumberjack, fisherman, market gardener, manure mixer." His testimony ended with the melancholy information that when he returned to Staung village after the Pol Pot regime was overthrown (at which time he had been assigned to a "fishing brigade" on the Tonle Sap, the "Great Lake"), he found it deserted.

> Everybody had left to camp along the national highway under the protection of the Khmer United Front for National Salvation, for fear of being taken off into the jungle by the Khmer Rouge. No one could tell me exactly what had happened to my wife and child. Until now, I have no news of them.

To be listed on the "profit" side of the Angkar ledger, those physically strong enough to survive the terrible privations of daily life had to become "pure and hard" revolutionaries. Thus, children were taught that to denounce their parents was a kindly service aiding in the latter's "purification" so that they could play a nobler role in the new society. One of the greatest built-in defects of the urban dwellers was their "tendency to individualism." The necessity of purging themselves of this was one of the most constant themes of the regularly held "political education" classes.

Pin Yathay, the author of a blood-chilling book entitled "L'Utopie Meurtrière" ("The Murderous Utopia"), has used the experiences of himself and his family to show how ideological "progress" was measured by the Khmer Rouge.[3] In less than one year after their deportation from Phnom Penh, he had lost nineteen of his immediate family's twenty-three members to disease and starvation. In the "cooperative" to which his family had been assigned at Don Ey, in Pursat province, Pin Yathay was at death's door after a heavy bout of malaria followed by hunger edema. His eldest son, Sadath, had a badly infected leg wound and was also suffering from edema. When a Khmer Rouge cadre came to take the boy away, Pin Yathay showed him the infected leg and begged that his son be allowed to rest for another day or two until the wound healed. The Khmer Rouge replied:

> You still have individualist tendencies. Because you are sick you want to keep your child with you. You have so far come through all the tests up to this one. You must, however, purify yourself. Free yourself from sentiments. The child belongs to Angkar. You should not desire to keep him for yourself.[4]

Young Sadath was dragged off and died five days later. Pin Yathay came in for further reproaches by demanding — in vain — to see the body.

On another occasion Pin Yathay was caught taking food and water to the widow of a friend from his Phnom Penh days after her husband and most of the rest of the family had also died at Don Ey. She was too weak to move from her bed so Pin Yathay and his wife, Any, did what they could to help. "It's not your duty to help her," said the Khmer Rouge who had stopped him. "It only shows that you still have not purged yourself of sentiments of pity, of friendship. You must get rid of such feelings and of your individualistic tendencies. Now get back to your own place!" The woman — a former employee of the Khmer Commercial Bank in Phnom Penh — died two days later. Her two children were taken off and not seen again.[5]

In one of their moves — frequent in the first year of deportation — Pin Yathay and his family, and others from the village where they had been located, were sent to Sramar Leav in Takeo province, south of Phnom Penh. The move was made on the lying pretext that they were all going back to their original homes. Hardly had they unloaded their belongings from the oxcart when the local Khmer Rouge chief informed them their departure for home would be delayed. It was the height of the agricultural season (July 1975) and they would be staying at Sramar Leav long enough to help get the crops sown.

> "Naturally, Angkar will house and feed you. It will take care of everything. For your part you must respect orders and discipline. You must try to purify yourselves."

The theme of ordeal and purification reappeared constantly in the homilies of the Khmer Rouge [reports Pin Yathay]. Our orator declaimed the litany of Angkar's ambitions for us. His torrent of words exalted transformation of man. "Angkar wants to make true revolutionaries of you. . . .

"Try to master yourselves and become responsible for your own destiny by working hard to produce for your own needs. It is indispensable to behave like good revolutionaries, washing away the stains of imperialism, capitalism and feudalism."[6]

The reference to "producing for your own needs" was part of the generalized scheme of lies. At no time did the slave laborers have access to what they produced. Their production went into the communal storage depots, and where it went from there was anybody's guess! I heard of no case in which there was any relationship between what was produced and what was consumed by "cooperative" or "commune" members. The penalty for trying to appropriate the fruit of one's labor was inevitably a public denunciation and an atrocious death.

Elections were supposed to be held in March 1976. In solemnly announcing the "results," the Khmer Rouge leadership reported that the country's population at that moment was almost 7.8 million, giving the number of "registered electors" and the proportion who had voted. I have never found anyone who took part in this election. Of this Pin Yathay writes:

We had expected to be consulted. In vain! Nobody in our area took part in the elections. In certain villages, single candidates had been presented. . . . The results were proclaimed in an atmosphere of general indifference.

The Khmer Rouge justified the absence of electoral consultation in certain regions by the mobilization of workers for the ricefields. They pretended they were too busy there or with their fishing boats to vote. In fact our voices did not count. We were of no importance. Perhaps we were not allowed to vote because we were the "new people."[7]

It was following these elections and the naming of a new government that Sihanouk "resigned" as Head of State and his old friend and adviser Penn Nouth "resigned" as prime minister. At the time it was announced that Sihanouk was to receive an annual pension of $8,000. Pin Yathay writes that this announcement led him and others to believe that Sihanouk and his family were going abroad "to some friendly country." Only after Pin Yathay escaped to Thailand in June 1977 did he learn that Sihanouk had been put under house arrest immediately after the "resignation" farce and was still inside the country.

There had been much hope among both "old" and "new" people that Sihanouk would take over and end the régime of terror and genocide. The reference to a money pension in a moneyless country was a typically devious Khmer Rouge method of insinuating that Sihanouk was quitting the country. Thus, they dashed any hope of salvation from that quarter, a hope which they had deliberately fomented in order to trap and exterminate those who showed enthusiasm for Sihanouk's return to real power. Pin Yathay notes that the régime became even more merciless after Sihanouk's elimination.

> During the political meetings, the Khmer Rouge barely veiled their threats. "You must work hard to become a good revolutionary. If you remain in the middle of the road, the wheel of revolution will crush you. In the new Kampuchea, one million people will suffice to continue the revolution. One million good revolutionaries will be enough for the society that we are building. The others we do not need. We prefer to kill ten friends rather than leave a single enemy alive." The warning was clear. The Khmer Rouge needed no proof to arrest a suspect, even if he was a friend of the new regime.

> Any village chief could make the decision to execute anybody at all. They were not averse to settling personal accounts or to robbing people. They camouflaged their crimes by political discourses. We had no defence against ideology. The Khmer Rouge promised us tears, blood, and despair....."You have to prove to Angkar that you do not hesitate to make certain sacrifices. You must work hard. If you fall, pick yourself up and start working again."[8]

Pin Yathay, and many of those with whom I spoke, said that the threats and exhortations which followed the pretended March 1976 elections were accompanied by an intensification of the terror and of the work required of the slave laborers. Threats to reduce the population to one million made nonsense of the official thesis that the targets of the terror were "only" class enemies.[9]

As famine conditions became widespread — generalized, in fact, when one compared the eyewitness reports from virtually every province — the living standards of "new" and "old" residents tended to be not too different. In the early days, the "old" could help themselves to more of what they produced and also to fruits and edible forest products. If the "new" residents did so, they were automatically and summarliy executed. But the "old" soon lost these privileges. As common suffering eliminated differences, the entire "new" population and an increasing proportion of the "old" — irrespective of their class status — represented an actual or potential threat to the regime.

Sporadic protests and uprisings spread throughout the countryside. Pin Yathay refers to an "incredible phenomenon" which took place in November 1975 while his family was at Veal Vong at the foot of the Cardamom Mountains. Hundreds of "new" residents, headed by five schoolteachers, marched to the local Khmer Rouge headquarters to protest against the tardy arrival — or non-distribution — of food rations. At the headquarters one of the schoolteachers stepped forward and made a short speech, summing up the grievances of the demonstrators but paying due tribute to the virtues of Angkar! The essence of the complaint was that:

> The rations are ludicrous! Neither meat nor vegetables. The work is too hard — there is no means of caring for our health. Neither medicine nor a medical clinic.[10]

The response of the Khmer Rouge village chief was to berate the spokesman for his "ingratitude" for all that Angkar had done for the community.

> Are these complaints the result of our daily education? Is this how you suppress individualistic tendencies? No, comrade! This is not the revolution. Go back immediately and remain calm. The rations will arrive.[11]

Within a week, the five schoolteachers had disappeared without a trace.

Pin Yathay remarked that from then on troops patrolled the outskirts of the village, taking their victims "one by one during the night." Villagers began to come across corpses in the surrounding forest.

> The Khmer Rouge had achieved their aim. They terrorized the village population by allowing them to find a few mutilated, rotting, human remains.
>
> No uprising was possible. The disappearance of the five school-teachers had deeply moved and wounded us. We were so vulnerable...How to revolt? We had no arms. And even if we had been able to procure some and kill fifty or so Khmer Rouge in the village, what would we do after such an uprising? Beyond Veal Vong, there was the jungle.... Difficult to take to the maquis with a dozen or so firearms, little reserve ammunition and extremely reduced food rations against a totalitarian organization.[12]

Important and successful resistance movements have been born under even less favorable conditions and were in fact already operating inside Kampuchea. But the difficulties of liaison and communication were formidable obstacles to forging a resistance movement on a national scale. Above all there was no leading organization to guide and coordinate such a struggle. Such armed struggle as was taking place was led by units of the armed forces which had mutinied against the Angkar leadership. By making inter-community contacts and travel along the roads capital offenses, the Khmer Rouge reduced the possibility of people's uprisings to a minimum.

The greatest ally of the Khmer Rouge was famine. By the time the slaves felt the need to revolt, their ranks had been so decimated and the survivors so weakened and emaciated that they had no more chance of turning against the Khmer Rouge than had the Auschwitz victims of revolting against their well-fed, splendidly armed Nazi guards. As early as May 1976, Pin Yathay estimated, eight out of every ten deportees at Don Ey had died of famine and disease or had been killed.

> We became more and more demoralized. The Khmer Rouge looked on unmoved at our distress and agonizing condition. Our clothes were in tatters, the fabric of our pants and shirts ruined by the primitive dyes.
>
> There had been so many deaths that only two camps were left of the original seven. Five had been set up at the time we arrived. These had been gradually abandoned as they were emptied. The greater part of the population had been decimated, the survivors coming to swell the

numbers of those in the two older camps, more or less spared by the epidemics and malaria. These two had best resisted the famine; they were above all inhabited by men and women from the original residents, who received decent rice rations....[13]

Pin Yathay left for a few months to serve with a fishing team on the Tonle Sap. When he returned:

Nothing had changed. People continued to die. Even the "old" ones were dying. Those of the latter who had retained their sensitivity — and above all their senses — shook their heads in sign of incredulity, of dismay and revolt. Disaster had engulfed us all.[14]

Desperation again drove a few of the hardier spirits to consider an uprising. During his work with the fishing team, Pin Yathay had picked up rumors of armed struggle and had heard the sound of small battles from rapidly shifting sites along the perimeter of the lake as if the Khmer Rouge were pursuing one or more resistance groups in the area. But he remained certain that in his region an armed uprising was impossible. Individual escape to try to join up with others in the maquis was almost equally so.

To discourage any attempt at flight, the Khmer Rouge had set up an extremely hierarchical organization. The villages, isolated in a hostile jungle, were fenced off. No contacts could be seriously and durably established between the different communities.... We did not have even the material possibility to consult with each other, to speak or conspire.... We were in no condition to stage a revolt.

At work the whole time, if we found a few moments of respite, we used them to garner some food. Attempts at rebellion were brutally put down. In a moment of anger one day at Veal Vong, a young member killed a Khmer Rouge guard. He was immediately killed by the other guards.... Without logistical support from outside, or a military revolt amongst the Khmer Rouge, all attempts to overthrow the Angkar dictatorship were in vain.[15]

Professor Keng Vannsak has made one of the deepest analyses of the Angkar system, based on hundreds of interviews with survivors and the study of such Khmer Rouge documents as have become available. The following is his summary of some of the essential Angkar guidelines and dogmas.

Education: Revolutionary, alongside the poor working peasants, not at school, but by the Party and through activities. "The true university is found in the ricefields, the worksites, the factories. The essential is neither Knowledge, nor Diplomas, nor Science, nor Technique but Proletarian Consciousness, that of the poor, working–peasants fighting for the ideas of the Party. On the basis of consciousness one can do everything, acquire everything, succeed in everything."[16]

Life: Not personal, but collective, in groups and to be conducted according to the Party slogans, which implies being at the entire disposal of Angkar.

Family: Dislocated. The family represents a milieu favorable to the reconstitution of clans and the differentiation of social classes. Thus family life is reduced to its simplest expression. Husbands and wives are separated, they can only meet through authorisation of Angkar. Parents and children obey the same collectivist requirements.

Work: Forced, collective labour under the surveillance of armed troops, accompanied by propaganda blasts on the theme of the "victorious offensive" on all fronts. It is a question of forced labour based on human energy. Thus men and women are yoked to ploughs in place of oxen and buffalo. Millions of people are used as animals, taking no account of their intellectual capacities, to do work that a machine could accomplish in a few days. The Khmer Rouge have conceived and organized work more as a punishment than for the liberation of man.

Cooperatives: This is the social and administrative unit, the economic and political organism, the "warehouse" of the collective; the point of the centralization of all powers, the concentration of property and for the distribution of foodstuffs, thus the point for control by the stomach. (Very effective.)

Inhabitants: Divided into two distinct categories: The Khmer Rouge, who are the masters, and the people, condemned as "war captives" to slavery and slow death. The Masters (Cadres, Committee members, especially the *Yothea* or armed combatants) have all rights and privileges. They feed themselves and act as they feel like acting. But the people have no right to touch anything at all, not even the rice they cultivate, nor the products of livestock raising.

The refugees often mention this type of case: "Having greatly suffered from lack of sugar, some residents succeeded in getting a few clumps of sugar-cane to grow in front of their huts. When stalks were about a metre high, armed Khmer Rouge arrived. They very carefully counted the number of stalks. Afterwards they hung up a sign which stated that 'all these stalks of sugar-cane belong to Angkar, which forbids anyone to touch them on pain of death'."

Isolation: The population are herded into forced labour camps. These camps are separated into squares of ten units, with a ban on people moving from one square to another. Refugees having lived in this concentration camp universe of the Khmer Rouge use a striking image in deploring this lack of liberty of movement, *Vos dei oy Doer,* which means that the Khmer Rouge measure off a portion of ground within which each person is authorised to move around.

Permanent Deportation: This is done to uproot people from the social — even agrarian — milieu to which they have started to become accustomed. The aim is to prevent the germination of any property instincts and the reconstitution of the family, clans or groups under any form whatsoever. The attachment to one's "cabin," to one's wife, husband, children, parents — is not this the root of all evil?

Meetings: The only ones authorised are the political education sessions, organized and imposed by the Party. The eternal self-criticism! But what is still more frightening is the "Biographical Examination"... Twice yearly, everybody becomes a "candidate" and must set forth the history of his or her life to uncover — cost what it may — and to denounce the "errors" committed in the past, the present and those intended for the future, based on intentions or thoughts. Khmer Rouge refugees swear that many "candidates" committed suicide, before or after the verdict of the Jury. After the "Biographical Examinations," naturally there were brain-washing courses and indoctrination. The principal theme was the infallibility of the Party, which was supported by the racist cult of a "small people having vanquished the great American imperialists."

Propaganda: Self-satisfaction! Superiority of the Cambodian Maoists! They boasted of having: "left the Soviet, Chinese and Vietnamese behind in the essential field — that of Doctrine and Revolutionary Practice." The only correct, "pure and hard" line is their own. Compared to them, other Communists appear as miserable revisionists! The majority, in their eyes, are vulgar opportunists. In their writings, intended for cadres and Party members, the Khmer Rouge never made any references to the "fathers" of Marxism-Leninism-Maoism, whose thoughts and texts they stole in order to appear before their ignorant compatriots as the only "demi-gods" to have invented true revolution.

Khmer-Rouge Society: This classless society would be formed exclusively by the Khmer Rouge. It is already functioning without money, with neither wages nor markets — thus no budget, no problem of balance of payments, of stimulating the economy, no inflation, no economic, social or political crises — at least so they claim! Without money or merchants, with no remunerated labour, there will exist no basis for such social evils as the cult of profit, individualism, personality conflicts, jealousy, rivalries, corruption, decadence and so on.

There will, on the one hand, only be the slave-labourers — to be killed or abandoned to die when they can no longer drag themselves to the fields. On the other, the watch-dogs, pointing their guns at the "poor, working peasants," starved to the most extreme degree. Thanks to the Revolution of the Cambodian Maoists, this "Promised Society" already exists. It is in the process of "liberating" the Khmer People by imposing on them a slow, but sure, atrocious death.[17]

Prince Sihanouk has written of the determination of the Khmer Rouge leadership to achieve "instant communism" in Kampuchea and of their contempt for the manner in which other countries undertook to slowly and patiently build socialism.

In 1976-78, Khieu Samphan was fond of telling me that Marshal Kim Il Sung's Koreans were "on the wrong track" if they wanted to make their country truly communist. Kim Il Sung, he said, had raised the standard of living and developed the economy "too much. Now the North Koreans have fine houses and cars, nice cities. The people are too attached to their new life," he said. "They will never want to start, or even fight in a new war, their only hope of liberating South Korea and reuniting their country."

In Peking in 1975, we visited Zhou Enlai — already seriously ill — in his hospital room. I heard him advise Khieu Samphan and Ieng Thirith (Mme. Ieng Sary) not to try to achieve total communism in one giant step. This wise and perspicacious veteran of the Chinese revolution stressed the need to move "step by step" toward socialism. It would take several years of patient work. Then and only then should they advance toward a communist society. Premier Zhou Enlai reiterated that China itself had experienced disastrous setbacks in the fairly recent past by trying to make a giant leap forward and move full speed ahead into pure communism. The great Chinese statesman counseled the Khmer Rouge leaders: "Don't follow the bad example of our 'great leap forward.' Take things slowly: that is the best way to guide Kampuchea and its people to growth, prosperity and happiness." By way of response to this splendid and moving piece of almost fatherly advice, Khieu Samphan and Ieng Thirith just smiled incredulous and superior smiles.

Not long after we got back to Phnom Penh, Khieu Samphan and Son Sen told me that Kampuchea was going to show the world that pure communism could indeed be achieved at one fell swoop. This was no doubt their indirect reply to Zhou Enlai. "Our country's place in history will be assured," they said. "We will be the first nation to create a completely communist society without wasting time on intermediate steps."[18]

This is a most revealing insight into the thinking of the inner core of the Khmer Rouge leadership. Had they followed the deathbed advice of one of the world's most experienced revolutionaries, millions of Kampuchean lives would have been spared and the Khmer Rouge leadership could have been in Phnom Penh presiding over the development of a flourishing economy. By 1975, in just over twenty years of organized labor, the Korean people under Kim Il Sung's leadership had rebuilt the country on the ashes of an infinitely greater destruction than had been inflicted on Kampuchea. They had introduced cradle-to-grave social benefits including general education up to university entrance standards, abolished taxes, achieved one hundred percent electrification of the countryside and total irrigation in the rice-growing plains, built up a modern heavy, medium, and light industry, and stimulated a great revival of traditional culture. In their infinite arrogance, the Khmer Rouge leaders were cocksure that ideas could be transformed into reality through "the barrel of a gun" and that they would provide a world model of "instant communism." Unfortunately, apart from Chou En-lai, there were other leaders in China who, for their own ends, encouraged them in this. The political, ideological, and moral degeneration of the Khmer Rouge leadership left them with smoking guns in their hands and skeleton-filled death pits all over their lovely country, grim monuments to their attempts to impose on Kampuchea their abstract concept of a new society.

1. Dith Munty, like all the other witnesses, was describing the conditions prevailing in the area where he lived and worked. The hours of work varied slightly but in all accounts which I heard they averaged from twelve to fourteen hours per day. The rice ration also varied considerably. According to my information, 150 grams per head daily was in excess of that provided in most provinces. The ration seems to have varied according to the whims of the local Angkar chief.

2. These were the people travelling back to their homes in the first months after the Khmer Rouge were overthrown. See Chapter 14 for the author's description of them.

3. Yathay, Pin, *L'Utopie Meutrière*. Paris: Robert Laffont, 1980. By far the most authentic and detailed account of the first two years of Khmer Rouge rule, this book contains invaluable personal testimony as to what really happened.

4. *Ibid.*, p. 222.

5. *Ibid.*, p. 226.

6. *Ibid.*, pp. 91-92.

7. *Ibid.*, pp. 235-6.

8. *Ibid.*, p. 237.

9. Some high-level Khmer Rouge statements over Phnom Penh radio spoke of "two million" as a satisfactory survival level after having eliminated the Vietnamese at the expense of the rest.

10. Yathay, *L'Utopie Meutrière*, p. 163.

11. *Ibid.*, pp. 250-1.

12. *Ibid.*, p. 163.

13. *Ibid.*, p. 250.

14. *Ibid.*, p. 251.

15. *Ibid.*, p. 164.

16. The passage in quotation marks is from a Khmer Rouge circular on education.

17. Vannsak, Keng, *Aperçu de la Revolution Khmer Rouge,* pp. 11-13. Montmorency, France, 2 March 1977. In a short introduction to this important work, Professor Keng Vannsak notes that the term "Pativattana," used by the Khmer Rouge to designate "revolution" in their official texts, in fact means "return backwards" or "return to the past." In popular Khmer language, "revolution" is expressed as "bâmbah-bàmbor," the first term meaning "uprising" and the second "reconstruction."

18. Sihanouk, Norodom, *Chroniques de Guerre et d'Espoir*. Paris: Hachette/Stock, 1979. It has been translated into English with some deletions from the French edition: Sihanouk, Prince Norodom, *War and Hope: The Case for Cambodia*. New York: Pantheon Books, 1980. All quotations in this work are from the French edition.

8.
HOW TO BE A
GOOD KHMER ROUGE

One of the difficulties in being a "good" Khmer Rouge was that of knowing the "right line" to apply or follow at any particular time and place. The Khmer Rouge leadership committed as little as possible to paper.[1] Most policy decisions were handed down orally, and village chiefs were often appointed on the basis of their ability to memorize the contents of what they heard at conferences where policy decisions were announced. As most of them were illiterate, perhaps there was no alternative. It certainly helps to explain the discrepancies occurring in eyewitness accounts of how the system worked in different geographical areas.

Contents of directives were obviously badly assimilated. By the time the village, district, and even provincial chiefs got back to their bases, the directives must have become even more blurred in their minds and application of them must have suffered accordingly. When possible, directives were issued in simplistic, slogan-type form: "All For Agriculture: Rice is Everything"....."Self-sufficiency Is The Key To Victory"...."Build Irrigation Systems in Every Province." "Wipe Out Class Enemies" hardly needed repetition, except when the process had to be stepped up or the category of victims widened.

The all-important rule for a "good" Khmer Rouge was blind and total obedience. It was also the essential prerequisite for survival. To question orders was implicit criticism of Angkar and, even at the highest level, this was equivalent to suicide. In "Comrade Ox," one of his most biting chapters, Pin Yathay delineates the ideal character not only of a citizen but also of a cadre.

The Khmer Rouge often used parables to justify their contradictory actions and orders. They compared the individual to an ox. "You see this ox which pulls the plough. He eats where one orders him to eat. If you lead him to another field where there's not much grass, he still browses at something. He can't go where he wants because he's guarded. When he is told to pull the plough, he pulls it. He never thinks about his wife or children." Such a humiliating and insane comparison might once have raised smiles, but smiles now would have to be dragged out of our tears and sweat!

It was based on such reasoning that the Khmer Rouge had let our families, our children die. The ox, docile *par excellence*, was the model we should imitate. Often in the meetings, the Khmer Rouge spoke of the bovines as humans. They frequently said: "Comrade ox." The ox had all the qualities that they demanded from a deportee. The ox never refused to work. It was obedient, never complained and never threw off its yoke. It blindly followed the Angkar directives.

The lesson of the parable was clear to everyone. Even for the rebellious, for the most recalcitrant citizens. We had neither the right to complain nor to reason. We had to put our intelligence to sleep. . . . A good revolutionary behaved like a respectful and servile animal, a tamed animal. He had no individualist tendencies, no feelings, no ambitions. The only initiatives tolerated were those judged good by the collective. These initiatives were exclusively practical. The labourer, for example, must know how to repair a damaged plough. . . .[2]

It is true, as stressed by Keng Vannsak and other authorities, that two thousand years of monarchies and slave systems of one sort or another in Cambodia had produced a built-in subservience to whomever was in power that could not be eradicated overnight. During Sihanouk's days it was symbolized by the ritual in which anyone approaching him on any matter whatsoever dropped on to one knee and touched the tips of the fingers of both hands together under the chin as a tribute to the Monarchy and Buddhism, the Diumvirate which Sihanouk personified. Oddly enough, it was Lon Nol in Phnom Penh and Ieng Sary in Peking — as I had many occasions to note — who were the most obsequious in this respect!

Blind obedience was particularly difficult for anyone who, like Pin Yathay, had been trained abroad in the exact sciences. When ordered to evacuate Phnom Penh, he had taken with him a few books from his library. They dealt with his specialty, the construction of dams, dikes, and roads. At the first roadblock it had been cameras, watches, transistor radios, and other such objects that Angkar needed to "borrow." At the second it was printed material. Pin Yathay pleaded for his technical books, showing diagrams and sketches to prove their utilitarian and non-political contents. In vain! "These books contain imperialist thinking!" They were hurled onto the road to be ground into the dust and litter by the vehicles which followed.

Ironically, one of the first tasks he and his family were given was to work day and night on an irrigation project in Takeo province. It was the sort of work — digging canals and building dykes — to which most deportees were assigned during the first months of their calvary. "The big work sites forge ideological solidarity," they were told. For specialists like Pin Yathay, they were "rule of thumb" exercises in frustration.

Sometimes physical laws were defied by the Khmer Rouge, dour builders though they were. One cannot define the slope of a field by the naked eye. The Khmer Rouge ridiculed technical help which could have corrected the errors of such guesswork. Vast undertakings were executed contrary to even common-sense rules. Each Khmer Rouge leader acted according to his own whims. There was no lack of labour power. Thousands of men and women obeyed the orders of the civilian cadres. The result of this Khmer Rouge amateurism was heart-rending. Canals running in the wrong direction. Dykes destroyed by the first rains, rebuilt and again swept away by the waters.... The result of all this work, incidentally, hardly seemed important in itself! The essential was to seize on how to learn lessons from experience. By learning from such mishaps we should bring our initiative into play to ensure that they would not be repeated....

I knew one could not dig canals of up to five kilometres by such rule of thumb methods. But I kept my mouth shut. The Khmer Rouge allotted precise tasks to each brigade of village workers. These limited sections were supposed to fit together, like parts of a puzzle, within the framework of a single, vast project. Such and such a village, for instance, should take care of a certain part of a road, dig its part of the canal, build its quota of dykes....

113

> The Khmer Rouge did not like to be bothered with intellectuals and specialists. They maintained that diplomas were useless bits of paper.... What counted was the concrete work that could be evaluated and approved — ploughing or digging. That was honorable work because it was visible, tangible....

Pin Yathay describes how the rains arrived, the rice seedlings were planted out by the women deportees, including his wife, and the water arrived at the required ankle level for the shoots to develop.

> Unfortunately, a month after planting out, the fields dried up. Lacking a rational irrigation system the rice plants died. The lack of water ruined all our work. The Khmer Rouge, demoralised by this setback, allotted other tasks to us, varying in their usefulness.

The main point that Pin Yathay makes about this is that in his first few months under the Khmer Rouge he had come to understand that blind, unquestioning obedience, even in matters which went against his professional training and expertise, was the essential ingredient for survival.

> I had found the key to survival. Pretend to be deaf! Pretend to be dumb! Understand nothing! Listen to nothing! I tried to feign ignorance and said very little.

He was able to cite innumerable examples of those who did speak up or who dared to question Angkar wisdom and were led off at night never to return.

The next big project in which Pin Yathay participated was the building of a huge dam at Veal Vong at the end of 1975. "Once again," he writes, "the Khmer Rouge were defying the laws of hydraulics and physics." But the young "pure and hard" Khmer Rouge insisted that "political consciousness" was what counted. They had only contempt for the laws of bourgeois science and for "book knowledge." Pin Yathay told me that he knew he was taking part in a disastrous enterprise but he dared not utter a word. To have questioned the wisdom of the methods or even hinted at the possibility of failure would be to commit the most heinous of crimes by suggesting that Angkar was something less than infallible! Security was stricter than ever. For the first time they worked under the surveillance of armed guards. The dam was being built in the dry season across a temporarily empty river bed.

We piled up all sorts of material, which we transported in our woven baskets — earth, mud mixed with grass, leaves, pebbles, branches. Anything went. We threw this debris on to the dam wall, without any security dispositions, any spreading out or compacting. I doubted that this improvised dam would last more than one year during the high water season, even if the dimensions were extremely great — gigantic in fact.

Thousands of men and women expended their energies day and night at this work site. The result was an inevitable bungle of revolutionary fervour. The Khmer Rouge had lost all their critical faculties, all sense of proportion.... The (new) caste of seigneurs and cadres could take all decisions. They had the right of life and death over us...

At the height of the flood season, the Veal Vong dam collapsed. The raging river swept away not only all vestiges of the dam but also the huts and shelters which lined its banks. Over a hundred deportees, mainly old folks and children, were drowned or disappeared. Below the dam site there was nothing but devastation. Fortunately for Pin Yathay, his work group was established on higher ground above the dam.

One could find the inspiration for most of the criminal absurdities perpetuated by the Khmer Rouge in the worst excesses of the Chinese Cultural Revolution, applied in an infinitely more primitive way. However, although "Politics in Command" was a favorite slogan of the Cultural Revolution, scientifically and technically sound irrigation systems — including complicated stone aqueducts and tunnels hacked through mountains — were built by the work forces of the Chinese communes. While paper knowledge was officially sneered at during the height of the Cultural Revolution, science and technique — and those who had mastered these subjects — were highly appreciated by the commune members. City intellectuals were sent by Mao Tse-tung to the countryside to be "educated by the poor peasants." By and large, they were put to good use by the commune members if they had demonstrable practical skills. Under the Khmer Rouge, city intellectuals were sent to the countryside to be exterminated; they had to exert considerable ingenuity to hide their talents in order to survive.

With unquestioning obedience to Angkar as one of the primary rules for a "good" Khmer Rouge and for those under his power, there had to be drastic sanctions for the disobedient. These were applied not only to the deportees, who were led out at night to have their heads bashed in, but also to the head bashers if they were imprudent enough to question an Angkar directive. Angkar represented the super-negation of the separation of state powers. Not only was it party, state, and government; it was also executive, legislature, and judiciary, against whose decisions there was no appeal. The local Khmer Rouge chief was the incarnation of all these powers.

In order to insure that the "poorest of the poor" would become the new masters, it was often the village "drop-out" — even by poor peasant standards — who was appointed local Angkar chief. (Just about any village in the world will have a few such "dropouts." Incapable of keeping steady jobs they often lapse into alcoholism, saved from prison or starvation by indulgent relatives keen to uphold family honor!) The Khmer Rouge endowed these village "marginals" with the powers of life and death over those in their charge. And the latter were not averse to imposing their will by the most murderous means as far as "new" residents were concerned, nor to settling accounts with "old" residents whom they felt had humiliated them in the past, nor to helping themselves to any material objects which could be appropriated in the name of Angkar's "needs." They were accountable — and automatically executable — only if caught *in flagrente delicto*, appropriating something coveted by a Khmer Rouge cadre of superior status!

A "good" Khmer Rouge — like all other husbands — had sexual relations only with his wife and only at times and places designated by the local leadership. But there were many pretty, sophisticated young women among the deportees, either unattached in general or separated from their husbands by work projects, starvation, or death. The lumpen-peasant Khmer Rouge chiefs were not indifferent to their charms. And they had the power — even without invoking Angkar — to press their demands. Pin Yathay relates a typical case at the Veal Vong work site.

A woman was caught by surprise by soldiers when she was making love with a Khmer Rouge. Her son, long before the incident, had been deported to a youth camp and she had been arbitrarily separated from her husband.... The Khmer Rouge with whom she had been surprised was not just anybody! He was the deputy-chief of Camp Two. During the interrogation to which she was submitted by the Khmer Rouge, she denounced two others. The *chlop* (official spy) and the secretary of Camp Two. The three Khmer Rouge implicated in the affair were real brutes, absolute butchers. They had numerous crimes on their consciences. All four, the young woman and the three Khmer Rouge, were taken into the jungle and executed.

The "new" residents considered the young woman as an authentic heroine of the passive resistance. She had denounced the *chlop* and the secretary — the most bloodthirsty (cadres) in the camp. Without doubt she had taken revenge for her husband and friends who had been tortured and killed by these two evil characters. We admired her gesture.... The combination of the ambitions of the chief of the camp and the heroism of the young woman rid us of dangerous elements....

One of the ironies of the system introduced by Angkar was that, in the name of establishing a "pure" and incorruptible society, it created a new administrative class which was just as corrupt in its own way as the old ones had been. "Power corrupts," and this could never have been more true than when a cadre at village or work site level had the power of life and death over those under his control. One of the most common forms of corruption under the Lon Nol regime was for high-level officers to draw U.S. dollars to pay and feed non-existent units. Lower-level officers did the same by not striking off the active list those who had died or deserted. Similarly, Khmer Rouge cadres only partially reported the daily deaths, or deferred reporting them for weeks or months, in order to store away their rice rations. Each condensed milk can of rice (the unit of measure by which it was doled out) had its specific value in terms of taels of gold, jewelery, or articles of clothing, this value fluctuating according to the capitalist law of supply and demand. Families like that of Pin Yathay remained alive and together as long as they did only because of the supplementary rations they bought on the black market from the secret Khmer Rouge stores. Of course, these were discreet operations which resulted in instant death for buyer and seller when they were discovered. Transactions were arranged through a middleman, whose life expectancy was short. He was the inevitable scapegoat, as it was on his person that the "black" rice was found. Occasionally, like the girl in the sexual offense case, he would denounce the principals before he was killed. Usually he kept silent, knowing that his family would be exterminated if he denounced the Khmer Rouge responsible.

Lies and deceit were part of the daily, hourly behavior of a "good" Khmer Rouge. How could it be otherwise when he was continually passing on lying and deceitful orders given by his superiors? There was no source from which he could acquire morality. The greatest of lies were justified by the cause of Angkar. He killed and stole in the name of Angkar. Pin Yathay relates the case of Uch Sam Sem, chief of the Phnom Penh Customs Service under Sihanouk. In January 1976, when the Angkar leadership announced a new Constitution, he was living alone (having been separated from his family) and was known as an indefatigable worker. One of the articles in the new Constitution stated that citizens were allowed to keep personal belongings. Uch Sam Sem noted that Khmer Rouge cadres started wearing watches. So he started to wear his own. A few days later, a member of the village Khmer Rouge committee said that Angkar "proposed to borrow" his watch. He replied that he needed it in order to be on time for work. The head of the group came and insisted: "You've worn that watch for years. You can leave it with me for awhile." Apparently naively believing in the Constitution — there had been many "political sessions" at which the Khmer Rouge cadres praised its contents, especially the passage about retaining items of personal property — Uch Sam Sem still held out. Ten days later he was sent into the forest to cut wood and never came back. A week after his disappearance, his watch reappeared on the wrist of a Khmer Rouge soldier. Pin Yathay heard this soldier boasting to his comrades about how he got the watch "from that traitor who often spoke in the language of the French imperialists."

The Constitution itself was a lie and every Khmer Rouge cadre soon knew it. Except for the setting-up of Chinese-type communes, none of its articles were ever implemented. Why not continue to lie and steal with impunity? The only one to whom the unfortunate Uch Sam Sem could turn in demanding his constitutional rights was the Khmer Rouge village chief, who had demanded the watch.

"Good" Khmer Rouge cadres learned to suppress any feelings of sentiment or humanity, even toward their own wives and children if they had any. Feelings of pity and friendship, or giving a helping hand to those in distress, were the stigmata of "individualist tendencies." They were "stains of a bourgeois past" and must be suppressed. If a Khmer Rouge couple wanted to be regarded as "models" they lived apart and met only with the approval of their immediate chief. Family life had to be stamped out as the nucleus of private property, the clan system, and eventually the capitalist state. Normal human sentiments were viewed as expressions of revolutionary weakness and had to be eradicated.

It is interesting to note that the Kuomintang Chinese had been vigilant for any signs of humane feelings among their prisoners, in order to detect which of them were Communists. Spies from the secret police were put in the prison cells to watch for anyone who shared a scrap of food with another, tended his or her wounds, murmured a few words of comfort after a torture session, or did anything which betrayed compassion or solidarity. That person was marked down as a Communist. For the Khmer Rouge, such a person was a reactionary!

The idea of a society comprised exclusively of the Khmer Rouge — that is, the military and civilian organizations of Angkar — was reiterated in numerous utterances from the top level of the leadership down to those who conducted the indoctrination sessions at the base. Only one or two million "pure and hard" militants would be needed to build this "new society." A "good" Khmer Rouge cadre was aware of this and acted accordingly. The task of the enslaved "new" residents — who, as they died out, were being replaced by the "old" residents — was to create the infrastructure of this "new society" for the master class to enjoy. When the slaves "old" and "new" had disappeared altogether, they would be replaced by the "pure and hard" themselves, who could be counted on to serve a tiny elite who would do their thinking for them. Angkar was the perfect organism to foster and execute such a monstrous concept. Oxen were castrated physically to make them docile and oblivious to their fate. The "pure and hard" were castrated mentally, spiritually, and psychologically to make them incapable of independent thought. As rigorous guardians of the "old" and "new" slaves, the Khmer Rouge cadres were well on their way to becoming slaves themselves.

1. There were two official journals: the "Revolutionary Flag," organ of the Communist Party of Kampuchea, and the "Red Flag," organ of the Communist Youth organization. Both were published irregularly and were not available to the general public. News was obtained — by those with the right to own a receiver — from Phnom Penh radio.

2. Yathay, Pin, *L'Utopie Meutrière*. Paris: Robert Laffont, 1980. All the rest of the quotations in this chapter are from this work.

9.
CONDITIONING THE PURE AND HARD

Had the Khmer Rouge remained in power for a few more years, there is a very real possibility that only the young "pure and hard" cadres would have survived. Survivors of the Khmer Rouge terror and foreign observers alike have remarked on the extreme youth of the Khmer Rouge cadres, especially the "vanguard units,"[1] and on the obvious pleasure with which they wielded knives, hatchets, and axes and vied with each other in devising more effective techniques of butchery. Documentary films about the youthful Khmer Rouge remnants in the Thai border camps — doing field exercises and push-ups — are visual indictments of the regime that formed them. Removed from the social influences of family and village life and conditioned to despise all religious, moral, and philosophical values (if they even know that such values exist!), their faces betray no emotions other than indifference, suspicion, and stony hatred.

In a talk at Columbia University on 4 March 1980 Sydney H. Schanberg of *The New York Times* — one of those who covered the entry of the Khmer Rouge into Phnom Penh and was held in the French embassy before being evacuated by road to Thailand — posed the question of what could be done with these teenage murderers. "Pol Pot's army of twelve- and sixteen-year-old boys cannot be allowed into normal society," he said. "They will kill normal people." To him it was clear that they had travelled too far along the road of inhumanity to be saved.

How could this have been brought about?

It was Prince Sihanouk's very articulate cousin, Lola, who first shed some light on this for me. During the period of her deportation, she succeeded in "taming" a few of these young savages to the extent that they shared some of their thoughts with her.[2] Lola explained that the first "harvest" of young assassins was reaped by the Khmer Rouge leadership in the remote mountain bases from which they waged armed struggle against Sihanouk in the last years of his regime. A standard catechism was prepared to answer questions relating to every detail of the truly hard and bitter life of the most underprivileged section of the community in the most remote and backward areas of the country. "Why do you work hard and live badly, while others do no work and ride around in cars?" "Why are some people educated but you cannot go to school?" The answers were predictable.

The guilty were the city dwellers; the exploiters and oppressors were the city capitalists. But capitalist, imperialist, and oppressor were applied to everyone who lived in a city. "Either we must kill them, or they will continue to oppress — and eventually kill — us." Repeated day after day, with infinite examples of the barbarous behavior of the city dwellers, the poison was effective. A hatred was built up against every aspect of city life from books, learning, and culture to automobiles and scientific laboratories. How does someone become a schoolteacher or university professor? "By stealing the fruits of the poor peasants' labor." Where did the rich get the money to buy their fine villas and automobiles? "From your rice, your fish, your bananas."

Keng Vannsak explains that the term used by the Khmer Rouge to designate their most implacable enemy — the bourgeoisie — is *sambor bep*, which literally means a tendency to consider comfort, well-being, and prosperity as a "better way of life." This was the ultimate sin and any thoughts in this direction had to be crushed for all time together with those who dared let their thoughts stray in this direction or who had the physical attributes of a *sambor bep*.

> In the category "bourgeois," who must be eliminated, first are all who have a fair skin, are in good health, well-fed, well-clad — for all these are the external signs of a *sambor bep*. And in fact the Khmer Rouge used such criteria to recognize their "class enemies" and summarily execute them. It suffices to turn up the palm of the hand — roughened it saved — if not it was death. . . .[3]

The Khmer Rouge took the Biblical doctrine that "the poor shall inherit the earth" and put it in even more idyllic terms: "The poorest of the poor shall inherit the earth — immediately.'' But first all the class enemies must be wiped out. That would be the main task of the ''pure and hard'' young combatants! They shouted the responses to the catechism questions in chorus until their reflexes were automatic. Then they were given guns.

''Giving illiterate kids guns after such indoctrination,'' exclaimed Keng Vannsak. ''Can anyone be astonished at the results?'' He continued:

> These were timid jungle boys who never had anything more lethal than a sling-shot to kill birds in their hands, who slipped out of sight when rare visitors came to their villages, scared of anything which smelled of Authority. Overnight, *they* became Authority, with arms at their disposal to enforce it, and no questions asked as to how or why they exercised their death-dealing power.

In an essay entitled ''A Vengeance-Seeking Passion,'' Keng Vannsak explained the effect of this indoctrination.

> More frightening even than the Khmer Rouge themselves is their faith in their Mission! The Angkar Leu had invested in them the power to act as ''the sole masters of their actions.'' They thus imagined themselves as real ''demigods,'' taking part in the collective creation of a ''New Man''!

> Slaves, degraded to the level of animals under the Monarchy of the God-Kings, again slaves more submissive and resigned than ever under the Monarchy of the Buddhist-Kings, continually hunted down, fugitives in the jungle, condemned to the double Nothing — on Earth as in Heaven — these men and women, these children and adolescents, having come forth from their miserable existence, liberated from their despicable existence until that moment.are all of a sudden promoted as Masters, Demigods! Imagine their conceit, their pride of power, in revealing themselves in the full light of day — and to exact obedience! Before, only princes, priests, the feudal class, the bourgeoisie and the rich could dispense life and death, misfortune and happiness. Now, thanks to the Revolution the sons and daughters of the worker-peasants, the poor, the weak, the pariahs, have arrived at their turn to be the only ones to decide on questions of life and death! One of the ''ancient predictions'' [very dear to the Kampuchean psyche—W.B.] had thus come true: ''Whilst the Great sink to the bottom, the Small flotsam rises to the surface!'' Further, the Khmer Rouge had the firm conviction that

they acted in the name of a Just Ideology. Attachment to a Just Doctrine — this is one of the constants among Khmer beliefs. They have always been passionately attached to doctrines and their sacred texts....

This explains, in part at least, the savage vehemence with which they relentlessly pursued their Revolution, on a field already prepared by traditional absolutism.[4]

Thus, teenagers with murderous weapons in their hands were convinced that theirs was a just and historic mission. Their task was to track down and murder their own and their country's "class enemies." With their aid, the Khmer Rouge succeeded in eliminating their Sihanoukist rivals and the veterans of the old Indochina Communist Party. The voices of reason were stilled throughout the land!

Later this reflex-fixing process of indoctrination was applied not only to cadres but also to citizens, beginning with the young children. In some areas, but by no means all, children from five to nine years of age received up to one hour's "education" daily. The Khmer Rouge considered children in this age group to be like blank sheets of paper, on which could be written whatever one liked. In the region where Pin Yathay lived, children ten and older no longer went to school. They were grouped in child brigades and worked the same hours as did the adults. The classes for the younger children lasted from 11:00 a.m. to 12:00 noon, the rest of the day they also worked. However, Pin Yathay notes, the determination of the children's ages could be done only by hit-and-miss methods.

The notion of age had in fact disappeared. There were no longer any vital records, no longer any possibility of getting a birth certificate. The age of a child was guessed at visually. The Khmer Rouge arbitrarily designated children who were between five and nine years. These were exempt from work between 11 a.m. and midday. Often, children of eleven pretended they were only nine, in order to study and have an hour's rest.

At school, the kids had a real break; they remained seated and listened to their lessons, learning by heart the songs of the revolution instead of planting out rice or clearing land. The greater part of Cambodian children, before the fall of Phnom Penh, could read and write. They learned to read, write and count at school, which was secular and compulsory in our country. As in France, there were primary and secondary schools and establishments of higher education.... But these children told the Khmer Rouge they were illiterate, in order to get an extra hour of rest.[5]

Chan Ven, a professor of physics who had headed the anti-Lon Nol resistance organization in Kompong Thom province, characterized the quality of the Khmer Rouge "hour-per-day" schools as follows:

> Because of the extermination of teachers with real pedagogical qualifications, these were replaced by persons who could hardly read or write. Their role consisted, above all, in interrogating their pupils to collect information on the backgrounds and activities of their parents, as well as other inhabitants of the cooperative. In this way, they were able to build up abundant and authentic information. The interrogation about the behaviour of their parents at home included the question: "Do you get anything extra to eat?" The children would reply truthfully.
>
> Children were grouped in classes according to their ages regardless of their level of education. This was done to be able to send them off to manual labour. They had neither exercise books nor chalk. They were all seated on the ground and some of them, girls as well as boys, were nude. There were a few textbooks for reading and arithmetic — they were the same for all classes, no others being available.
>
> The basis of this education, apart from the manual labour of gathering manure and building ricefield dykes, concerned the hatred which must be maintained against the former city-people, the discovery and wiping out of hidden enemies and anyone from Vietnam — the hereditary enemy. The true friend of Democratic Kampuchea is Peking. Angkar is the benefactor of children et cetera.
>
> The classes were only open for about half an hour daily — between midday and 1 p.m. Outside class hours, the children were employed in looking after herds of oxen and buffalo, collecting their dung (20 to 30 kilograms daily for each child of 8 to 10 years)....
>
> The method of education...consisted of memorising phrases and slogans, the sense of which they did not understand. In other words education of our children consisted essentially of learning to love Angkar; to despise the sacred links which united them to their parents and become capable of killing with their own hands their father, their mother and other relatives in case the latter were

suspected of acts likely to harm the revolution. The traitors wanted to transform our children into robots, thinking only what Angkar had inculcated into them, acting only according to the orders or the slogans of Angkar.

It should be noted that if children did not achieve the norms set for them, they were deprived of rations, they were whipped, they were punished by all sorts of methods in front of their friends. Sometimes a child would be killed in front of his or her friends to serve as an example.

The youth of the "new" urban evacuees were not eligible for membership in the "elitist" Khmer Rouge or for enlistment in the armed forces, even if they volunteered. Their non-revolutionary, urban backgrounds were considered to be a source of "corruption" of the "pure and hard," and their fate was to become extinct by direct or indirect extermination.

Those who were enrolled in the revolutionary forces began their military careers at the age of twelve. They were separated from their families and removed from their native villages to be indoctrinated in the mold of Pol Pot. At an early stage they were conditioned to what Sihanouk defines as a "cult of cruelty."

Pol Pot and Ieng Sary believed, quite correctly, that by getting them used to the "cruelty game" quite early, these *yotheas* (soldiers) would end up by delighting in massacres and thus in waging war.

During the three years of my "house arrest" in Phnom Penh, I watched the *yotheas* entrusted with guarding my "camp" repeatedly delight in practicing the "cruelty game" at the expense of animals (dogs, cats, monkeys, geckos et cetera) and at the same time I often heard them complain at not being sent to the front "to bash the Viets"![6]

Sihanouk's blood-curdling details help to explain the mentality of the Khmer Rouge leadership and the sadism of their young robot killers.

Among the means conceived to toughen the *yotheas*, in first place was the "cruelty game." The young recruits started to "harden their hearts and minds" by killing camp cats, dogs and other "edible animals," by clubbing or bayonetting them. Even after the victory of April 17, 1975, the Khmer Rouge, when they had no human beings to kill or torture, kept themselves "in form" by plunging animals into the "flames of hell." I witnessed an example at the Royal Palace where I was held under "house arrest." The *Kammaphibal* — political commissar charged with looking after the "royal prisoners" — and his team took great pleasure in catching mice, locking them up in a cage and setting fire to it. They greatly enjoyed the spectacle of the mice rushing in all directions trying to escape, then the agony of the little beasts being burned alive. This was a daily spectacle....

Another "game" consisted of torturing monkeys, of which "the suffering resembled that of humans." They cut off their tails with axes. They put them in chains, the chain placed around their necks gradually strangling them as they were forced to run behind their torturers who gradually pulled harder on the chain. The poor monkeys uttered heart-rending cries. The spectacle and the cries were insupportable, but the young *yotheas* thought it all highly amusing.

Not far from the Royal Palace there was a special crocodile-raising farm run by a company of *yotheas*. The crocodiles were fed with live monkeys. Every day the *yotheas* threw the monkeys into the pit and were delighted with the spectacle of the unfortunate simians, uttering terrified screams as they vainly tried to clamber out of the pit and were then subdued, hypnotised by the fixed stare of these monstrous reptiles, snapped up and devoured by them.[7]

At the Phnom Penh genocide trial, evidence was given of young children having been fed to crocodiles at a breeding center at Siem Reap. During a visit to the site of this grim enterprise we met witnesses who claimed to have heard the terrified screams after truckloads of children were driven to the spot. The mind refuses to accept many such accounts. I myself would not have given credence to the children and crocodiles story, had I not read Sihanouk's account of the sort of conditioning to sadism he had witnessed. After that, anything was possible!

Up until early 1977 most killings were carried out by taking people off at night, one or two at a time. But from April 1977 on, because of the widespread unrest and armed uprisings, the order went out for wholesale executions. The killer-robots were in their element, carrying out the task they had been conditioned for with zeal and probably the closest thing to joy that they were capable of feeling. The only times when these youthful assassins were seen with smiles on their faces were when they were killing their compatriots, flexing their muscles and competing to see who could kill with just a single blow of an axe or spade or hoe.[8]

One of the places where massacres on a huge scale took place in 1977 and 1978 was near Chup, Kampuchea's biggest rubber plantation, in the country's most revolutionary province of Kompong Cham. Investigation teams appointed by the Genocide Tribunal estimated that about twenty thousand people had been killed in the immediate vicinity of Chia Po Ri village alone. One of the numerous witnesses from that area was 26-year-old Man Bien, a Chia Po Ri resident, whose evidence was as follows:

> Among the victims, some were Chup rubber plantation workers, others were brought from Ka Rach district of Kompong Cham and others were soldiers from the Pol Pot armed forces and cadres from the Eastern Region. They were killed from 4 o'clock in the afternoon until the small hours of the next morning for ten consecutive days. With their arms tied behind them, they were brought in trucks. The butchers then bound their eyes and led them in groups to the execution site. They were killed by thrusts from bayonets or blows from hammers; those still surviving were pushed into the open graves. Near Chia Po Ri village there are about forty of these craters formed by bombs dropped by the Americans in 1973. There were others from 8 to 12 feet deep, about 30 feet long by 15 feet wide, scooped out by the Pol Pot forces with the aid of bulldozers. The victims uttered lamentable cries which the local people could clearly hear at five hundred metres from the execution site. I heard their screams while looking after buffalo, three hundred metres from there.

Another witness, who had collected an axe and a hammer from one of the execution sites, said that "around July-August 1978" he had seen convoys of trucks, each loaded with about one hundred persons, arriving at the outskirts of Chia Po Ri.

> The victims were men and women, most of them plantation workers, but there were also Pol Pot cadres and militia. Others were brought from I don't know where, but from the direction of O Rang Au village. The Pol Pot agents loaded those with bound arms on to vehicles which took them to the plantation. On getting down from the trucks, their eyes were bandaged. The assassins then killed them with blows from hammers and iron bars. Lads of 15 to 18 years, the butchers didn't have enough strength to kill with one blow, but had to strike two or three times. They buried alive those who were in their

death throes in five big pits on the plantation. These were craters made by very big American bombs, of which one was about 18 feet deep and 60 feet in diameter. The butchers filled these craters with corpses, then covered them over with earth.

There were many eyewitnesses to the Chup massacres and to others of similar magnitude in Svay Rieng, Siem Reap, Battambang, Pursat, and other provinces. All of those with whom I spoke stressed the demented glee with which the young executioners went about their gruesome, physically exhausting tasks, cracking jokes about the toughness of this or that victim's skull and speculating about how many blows it would take to crack it. Pleas for mercy, especially from women victims, produced roars of laughter.

To bring teenagers to this state of mind clearly required that everything relating to humanist culture, education, religion, philosophy, and morality had to be suppressed and even, whenever possible, eliminated. There was a Four-Year Plan for the development of culture. But like the term used for Revolution, which in fact meant the opposite, the Four-Year Plan was aimed at the dismantling of culture as it had been expressed until then in Kampuchea. "In the Four-Year Plan, 1977-80 concerning culture, literature and art," states the Angkar directive, "we must continue to eradicate from culture and art, all vestiges of imperialism, colonialism, feudalism and all other former classes in power." It was within this framework that Phnom Penh's Catholic cathedral was completely dismantled, stone by stone.

Libraries, research centers, museums, monuments — anything which reflected the millenia of rich contributions by Kampuchea to national and world culture — had to be abolished. And those active in any form of traditional or contemporary art had to be exterminated. It would be left to the robot-killers, bereft of any human sentiments and concepts of art or beauty in any form, to create a new Angkarian art, literature, and culture!

From its ancient Angkor monuments to its traditional handicraft workers in silver, ivory, precious woods, and other materials, from its world-famed classical ballet to its village forkloric dance and musical groups, Kampuchea was a cultural treasure-house until the seeds of destruction were sown by the Khmer Rouge! Statistics are a very inadequate means of describing what happened but at least they tell part of the story.

Of the 54 members of the world-famed Royal Ballet, 4 survived.

Of 195 classical dancers from other groups of traditional ballet, 48 survived.

Of 199 dancers, musicians, and learners of the folkloric dance group, 38 dancers and 9 musicians survived.

Of 416 students of the plastic arts, 14 survived.

In presenting the balance to the Genocide Tribunal, a representative of the Ministry of Culture gave the following summary of what happened to culture and the arts under the Khmer Rouge.

> Immediately after they took power, the Pol Pot-Ieng Sary clique ordered the destruction of all musical instruments, all the traditional theatre costumes, all documents regarding the arts. The places where the artists exercised their arts, such as the Phnom Penh and provincial theatres, the University of Fine Arts, and the Faculty of Music, were almost all destroyed or damaged with a few, very rare exceptions.
>
> The artists, men and women, old or young, were pitilessly massacred by blows from hoes, lengths of bamboo, metal rods. They were stabbed with bayonets or sharpened bits of iron. Many had their eyes gouged out, were disembowelled or were buried alive. The least unfortunate, if one can use such an expression, died gradually through the hard labour demanded of them in exchange for completely insufficient food. Thus died....

There followed a long list of some of the most renowned actors and actresses, musicians, dancers, and others prominent in all fields of contemporary Kampuchean culture. What power those young savages must have felt when, with a blow or two of a hoe, they could fell a famous actor of member of the Royal Corps de Ballet. Now the farmyard had really triumphed over the "class enemy"!

Approximately one thousand students, technicians, engineers, doctors, diplomats, and others returned to Kampuchea after April 1975 when the Khmer Rouge appealed to them to help reconstruct the country. Only eighty-five survived, mainly by hiding their true identity. Most of the rest were killed at the Tuol Sleng torture extermination center. In the days of Sihanouk, Tuol Sleng had been a school, the Lycée Ponhea Yat. Its name was changed to Lycée Tuol Sleng after Lon Nol's coup in March 1970. At the end of 1975

Pol Pot transformed it into the principal torture-extermination center in Phnom Penh. An important subsidiary center was located at the Lycée Descartes, where my three children had been enrolled during our family's four years of residence in Phnom Penh.

Chan Ven, now Minister of Education in the Heng Samrin government, gave the Genocide Tribunal a detailed account of what had happened to education under Angkar rule. Based on a nationwide study, he presented the following statistical table of human losses. The first set of figures is from 1968; the second set comes from a census taken on 1 August 1979.

	1968	1979
Higher Education		
Professors and Lecturers	725	50
Students	11,000	450
Secondary Education		
Teachers	2,300	207
Pupils	106,000	5,300
Primary Education		
Schoolteachers	21,311	2,793
Pupils	991,000	322,379

Phnom Penh's only televison station was destroyed, as were some forty thousand television sets. Of sixty-six technicians and employees at the station, seven survived. Five journalists out of some three hundred were found alive.

Visiting libraries and museums was not only considered useless, but as a waste of time, illicit for it only enabled readers, visitors, to discover beauty, or ideas which they (the Khmer Rouge) had never considered as orthodox. It was thus that hundreds of thousands of books classified in the Phnom Penh National Library, the Library of the Buddhist Institute, the Khmer-Mon Library, of the Pedagogical Institute and other institutes of learning were sacked and thrown pell-mell into the gardens and onto the footpaths. The greater part of the personnel from the libraries were assassinated — 35 of the original 41 of the National Library were killed....

Antiques attesting to the glorious civilization of the Khmer people, in gold and silver, were stolen by the ruling clique; those in bronze, copper and various alloys were seized up to 70 percent. It was the same for statues in wood and stone. Very beautiful monuments had thus been destroyed in the University of Fine Arts, centre for training archeologists and of archeological research. The majority of archeologists, sculptors and students of the Faculty of Archeology were assassinated. Monsieur Ly Vu Ong, dean of the Faculty and at the same time Curator of the National Museum, was killed at Kien Svay immediately after having been forced to leave Phnom Penh. The victim had to dig his own grave before being killed by blows from a pick. Phim Neon, at present working at the National Museum, was an eyewitness.[9]

Those champions of the "revolutionary left" who defend the sweeping away of all traces of feudal and bourgeois culture would do well to recall the remarks made by Lenin when such views were put forward by Bogdanov in the name of "Proletcult" shortly after the Bolshevik Revolution.

Marxism has won its historical significance as the ideology of the revolutionary proletariat because, far from rejecting the most valuable achievements of the bourgeois epoch, it has, on the contrary, assimilated and refashioned everything of value in the more than two thousand years of the development of human thought and culture. Only further work on this basis and in this direction, inspired by the practical experience of the proletarian dictatorship as the final stage in the struggle against every form of exploitation, can be recognised as the development of a genuine proletarian culture....[10]

One does not need to be a Marxist or a Leninist to accept this formulation as a crushing denunciation — in advance — of the burners of books and the destroyers of museums and libraries, of those who spurned their own culture and traditions and deliberately set out to transform their youth into cultureless, dehumanized robot-killers.

In his summing-up statement to the Genocide Tribunal, the Ministry of Culture's representative made a significant point concerning the attitude of the new Kampuchean government toward what at first sight seems to be an irrevocably lost section of the present generation of young Kampucheans.

All culture was to be abolished and in fact was abolished during the regime of Pol Pot and Ieng Sary. The resulting consequences are numerous. Apart from the immense losses in artists and scientists and the considerable material losses, we must insist that losses from the human viewpoint are incalculable. Children and young people who have been gravely poisoned by the Pol Pot-Ieng Sary "cultural revolution" must again become Cambodians with an authentic Khmer culture.

The simplistic solution of killing ten thousand or so of them has been rejected in a generous demonstration of faith in human nature and the possibility of recuperating the seemingly most hopeless of the "lost souls"!

1. "Vanguard units" or "shock brigades" were comprised of youth conscripted for particularly difficult emergency tasks such as building military fortifications or urgent irrigation works. These youth were worked to death at a slightly faster pace than the ordinary slave laborers and were subject to more rigid, military-type discipline.

2. Luckily for Lola, she is dark-skinned (skin pigmentation being one of the criteria for spotting a "bourgeois") and by the time she started the "taming" process her hands and feet were as calloused by field work as those of the "old" residents. Dark skin and calloused hands and feet were *prima facie* criteria of class respectability.

3. Vannsak, Keng, *Aperçu de la Revolution Khmer Rouge*, p. 18. Montmorency, France, 2 March 1977.

4. *Ibid.*, pp. 19-20.

5. Yathay, Pin, *L'Utopie Meutrière*, pp. 303-4. Paris: Robert Laffont, 1980.

6. Sihanouk, Norodom, *Chroniques de Guerre et d'Espoir*, p. 69. Paris: Hachette/Stock, 1979.

7. *Ibid.*, pp. 136-7.

8. There was certainly something symbolic in the choice of the death-dealing weapons. Hoes and spades are the tools of the poorest of the poor peasants, as is a length of bamboo. In the numerous cases in which torture preceded execution, I was told, the torture was done by sawing at the throats of the victims with razor-edged reeds or the serrated fronds of certain palms. The victims' agony was prolonged, sadistic pleasure was intensified for the torturer-executioners, and such exercises in rustic "self-

sufficiency" were meritorious in the eyes of Angkar!

9. Testimony given at the "Trial for Genocide of the Pol Pot-Ieng Sary Clique," Phnom Penh, 17-19 August 1979.

10. Lenin, V. I., *Collected Works*, Volume 31, p. 317. Moscow: Progress Publishers, 1966.

TRIANGULAR
RELATIONS

10.
THE FRONTIER WAR

In late March 1964 I was in Phnom Penh, awaiting a meeting with the Head of State, Prince Sihanouk, with mixed feelings. A few days earlier I had illegally crossed into Cambodian territory from the Liberated Zones of South Vietnam, my second illegal frontier crossing within a couple of months. (The first had been in the opposite direction.) There was no way in which Sihanouk could have known officially that I was even in Cambodia had I not called on his prime minister, Son Sann, a few days earlier to show him a map. This map — which the President of the National Liberation Front, Nguyen Huu Tho, had authorized me to show to Sihanouk — portrayed in red the areas solidly occupied by the National Liberation Front (NLF), in blue those occupied by the Saigon regime, and in yellow the contested areas. Most of the area on the Vietnamese side of the border was red in considerable depth. Sihanouk was away for a few days but Son Sann begged me to await his return. As I had another set of documents of interest to Sihanouk, I decided to stay.

Starting up the steps to Sihanouk's Chancar Mon residence a few days later, I was still in doubt as to how I would be received. He was, quite rightly, very sensitive to any infringements of his country's neutrality. In fact, it was to avoid putting him in a compromised position that I had entered the country under another name and had not asked for permission to leave and re-enter. Thus I felt that Sihanouk could answer any Saigon or U.S. charges that he was allowing "neutral Cambodia" to become a base for clandestine frontier crossings into South Vietnam by jailing or expelling me as someone who had illegally entered Cambodia and twice

137

violated her frontiers with South Vietnam. This was very much in my mind as I was ushered up the steps into the reception salon. But there was a smiling Sihanouk advancing toward me, taking both my hands in his and saying: "Monsieur Burchett, I understand you have accomplished a fabulous exploit. My warmest congratulations." An attendant appeared with a tray and two glasses of champagne; then a photographer snapped us clinking glasses. "I understand you have a most interesting map," Sihanouk said. I spread it out on a table and he was fascinated, his eyes round with surprise.

"I see with whom I have to discuss frontier questions," he said. "Not with Saigon, but with Maître Nguyen Huu Tho." A few days earlier, just before my last discussions with Nguyen Huu Tho at his jungle headquarters in Tay Ninh province, the Saigon government had laid claim to a group of seven small Cambodian islands just opposite Kep, a holiday resort on Cambodia's southeast coast. For years previously, the Saigon regime — and U.S. planes — had bombed, strafed, and shelled Cambodia's frontier villages on the grounds that the frontier had not been defined. I was authorized to inform Sihanouk that the NLF recognized the islands as Cambodian territory and considered the frontier, at least in the regions where the violations were taking place, to be clearly defined and recognized by Vietnamese and Cambodians living in their respective frontier villages.

Another "present" I had for him from Nguyen Huu Tho was in the form of some documents — including training manuals for subversion, espionage, and sabotage — captured when NLF forces overran a Khmer Serei headquarters in the Mekong Delta. (Captured with the documents were four U.S. master-sergeants. They were advisers to the CIA-created Khmer Serei forces, which were then being groomed to overthrow Sihanouk.) Nguyen Huu Tho also charged me with informing Sihanouk that if the Saigon troops launched any large-scale attacks against Cambodia, the NLF would attack them from the rear. As the map indicated, they were well placed to do so.

Sihanouk asked detailed questions about my experiences. He was clearly impressed by my accounts of the strength and widespread organization of the "Vietcong" and the support they enjoyed from the local population everywhere I went, including up to the outskirts of Saigon. He cut short my attempted apology for having violated his frontiers: "The other side is violating our frontiers every day, killing our peasants."

He advised me, however, on future occasions to inform him so that he could give me a military escort to a frontier crossing point. I took advantage of that offer on three subsequent visits. Indeed, one of the most perilous moments on my first visit had been my return frontier crossing. I hid in the high grass in a roadside ditch while a Cambodian motorized patrol went by. The troops had their guns at the ready and spotlights slowly swept the few yards between the road and the frontier at that point. The frontier guards were known to be "quick on the trigger" and shot on sight any marauder, which I clearly was!

Sihanouk was also "quick on the trigger." Within three months of our meeting (on June 20 to be exact), he sent a letter to Nguyen Huu Tho. Having given due attention to what I had told him of the friendly feelings towards him shared by all the NLF leaders with whom I had talked and their respect for the courageous way in which he had defended his country's neutrality, he expressed a desire to meet Nguyen Huu Tho. As for the border question:

> We give up all territorial claims in exchange for an unambiguous recognition of the existing borders and of our sovereignty over the coastal islands illegally claimed by the Saigon administration....

In a subsequent letter, replying to one from Nguyen Huu Tho, Sihanouk clarified his position still further.

> For its part, Cambodia only demands recognition of its existing land border as drawn on the maps commonly used up to 1954[1] and recognition of its sovereignty over the coastal islands illegally claimed by the Saigon regime without any justification whatsoever....[2]

The exchange of the Sihanouk-Nguyen Huu Tho letters, the contents of which were confirmed to me in a meeting with Nguyen Huu Tho (by then vice-president of the Socialist Republic of Vietnam) in Hanoi in December 1978, was followed by secret meetings between Cambodian and NLF representatives in Peking in October and again in December of 1964. Sihanouk must be given full credit for having been convinced as early as 1964 that the NLF would emerge as the victor in South Vietnam. Otherwise, why bother to negotiate? In this he was more foresighted than his opposite numbers in

Saigon and Vientiane.

Sihanouk's diplomatic skill was considerable but he often failed in his aims by over-estimating the value of his cards. He believed he held an ace — even a joker — in the conflict in South Vietnam. He could offer sanctuary to hard-pressed NLF guerrillas, hospital and supply facilities, including the use of the port of Sihanoukville to receive shipments of military equipment from the Soviet Union and China, and rice delivered to the frontier. For this Sihanouk felt the NLF should pay something over and above top world prices in hard currency.

On the map presented at the first round of the Peking talks, the Cambodians had amended the pre-1954 map in nine places. In each case the "corrections" were at the expense of South Vietnamese territory. The Cambodians also claimed two islands which clearly lay to the south of the Brévié Line and asked for special privileges for Khmer ethnic minorities living in South Vietnam and for the use by Cambodia of Saigon as a port of trans-shipment. Apart from any other considerations, the yielding of such concessions by the NLF would have laid it open to charges of "selling out the national patrimony" by the Saigon regime, with whom the NLF was locked in a life-and-death military and political struggle. The Peking talks resulted in nothing except expressions of friendship and solidarity between the two sides. The NLF position remained that of "recognition of existing frontiers as drawn on maps commonly used up to 1954."[3]

In March 1965 a Conference of the Indochinese Peoples was held in Phnom Penh at Sihanouk's initiative. By this time the United States had started its air war against North Vietnam and was landing combat troops in the South. The delegation of the Vietnam Fatherland Front from the North and that of the NLF from the South used the Conference to reiterate their position of "respect for the sovereignty, independence, neutrality, and territorial integrity of Cambodia and undertook to continue to do so and to avoid any action inconsistent with these principles."

The American build-up in South Vietnam continued; combat action with the use of U.S. troops intensified; and the war continued to spill over into Cambodian frontier villages. Sihanouk proposed an international conference to guarantee the inviolability of his country's frontiers. The proposal was treated with contempt by the United States and her Western allies.

In August 1966 I made my fourth visit to the Liberated Areas of South Vietnam, arriving back in Phnom Penh a few hours before the arrival of French President Charles de Gaulle. In my pocket I had the text of an interview made two days earlier with Nguyen Huu Tho, in which he stated that the NLF "recognized the sovereignty, independence, and territorial integrity of Cambodia within the limits of its present frontiers." Sihanouk and de Gaulle each received a copy of the interview in the form in which I was publishing it and Sihanouk persuaded de Gaulle to include France's endorsement of this principle in his famous Phnom Penh speech of 1 September 1966.[4]

After de Gaulle's departure, Sihanouk gave a luncheon for the local foreign correspondents and the few who had accompanied the French president but had stayed on a few extra days in Phnom Penh. Sihanouk declared himself to be very satisfied with the results of the visit — and especially with de Gaulle's acceptance of the formula on Cambodia's independence. He paid tribute to Nguyen Huu Tho for having been the first to propose a formula coinciding exactly with his own concepts and to myself for having produced this formula in my interview. He also solemnly announced that in the future any country wishing to establish diplomatic relations with Cambodia would have to affirm acceptance of this formula and any countries already having diplomatic relations would have to do the same if they wanted to maintain diplomatic representation in Phnom Penh.

At the time of the de Gaulle visit to Phnom Penh there was also a delegation of the NLF headed by Tran Buu Kiem, a member of the Presidium of the NLF's Central Committee, in Phnom Penh at Sihanouk's invitation to discuss the border problems. Again Sihanouk sought to exploit an advantage which the NLF had presented to him. He used the NLF formula defining the basis of Cambodia's sovereignty, which he had sought for so long, to secure de Gaulle's endorsement. Then he turned the latter into a weapon to seek further concessions from the Vietnamese. This was smart tactics but poor politics. In the talks with the NLF Sihanouk's delegation presented the same demands as at Peking, added its rejection of the Brévié Line on the grounds that acceptance of it would confirm Vietnamese ownership of Phu Cuoc Island,[5] and insisted that the whole lot was a "take it or leave it" package deal. The NLF opted to "leave it" and after a few weeks of fruitless exchanges the Cambodian delegation proposed that the talks "be suspended for the time being."[6]

Some nine months later, on 9 May 1967, the government of the Kingdom of Cambodia issued a formal statement calling on all countries wishing normal relations with it "to recognize the independence, sovereignty, and territorial integrity of Cambodia within its frontiers as defined in maps used in 1954." The first NLF response to Sihanouk's statement came three weeks later. It stated that the NLF:

(1) Reaffirms its consistent stand to recognize, and undertakes to respect, Cambodian territorial integrity within its existing borders.

(2) Recognizes, and undertakes to respect, the existing frontiers between South Vietnam and Cambodia.

A week later Hanoi made a similar statement. Sihanouk was delighted and immediately began using these two declarations to pressure other countries having diplomatic relations with Cambodia to do likewise. Eventually they all did, some of them with obvious reluctance. Even the United States, in its eagerness to restore diplomatic relations (severed at Sihanouk's initiative in May 1965), eventually swallowed its pride and endorsed the formula. This paved the way for restoring diplomatic relations in June 1969.

Except for further pledges of "respect for the territorial integrity of Cambodia within its existing borders" given by the DRV and the PRG at the April 1970 Summit Conference of the Indochinese People, the border question remained in abeyance until the Khmer Rouge forces took over in Phnom Penh. Sihanouk was overthrown in March 1970 by Lon Nol. Subsequently, both Cambodia's border and its territorial integrity were violated openly by the United States[7] and South Vietnam on the pretext of destroying NLF sanctuaries and supply routes. Throughout this period the Vietnam Fatherland Front and the NLF struggled in solidarity with the Khmer Rouge to defeat U.S. aggression in Indochina.

The struggle against Lon Nol was led by the National United

Front of Kampuchea (FUNK) which had been formed by Sihanouk soon after he was ousted and to which the Khmer Rouge immediately rallied. In his book "Chroniques de Guerre et d'Espoir" (published in Paris after the Chinese persuaded Pol Pot and Ieng Sary to allow him to leave the country), Sihanouk gives the Vietnamese full credit for having borne the brunt of the fighting in the most decisive battles against Lon Nol. He pours scorn on Pol Pot and his clique for attempting to take the credit for all of this:

> In all seriousness, Pol Pot, Ieng Sary, Khieu Samphan, and Nuon Chea (President of the Popular Assembly) asserted over the radio (first from the *maquis*, then in Phnom Penh) that with rudimentary and primitive weapons their troops succeeded in wiping out almost all of the enemy infantry divisions, armoured divisions and air power.

> There is nothing wrong with being patriotic, but deliberately adopting a chauvinistic and dishonest attitude, to the point of denying that the North Vietnamese allies and comrades-at-arms played a preponderant role, to say the least, in stopping, then pushing back the American and South Vietnamese invaders in 1970, 1971 and 1972, is not only insulting to those allies but also an insult to history....[8]

Given the dates Sihanouk uses as illustrations for the decisive role of the Vietnamese forces, it is clear that he is referring to the actions which presented the FUNK forces with a huge liberated area cleared of all Lon Nol military or administrative forces by stopping the U.S.-Saigon invasion of May 1970 and by smashing Lon Nol's Chenla 1 and Chenla 2 offensives. Sihanouk was apparently unaware of the role that Vietnamese artillerymen played in the final offensive which put the Khmer Rouge into Phnom Penh on 17 April 1975. But he does refer to key engagements in which it was the Vietnamese artillery, tanks, and infantry units which played the decisive role.

> Right up to the end of the war in April 1975, the Khmer Rouge armed forces were not able to set up any armoured units or any artillery worthy of the name....[9]

Sihanouk cites many exploits — for example, commando raids on Phnom Penh airport and against oil storage depots in the port of Kompong Som — for which the Khmer Rouge claimed credit but which were in fact the work of Vietnamese special units carrying out plans worked out together with the Khmer Rouge High Command. Time and time again he refers to the insane illusions of Pol Pot and his cronies that they, and not the Vietnamese, were the real architects of the American defeat, not only in Cambodia but the whole of Indochina!

> Unfortunately, Pol Pot allowed his head to be turned somewhat too soon about his "victories" to the point of comparing himself with the great conquerors of the past (Alexander of Macedonia, Rome's Caesar, the Corsican — Napoleon — and the Nazi, Hitler)....

> In September 1975, returning for the first time to "liberated" Cambodia at the invitation of the Khmer Rouge leaders, I was astonished to hear Khieu Samphan, Son Sen and others tell me — with broad smiles and very satisfied airs — that their troops were "dissatisfied" with the "Party" because the latter was not giving them the "green light to recover the Kampuchea Krom" and the frontier districts with Thailand....

> According to Son Sen, then Deputy Defence Minister, his glorious "Kampuchean Revolutionary Army" reckoned that Giap's army represented only a "mouthful" for them and the miserable army of Kukrit Pramoj and Kriangsak Chamond (Thailand) even less![10]

In fact, without the substantial assistance of their Vietnamese comrades-in-arms, the Khmer Rouge would have been fighting on in the jungles of Cambodia long after the Vietnamese had liberated Saigon. Towards the end of 1974 Pol Pot had visited Peking, revealing that he intended to launch a war-winning offensive at the beginning of the following year. To do so, he needed heavy artillery. Mao Tse-tung personally advised him to carry on with guerrilla warfare. "You have already fought for nearly five years," said Mao, "you must fight another five years and rely on your own forces." Pol Pot became very downcast. During his transit through Hanoi on his way home, he asked the Vietnamese for help. The leadership told him: "We will liberate Saigon; we will help you liberate Phnom Penh." The Vietnamese then contributed 130 mm and 122 mm artillery pieces together with the gun crews to handle them, the Khmer Rouge having trained none of their own.

On 17 April 1975 the victorious Khmer Rouge entered Phnom Penh. Two weeks later, on May 1 — the day after the liberation of Saigon and the day on which the victorious forces swept on to liberate the whole of the Mekong Delta — Khmer Rouge forces launched small-scale but violent attacks along the entire Cambodian frontier with South Vietnam's Mekong Delta provinces, from Ha Tien province in the extreme south to Tay Ninh, well to the north of the Mekong Delta area.

On May 4 Khmer Rouge troops landed in force on Phu Cuoc island. It was politely explained to them that they were on Vietnamese territory but they showed no signs of withdrawing. "We made a demonstration of force," the Phu Cuoc commander told me later, "and they left. No shots were fired."

Six days later Khmer Rouge forces from the mainland and from their island of Hon Troc (Poulo Vai) invaded the Vietnamese island of Tho Chu (Poulo Panjang). On May 25 the Vietnamese People's Army (VPA) counter-attacked and drove the Khmer Rouge forces off Tho Chu, chasing them back to Hon Troc. A lot of the Tho Chu people had been killed and the Khmer Rouge took with them 515 of the island's inhabitants. After receiving assurances that there would be no more attacks in the area, Vietnamese troops withdrew from Hon Troc, returning 500 Khmer Rouge prisoners captured during the various attacks. But the 515 Vietnamese seized by the Khmer Rouge on Tho Chu island were never seen again. The Vietnamese landing party found no trace of them on Hon Truc. Their most probable fate was to have been killed on board the boats that took them away, their bodies being thrown into the sea.

On June 2 at a meeting with Nguyen Van Linh, a member of the Central Committee of the Vietnamese Workers Party, Pol Pot explained that the island incidents (as well as those which had occurred along the land border) happened because the Khmer Rouge forces were "ignorant of local geography." But it is inconceivable that such an important action as the landing on Phu Cuoc, just seventeen days after the "liberation" of Phnom Penh, could have been the result of some spontaneous decision. Apparently these actions had been planned well in advance.

In early exchanges at government and party levels aimed at halting the fast deteriorating situation along the frontier, it was agreed to hold a top-level conference in June 1976. Preparatory talks were held in Phnom Penh May 4-8 to fix an agenda and settle seemingly easy matters. Agreement was quickly reached on tracing the land frontier on the basis of a 1:100,000 scale map of the Indochinese Geographical Service which conformed to what Sihanouk had stipulated should be "maps commonly used prior to 1954." Then the Phnom Penh delegation turned up with a map which had been clumsily faked. A bit of paper pasted over the original showed an additional score or so of square miles on the Kampuchean side of the border, where the Khmer Rouge apparently believed that there were mineral deposits. To get a settlement, the Vietnamese ceded the area. On May 8 it was agreed that the Brévié Line would be used to define the land territories of both sides but would not be used to determine the maritime frontier. The Vietnamese planned to make a compromise proposal at the following session, but the Khmer Rouge delegation abruptly adjourned the talks. Innumerable requests by the Vietnamese for resumption of the talks, either at the same level or at the originally proposed higher level, were rejected by the Khmer Rouge leadership.

Before the talks ended, a three-point agreement was reached, the essential part of which stipulated "that all conflicts must be settled in a spirit of solidarity, friendship, and mutual respect and that the liaison committees of the two sides must investigate and meet to settle them." I was later given the following account of the working of the various limited agreements — similar to that of May 1976 providing for joint investigations and settlement of frontier incidents — by Huynh Van Luan, a member of the People's Committee of Tay Ninh province (one of those most frequently attacked).

Our province has 240 kilometres of frontier with Kampuchea. The southern part leading north follows a track built by the peasants of both sides up to a river which marks the border to the east and which joins up with another well-defined track. For generations this has been the recognized frontier. Relations between the peasants on both sides have always been good. They spoke each other's languages — there were no problems. During the anti-U.S. resistance war, there was always famine in this area. Our peasants were forcibly evacuated by the U.S.-Saigon regime and herded into concentration camp "strategic hamlets." Immediately after Liberation people went back to their villages and started to cultivate their land. An anti-illiteracy campaign was launched; everybody thought only of peaceful reconstruction.

But the Khmer Rouge started building military posts along their side of the frontier. They sent regular forces to man defensive positions, pushing their own population back ten to twenty kilometres from the frontier to create a buffer zone and halt any contact with our people, in whose development the Cambodians were showing great interest. Then the Khmer Rouge started planting mines and setting up "hedgehog" lines of bamboo spikes on our side of the frontier....

Between 17 April 1975 and June 1976 the Khmer Rouge violated our territory several times, on one occasion occupying 302 hectares of Donh Phu and also carrying out espionage. During that period we captured some sixty Khmer Rouge commandos. They said they had two main tasks: (1) to set up bases on Vietnamese territory and study our military dispositions in the frontier area and our methods of consolidating revolutionary power; (2) to gradually expand a network of bases in Tay Ninh and down towards Ho Chi Minhville.

We proposed negotiations several times. Between August 1975 and June 1976 there were two meetings at Central Committee level, two at provincial level, five at district level, and twenty-odd at the level of frontier posts. At each of these meetings the Khmer Rouge comrades acknowledged the incursions and promised to "correct their mistakes." Our instructions were at all costs to preserve friendship and avoid further incidents, right up until June 1976 when the Khmer Rouge attacked Tien Thuan commune, three kilometres on our side of the frontier. Our forces counter-attacked, pushing the Khmer Rouge back and capturing 42 of their troops. As proof of our goodwill, we released them that same afternoon. At a meeting at the provincial level — Tay Ninh with Cambodia's Svay Rieng — the Khmer Rouge acknowledged their "error" and promised that it would not be repeated. In fact the attacks and incursions were intensified.

After that "apology" the Khmer Rouge refused further contacts. To protest further attacks we could only send letters — ten in all, before we gave up — to be transmitted through their frontier posts. There were no replies. Despite all our efforts, trying to use the agreed channels, there were no further contacts and the Khmer Rouge stepped up their attacks.

By the beginning of 1977 the Khmer Rouge were carrying out ongoing, usually large-scale attacks — with two or three regiments employed at a single point on the frontier. These were aimed at seizing positions, digging in, and using each point gained to advance a line ever deeper into Vietnam. After a series of violent attacks against the Mekong Delta provinces,[11] the Vietnamese People's Army (VPA) launched a limited counterattack in April 1977, throwing the Pol Pot forces out of Vietnam and proposing negotiations. For some months afterwards, the Khmer Rouge response was in the form of shelling border villages by long-range artillery. On June 7 Hanoi again proposed to reopen talks. The reply from Phnom Penh on June 18 rejected the offer on the grounds that such talks, "while necessary, should only be held when the situation returns to normal and there are no further border conflicts." In other words, as long as the Khmer Rouge wanted to continue the attacks, there would never be talks!

The situation deteriorated rapidly during the second half of 1977. Hardly a day passed without an attack somewhere along the Svay Rieng-Tay Ninh frontier. And it was the same from Tay Ninh all the way down to Ha Tien on the Gulf of Siam. Many of the attacks into Tay Ninh were of divisional strength (a Cambodian division then being about 10,000 troops). By November 1977 three divisions were permanently operating along the Tay Ninh frontier. According to Huynh Van Luan, there were not only incursions by regular units but also artillery shelling by day and commando attacks by night. It was in that context that the Vietnamese launched a counterattack in late 1977 and drove the Khmer Rouge troops out of Vietnam, hurling them back to the Mekong River and across it to take up defensive positions around Phnom Penh.

In a discussion in Paris at the end of October 1978 Nguyen Co Thach, then deputy foreign minister[12] of the Socialist Republic of Vietnam, described the rapid evolution of relations with Kampuchea as follows:

During 1970-75, the Khmer Rouge considered Vietnam as No. 1 friend, the North Koreans as No. 2 and the Chinese, No. 3. Enemy No. 1 was the USA-CIA; No. 2, the remnants of the Lon Nol forces; No. 3, the influence of Sihanouk. After the April 1975 victory, the Chinese moved up to No. 1 position among friends and Vietnam fell back into 7th place. Enemy No. 1 was still the USA-CIA with Lon Nol remnants No. 2, but Thailand had replaced Sihanouk's influence as No. 3! By April 1977, enemy No. 1 had become Vietnam, followed by Lon Nol remnants and the Soviet KGB in second and third places. The Chinese remained No. 1 and the Koreans No. 2 among friends.

He also asserted that the Khmer Rouge propaganda line of April 1977, naming Vietnam as the "main enemy," was followed by a formal resolution of the Khmer Communist Party's Central Committee in June 1977 naming "Vietnam as our enemy number 1, our eternal enemy. We must prepare to attack Vietnam." According to Nguyen Co Thach, this resolution was sent to all levels of the armed forces and was followed by cross-border attacks on an increasing scale from then on.

Why was a negotiated solution to problems between two neighboring states, headed by supposedly comradely Communist Parties, impossible?

It is now clear that by then Peking was running Khmer Rouge affairs. The Chinese leadership that had exerted pressure on Vietnam in 1967-68 to renounce peace negotiations with the United States would have had no inhibitions about ordering Pol Pot to reject any meaningful relations with Vietnam. Whereas Vietnam had stubbornly refused to be placed in China's pocket, Pol Pot had jumped into it himself. China has been charged on many occasions with being interested in fighting the United States to the last Vietnamese and was certainly no less averse to fighting Vietnam to the last Kampuchean.

But how could Kampuchea with a population of (by then) 5-6 million dare to take on a battle-hardened Vietnam with a population of over 50 million? I asked Nguyen Co Thach. He countered with: "Why would an Israel with a population of 3 million dare to invade Egypt with its population of 35 million? Because the Khmer Rouge are assured they have 800 million Chinese behind them, as Israel has the might of the United States to rely on."

At the time of our conversation, Western intelligence sources estimated that there were 7,000-8,000 Chinese military "advisers" in Kampuchea. Nguyen Co Thach believed the number was more than twice that and they were operating down to platoon level in combat operations. They handled all artillery and other complicated weapons, mastery of which was beyond the educational level to which Khmer Rouge cadres had been reduced.

In its Statement of 31 December 1977 the government of Democratic Kampuchea (the Khmer Rouge) "went public" for the first time concerning the war situation along the Kampuchea-South

Vietnam frontier. In many respects the Statement is a remarkable document. What was purported to be the original text was released in French by the Embassy of Democratic Kampuchea in Peking on December 31. The extracts I have used are from Hanoi's English translation of that text. The editors, however, add this note:

> On the whole the French translation of the Statement is faithful to the original text in Khmer delivered on the same day by Head of State Khieu Samphan over Phnom Penh radio.... However, the Khmer and French texts of the ninth [and last—W.B.] part of the Statement are completely different. We try here to give a faithful translation of the Khmer text into English.

The Statement itself is a most virulent tirade against Vietnam, its party, and its people. It exhorts the Kampuchean people "to wipe out the expansionist and annexationist enemy" and declares that "shameful defeats" will be inflicted upon them. The Vietnamese are referred to by the perjorative terms "Yuon" and "Annamites." To beef up the morale of the youngsters who represented an ever-growing proportion of the Khmer Rouge armed forces — especially the assault troops — the following summary of casualty rates in the frontier conflicts was given.

> In 1975, the enemy's casualties were 100 killed or wounded against 5 killed or wounded on our side. We wiped them out and prevented them from occupying our territory.

> In 1976, the enemy's casualties were 100 killed or wounded to our 5 killed or wounded. We completely wiped them out and did not let them encroach upon Kampuchean land.

> In 1977, during their large-scale attacks from January to November, the enemy casualties were 100 killed or wounded to our 3 to 5 killed or wounded. We safeguarded our country totally. Since (the beginning of) December 1977, the enemy casualties so far have amounted to 100 killed or wounded to our 3 to 5 killed or wounded. We have completely safeguarded our country. We are continuing to strike and destroy them and drive them out of Kampuchea....[13]

Based on this product of obviously demented minds, Khieu Samphan arrived at the following conclusions.

> First: If they invade our country they will certainly suffer political setbacks and will suffer ever more serious ones.

> Second: They have been suffering from serious food shortages for

the past few years.... They are short of millions of tons of food. They are begging for food, even from the imperialists; they have lost all sense of dignity.

Third: Their people are against them and there is insecurity everywhere in South Vietnam.

Fourth: The Yuon enemy cannot produce his guns, tanks, ammunition and aircraft. They cannot match even a small part of the United States. If they follow in the U.S. footsteps they will bring only ruin upon themselves. Theirs is an adventurous policy which will lead them into an impasse....[14]

The Statement was clearly designed to kill two birds with one stone. On the one hand, it was to inform the outside world about Vietnam's "large-scale surprise acts of aggression and invasion" and on the other hand, by the specially doctored Point Nine, to boast to their own people that the Khmer Rouge had "completely safeguarded our country" and were continuing to "strike and destroy" the invaders. In fact, by the time the Statement was issued the VPA had struck in force, driving Pol Pot's forces out of positions they had taken inside Vietnam and chasing them back to the other side of the Mekong River at Neak Luong. When the VPA then totally withdrew from Kampuchean territory, Pol Pot seized on this to claim "the greatest victory in Khmer history," stating that for a loss of some 100 Khmer Rouge troops over 29,000 Vietnamese had been wiped out!

In his book Sihanouk quotes a Phnom Penh radio broadcast aired shortly after the 31 December 1977 Statement, in which the Khmer Rouge leaders claimed that Kampuchea was in a position to wipe out the entire population of Vietnam! How?

The Khmer Rouge leaders, in all seriousness, ordered their troops and people to kill Vietnamese in the ratio of 30 Viets for one Kampuchean. The Khmer Rouge leaders based themselves on the following calculations. "By sacrificing only two million Kampucheans, we can wipe out up to 60 million Vietnamese and there will still be 6 million Kampucheans to build up and defend the country."[15]

Those governments that still champion the cause of the Khmer Rouge at the United Nations and other international organizations would do well to ponder this sort of criminal insanity, evidence of which is easy to obtain. Sihanouk, who undertook to defend the regime at the UN and to condemn Vietnamese participation in overthrowing it — in exchange for permission to flee the country — nevertheless makes the following assessment of the intolerable provocations which Vietnam endured. As he wrote the book in which the assessment is made in mid-1979 while in Peking as a guest of the Chinese government, his words have even greater weight.

So-called "Democratic" Kampuchea took over...on April 17, 1975. How did it act toward Communist Vietnam which, like it, had emerged as a victor in the anti-American struggle?

(1) From 1973 onwards, the Khmer Rouge massacred tens of thousands of Vietnamese residents accused of being "spies" and a "fifth column" of the Viet communists. The remaining residents were expelled to South Vietnam.

(2) They assassinated on a large-scale pro-Viet Kampuchean communists, including Khmer Rouge suspected of being pro-Viet.

(3) They ordered the Kampuchean people not to sell anything to the Viets, not to help them in any way whatsoever. And this, at the height of the "common struggle" against American imperialism and its vassals in Saigon and Phnom Penh.

(4) Immediately after the signing of the Vietnamese-American agreements (Henry Kissinger-Le Duc Tho in Paris, 1973) the Khmer Rouge ordered all Vietminh-Vietcong stationed in Kampuchea to dismantle their bases and trails and leave the country. The Khmer Rouge units thus wanted to "punish" Viet units whose government had "betrayed the common cause."

(5) After their victory of April 17, 1975, the Khmer Rouge tried to seize parts of Kampuchea Krom, committing horrible atrocities on large numbers of Vietnamese civilians (including old people, women and children). Western journalists confirmed *a posteriori* these atrocities on the spot in South Vietnam.

(6) The Pol Pot government rejected all proposals for a peaceful settlement, repeatedly presented (especially that of February 5, 1978) by the government of Hanoi. [On February 5, 1978, following the removal of the immediate Khmer Rouge threat to their frontier, the Hanoi leadership proposed a withdrawal of the armed forces on both sides of the mutually recognized border, with joint or international supervision of the demilitarized zone thus created while high-level talks were held, in Phnom Penh, Hanoi, or any other mutually ac-

ceptable site, to settle frontier and other problems—W.B.]

(7) The Pol Pot regime stubbornly refused to use the services of Norodom Sihanouk who, in the opinion even of the People's Republic of China, appeared to be the only one capable of "putting the Vietnamese against the wall" and obtaining their respect for Kampuchea's land and sea frontiers and for her sovereignty. [16]

(8) The policy of genocide, of massacre, of forced labour, of slavery, of concentration camps, of political purges carried out by the Khmer Rouge leaders against their own people, even their own supporters, has horrified the whole world and has isolated every day more completely "Democratic" Kampuchea. [17]

It was very difficult at first to believe the reports of unspeakable atrocities committed by the Khmer Rouge troops in their cross-border attacks into Vietnam and Thailand. For a long time — too long — the Vietnamese authorities were silent about what was happening in their frontier areas. When travellers did come upon evidence — a burned-out hamlet, ox-cart convoys of bewildered Vietnamese peasants moving back from the border villages, the distant sounds of gunfire — the official explanation was usually a vague statement about "undisciplined local Khmer Rouge units." One was left with the impression that, while the Khmer Rouge leadership did not have firm control over their troops in some areas, what was happening was not official Khmer Rouge policy.

The Thai authorities were not so reticent. They published full details of the atrocities committed against their border villages and allowed journalists to visit the sites and see for themselves. The Thai Ministry of Foreign Affairs published a "White Book" on these events and sent an official protest to the Khmer Rouge government for a particularly atrocious incident which took place on 28 January 1977 in three Thai frontier villages. In the version released by the Permanent Mission of Thailand to the United Nations on 3 February 1977, the following points were made.

(1) On 28 January 1977, at approximately 2 a.m. about 300 armed Cambodian soldiers entered Thai territory and attacked the villages of Baan Nong Dor, Baan Klong Kor and Baan Noiparai which are situated inside Thai territory.

(2) The Cambodian forces, employing weapons of deadly destruction, raided the three villages without warning in the middle of the

night. The degree of unprecedented savagery displayed by the attacking Cambodian forces on the unarmed Thai villages was a great shock to all those who witnessed the scene after the attack. Preliminary surveys of the casualties and damages sustained are as follows:

At Baan Nong Dor, 21 Thai residents were killed, including a pregnant woman. Children and babies were badly mutilated. All houses were burned down.

At Baan Klong Kor, 9 Thai residents were killed and all houses burned down.

At Baan Noiparai, all 200 residents were forced to abandon their homes and a large number of people were seriously wounded.

(3) The Government of Thailand wishes to lodge a strong protest with the Government of Democratic Kampuchea for the abovementioned brutal acts of savagery which constitute a flagrant violation of Thai national sovereignty and territorial integrity, as well as being in contravention of the Thai-Kampuchea Joint Communiqué of 31 October 1975, to which Thailand gives strict adherence. The Government of Thailand regards the incident as inhuman and in serious breach of civilized international law and morality. . . .''

The complete protest note, as distinct from the version released at the United Nations, included these additional details.

These murderers did not only gun down everybody in sight, including helpless women. They also disfigured the bodies and slashed the throats of the children and babies. Before they were driven back across the border, the Khmer Rouge murder squad managed to set fire to the crops and slaughter animals to complete their bloodthirsty mission. . . .

The note also quoted on-the-spot reports of journalists from *Time Magazine, Newsweek,* and others. Thus, from *Time* came the following quotation from a Thai peasant whose wife and five of his eight children had been killed.

A Khmer Rouge soldier shot her though the right shoulder, seized a month-old baby from her arms and cut its throat. In almost every case, their throats were slashed with a jagged knife edge.[18]

The Khmer Rouge reply note of 11 February 1977 did not deny the atrocities. However, it claimed that the three villages were on Kampuchean territory and that the Thai protest amounted to ''an act of interference in Kampuchea's internal affairs,'' as Kampuchea had "every right to rearrange its internal affairs"! (The totally justified Thai official indignation at that time was in sharp contrast with Thailand's later policy of collaboration with and protection of the Khmer Rouge remnants who fled into the Kampuchea-Thai frontier areas and continued to exist solely as a result of Thai protection and Chinese-Thai logistic support.)

That the Thai government deemed the atrocities committed against its villagers horrifying enough to publish a White Book on the subject speaks for itself. But what happened to the Thai frontier villages was infinitesimal compared to the crimes committed against Vietnam's frontier villages, about which the world public knows virtually nothing. Had Hanoi been as explicit as Bangkok (and this applies equally to Laos) regarding Khmer Rouge cross-border attacks from 1975 on, Vietnam's role in helping to overthrow the Pol Pot-Ieng Sary regime would have received far more international support, especially from those who stood by the Vietnamese people during their anti-French and anti-U.S. liberation struggles. Hanoi's long silence as to what was going on along the frontier was a case of misplaced loyalty to the international revolutionary movement. It was well exploited by Vietnam's enemies and has caused great confusion among her friends.

It was not until 6 January 1978 — six days after the Khmer Rouge leadership released its "Statement to Its Friends" denouncing what was in fact a Vietnamese counter-offensive — that Hanoi's press department arranged for foreign correspondents to visit the scene of one of the massacres. But this was four months after the attack had taken place! Nevertheless, the journalists collected detailed accounts from survivors that left them with no doubt as to what had happened: babies torn in half, pregnant women disembowelled, heads, arms, and legs hacked off, livers ripped out, fried, and eaten. Iron bars, hatchets, knives, and clubs — anything which could deal lethal blows was used. The attack, which left 500 villagers dead (including 25 families entirely wiped out), took place just after midnight on 25 September 1977 at Tan Lap village in Tay Ninh's district of Tan Bien, about seven kilometers inside Vietnamese territory. The accounts of the survivors corresponded with details contained in the Thai Foreign Ministry's White Book. The five hamlets which made up the village were burned down. There were no military installations there — or in any of the other frontier areas to which I made extensive visits. But what took place at Tan Lap and in innumerable other villages along South Vietnam's frontier with Kampuchea, especially in 1977 and 1978, was an orgy of sadism hard to match in modern times.

According to Vietnamese accounts, illustrated by military maps showing the disposition of Khmer Rouge units, at the time of the Tan Lap massacre there were three Khmer Rouge divisions operating permanently along the 240 kilometers of the Tay Ninh-Kampuchean border; in some places they had penetrated to a depth of 10 kilometers inside Vietnamese territory. About one thousand Vietnamese had been killed or wounded in such attacks and at least an equal number had been dragged off to the other side of the frontier. When I visited Tay Ninh in December 1978, I was informed by Huynh Van Luan of the provincial People's Committee that between September 1977 and November 1978 more than two thousand Vietnamese had been killed in the cross-border attacks and seventy-one thousand people had been evacuated from the frontier villages, abandoning some thirty-seven thousand acres of cultivable land. On one occasion when Huynh Van Luan and I were travelling through Tan Bien district, along Highway 22, we were subjected to artillery fire from the Kampuchean side of the frontier. Fortunately, we had just skidded to a stop after I had asked to interview some peasants at the tiny hamlet of Tra Rong, which had been burned out by Khmer Rouge commandos a few nights earlier. The first shell, intended for our command car, landed on the road exactly where we would have been but for our sudden stop.

Although the raiders at Tra Rong had been driven off by local self-defense militia before they could perpetrate the type of atrocities that occurred at Tan Lap, there were enough survivors of earlier attacks into Tay Ninh province to describe other savage slaughters and orgies of mutilations comparable to those at Tan Lap. In all cases, the most zealous of those wielding knives, hatchets, and axes and vying with each other in devising techniques of butchery were said to have been teenagers, hacking and slashing with broad smiles on their faces. This was consistent with remarks all foreign observers have made on the extreme youth of the Pol Pot soldiery, especially in the "vanguard units."

Some of the worst atrocities committed in Vietnam by the Khmer Rouge troops occurred in the Mekong Delta province of An Giang[19] between 14 and 18 April 1978. After a visit to the area in early December 1980 I was able to piece together what happened at the Ba Thuc commune. Ba Thuc is located in what is known as the Seven Mountains area of An Giang province, which has a common frontier with Kampuchea's Takeo province. On 14 April 1978 two Khmer Rouge divisions invaded the area from bases in the Elephant Mountains (which reach down to within a few kilometers of the Khmer-Vietnam frontier). They encircled the Ba Thuc commune and massacred everyone on whom they could lay their hands. I talked with an incredibly tragic-faced woman, Ha Thi Nga.

> We learned around midnight that the Pol Pot troops had arrived. It was not the first time, so people fled in all directions. The Khmer Rouge commander used loud speakers to order everyone to gather in the Phi Lai pagoda where he would make a speech. Any refusing would be killed. Many of us came out of our hiding places and went to the pagoda. Most were shot there, the children being clubbed to death. My husband and our six children were killed, but I was taken with some other women to another place close to the frontier. There we were all shot down at 8 a.m. on the morning of the 18th. I pretended to be dead and lay under a heap of bodies until nightfall. Of about one hundred relatives, I have just three cousins left.

At the Buddhist Phi Lai pagoda the surviving bonze Di Van Hanh, with a wispy beard and piercing eyes, explained that he had been absent from Ba Thuc that week but that his wife and three children had been killed. He showed me blood stains on the walls of the pagoda, the floor of which was "awash with blood" (as he expressed it) when the Khmer Rouge withdrew. On the pillars and walls were the blood-stained handprints of the children who had been butchered there.

Among those who miraculously survived was a girl, Nguyen Thi Ngoc Huoy, who had been 12 years old at the time of the attack. She was abandoned for dead in a heap of bodies which included her father, mother, and two sisters. The massacre took place at midday on April 16 and was just one of many in which batches of sixty to one hundred people were murdered. As she described it:

> When we knew the Pol Pot troops had arrived, father ran to the

pagoda to pray. Many people were already there praying. Troops entered the pagoda and asked for the chief bonze. He was ordered to call all the faithful to come out of their hiding places and line up in the nearby ricefields. One old chap went to drink some water from the river. They kicked him hard in the behind and he fell in the river and was drowned. The Khmer Rouge roared with laughter. Then they divided men, women and children into groups and started shooting. Father was killed immediately. I was also shot and fell with others falling on top of me. [A bullet went through her from below her right shoulder to emerge above her right breast. Another grazed her scalp.—W.B.] I was sure I was dead. But after sunset I woke up and together with another girl struggled out from under the bodies and hid until our troops came and the Khmer Rouge went away.

Among the members of the An Giang provincial People's Committee I was delighted to find Hu Duy Ke, an old friend from the Saigon district of Cu Chi whom I had met during my first visit to the Liberated Areas at the turn of the years 1963-64. With him was Nguyen Van Uc, chairman of the Ba Thuc People's Committee. They explained that 75 percent of the An Giang population of 1.5 million are Vietnamese of Khmer origin. The aim of attacks such as that against Ba Thuc was to exterminate the ethnic Vietnamese and stimulate those of Khmer origin to rise up and declare An Giang a 19th province of Kampuchea.

The Ba Thuc attack of April 1978 was only one of many which had started in An Giang as early as 5 May 1975. It was estimated that at least twenty-five hundred people were killed in the Ba Thuc attack alone, skulls and skeletons of over two thousand having already been recovered at the time of my visit. But the "Seven Mountains" area is riddled with caves into which people fled for shelter, pursued by Khmer Rouge using hand grenades to finish them off. Parents suffocated their babies so that their cries would not expose large groups to extermination. Entire hamlets were wiped out to the last human being.

During the operation twenty thousand ethnic Khmers (Khmer Krom) were shepherded back into Kampuchea. It is known that four thousand were killed or died of starvation and illness and two thousand escaped back into Vietnam. The fate of the rest is unknown. Once across the border in Kampuchea, older people were concentrated in special areas with the customary starvation diet and no medicines; the rest were classified according to their estimated military or work capabilities. Those who objected were summarily executed. The escapees from among those who were escorted across the frontier, like the survivors of the Ba Thuc massacre, were unanimous in describing the glee with which youngsters, hardly into their teens, went about their work of mutilating and killing.

Hu Duy Ke, who had interrogated some of those taken prisoner, said they were conditioned to believe that killing "plenty of Vietnamese" was a sure road to high rank in the Khmer Rouge forces.

> They were taught to believe that capture by the Vietnamese meant death but they knew that retreat also meant death. They could kill, mutilate, rape, and plunder to their hearts' content — anything except retreat which meant death for their families as well as themselves. There were rewards for "high kill" performances and inventiveness in savagery, especially in speedy mass killing without expenditure of bullets and grenades. There were "summing up" sessions after each day's activities at which experiences in "low cost" killings were exchanged. Perpetrators of the most barbarous killing methods were the most highly praised by the Khmer Rouge commanders and were presented as examples for other unit members to emulate.

Pham Van Ba, the leader of the Communist Party group to which Pol Pot was attached in 1954 and later Vietnam's first ambassador to Khmer Rouge Kampuchea, told me that in his occasional official meetings with Pol Pot during the 1975-77 period Pol Pot always brushed off the frontier "incidents" as "regrettable errors" due to "enemies within our ranks" or to the ignorance of his troops in such matters as topography and map-reading. Pham Van Ba specifically referred to a meeting on 2 September 1977 between himself and Pol Pot, Ieng Sary, and Nuon Chea. "In our exchanges, Pol Pot always addressed me with respect, as far as form was concerned, as his former cell leader, but in practice he violated all norms supposed to be respected between Party comrades." Referring to the increasing gravity of the frontier incidents, Pham Van Ba told me that his brief dialogue with Pol Pot had gone as follows:

Pham Van Ba: Vietnam has no intention of dominating, of committing any aggression, or of maintaining any Vietnamese presence in Kampuchea. We want Kampuchea as a friend of Vietnam. We still have to take into account U.S. imperialism and other reactionary forces which would like to swallow us up. That is why we need friends — not enemies — in our rear. We want Kampuchea only as a friend.

Pol Pot: Do you really believe that Kampuchea can conquer or dominate Vietnam?

Pham Van Ba: I note your question. But we have proof of your attempts to seize Phu Cuoc island. We have documentary evidence that you intend to take over Saigon, that you dream of dominating South Vietnam.

Pol Pot: That would not be in our real interests. The problem is that we have enemies in our ranks.

Prior to this meeting Pham Van Ba had been restricted in his movements to 50 to 100 yards from his residence, as were the ambassadors of the handful of other countries represented in Phnom Penh (with the notable exceptions of China and North Korea, whose ambassadors were relatively free to move about as they pleased). After it Pham Van Ba was placed under house arrest. Following the Vietnamese counter-offensive at the end of 1977, he was expelled from Kampuchea and diplomatic relations between the two countries were severed.

Hanoi's major effort to ward off the otherwise inevitable full-scale confrontation was its three-point proposal of 5 February 1978. It stated:

(1) An immediate end shall be put to all hostile military activities in the border region; the armed forces of each side shall be stationed within their respective territories, five kilometres from the border.

(2) The two sides shall meet at once in Hanoi, or Phnom Penh, or at a place on the border, to discuss and conclude a treaty on mutual respect and a border treaty between the two countries.

(3) The two sides shall reach an agreement on an appropriate form of international guarantee and supervision.

Copies of the proposal were sent to UN Secretary-General Kurt Waldheim and to governments represented on the Coordinating Committee of the Non-Aligned Movement, then under the chairmanship of Sri Lanka (Ceylon). There was no reply from Phnom Penh but immediately following the proposal — between February 9th and 11th — the Tay Ninh capital was shelled by Chinese 122 mm and 130 mm artillery and district centers were bombarded in the three Mekong Delta provinces of Long An, An Giang, and Dong Thap.

In May 1978 Hanoi proposed that the UN appoint a mission to mediate frontier and other outstanding problems between Vietnam and Kampuchea. This move was blocked by China.

Then at the Belgrade Conference of Foreign Ministers of the Non-Aligned Movement in July 1978 — which I attended — Vietnamese Foreign Minister Nguyen Duy Trinh asked that the appointment of a "good offices" mission, composed of Non-Aligned members, to mediate Vietnam-Kampuchea differences be placed on the agenda. Sri Lanka's foreign minister A. C. S. Hameed, as Chairman of the Movement, was willing, as was India's foreign minister, A. B. Vajpayee, who chaired the Political Committee where the agenda was decided. But Yugoslavia's foreign minister, Josip Vrhovec, acting as the delegate of the host country and under intense pressure from China — which was not a member but was extremely active in the lobbies — persuaded Sri Lanka's Hameed that this would be a "divisive move" because only one of the two parties to the dispute sought mediation. To force the proposal through — assured as it was of overwhelming support — would be "interfering in the internal affairs" of Pol Pot's Kampuchea! Under pressure from Sri Lanka, Vietnam withdrew the proposal in the interests of "maintaining Non-Aligned unity"!

On the opening day of the Belgrade Conference I met Milan Marcovich, head of liaison with foreign delegates and a friend from my days in Phnom Penh when he had been Yugoslavia's Chargé d'Affaires there. His first question was: "Do you know what's going on in Cambodia?" I replied that I did not and that it was just this lack of information that was most troubling. All of my requests to make a visit had been ignored. "It is simply awful," said Marcovich, "and we are the best placed in the West to know because we have maintained an embassy there all the time. All our mutual friends have been killed." He then ticked them off on his fingers, starting with Huoth Sambath who had headed several ministries under Sihanouk and as ambassador at the UN had immediately rallied to the resistance government. He had been appointed by Pol Pot as the Khmer Rouge ambassador to Belgrade. "He returned for a so-called conference of ambassadors and like all others who responded he was arrested and executed."

He asked if I had met Vittorovich, a Yugoslav filmmaker who had made the only Western film inside Pol Pot's Kampuchea. I had, but had not seen him since he visited our home in Phnom Penh years earlier. Marcovich said he would be at the conference the following day — and he was. After greetings, his first question to me was: "Did you see my film?" I had not but my wife Vessa, who was standing alongside me, said she had seen it on French television. Asked what she thought of it, Vessa replied: "For anyone who has lived in Cambodia, it was terrifying. The only smiling face was that of Pol Pot." Vittorovich seemed relieved. "Then my message got through," he said. "What we saw was a hundred times worse than we could put on film or I could express in my commentary." It was clear that diplomatic considerations were an inhibiting factor!

What was extraordinary at Belgrade — and in February 1979 at a meeting of the Non-Aligneds' Coordinating Bureau in Maputo (Mozambique) and even more so at the Non-Aligneds' summit in Havana in September 1979 — was that Yugoslavia took the lead in stubbornly defending the Pol Pot regime. It continued to do so later at the United Nations. That the "best informed" Western country would do this is explainable only by Yugoslavia's intimate relations with the United States and its new-found friendship with China.

It was at the Belgrade Conference that the Pol Pot delegation proposed that Vietnam be expelled from the Non-Aligned Movement. This move did not get a single supporting vote, despite intensive lobbying by Chinese diplomats and journalists. At the closing session, as the protocol congratulatory speeches were being made to the Chairman for the success of the conference, the Pol Pot delegation ostentatiously stalked out. Ieng Sary, who headed the delegation and whom I had met several times, refused my request for an interview and glared at me as we passed in the corridor, as if he regretted not having an axe or short-handled spade to deal with me as he had done with so many of his closest "comrades."

1. Sihanouk's reference to "maps commonly used up to 1954" (as a basis for defining the land frontiers between the former three components of Indochina at the Geneva Conference) is significant in light of claims advanced later by Sihanouk and in an infinitely more extravagant way by Pol Pot. There was general agreement as to where the frontier ran along the land border. As to the sea frontiers, Pol Pot made a *casus belli* out of a dispute revolving around what was known as the Brévié Line. On 31 January 1939 Jean Brévié, in his capacity as Governor-General of Indochina, gave a ruling on "the question of islands in the Gulf of Siam, the possession of which is disputed by Cambodia and Cochinchina [that portion of Vietnam south of the junction of the Mekong and Dong Hai Rivers-W.B.]. The position of this string of islands, scattered along the Cambodian coast and some of them located so close by this coast that the continuing alluvial deposits must join them to the Cambodian coast in the relatively near future, makes it necessary from a logical and geographical point of view for these islets to be placed under the administration of the latter country." For the rest he drew a line attached to all official maps, stipulating that all islands south of the line "including the whole island of Phu Quoc" would be administered by Cochinchina, those to the north would be administered by Cambodia, the question of territorial ownership remaining open.

2. *Kampuchea, Dossier I*, p. 121. Hanoi: Vietnam Courier, 1978.

3. After 1954, the Saigon regime published maps with frontiers "corrected" at Cambodia's expense.

4. In this speech de Gaulle stated that the war in South Vietnam was due to a U.S. attempt to replace the French presence in Indochina, that the war itself was a national liberation struggle, and that the solution was an American withdrawal.

5. I had been with Sihanouk and Chou En-lai — during the latter's state visit to Cambodia in December 1956 — at Kep, looking across the water to the seven Cambodian islands claimed by the Saigon regime. "We will support you in defending them," said Chou En-lai. Then, pointing to the vastly bigger silhouette of Phu Cuoc to the southwest in the Bay of Siam, he added: "We will help you recover that also." A visibly embarrassed Sihanouk murmured: "We will be quite satisfied to defend our present territory." It crossed my mind at the time that it was curious that Chou En-lai — one of the world's most experienced diplomats — should be inciting Sihanouk to raise his sights for something which he had never claimed until then! It also posed the question as to how China — which had no common frontier with Cambodia — would help in the conquest of Phu Cuoc!

6. These seemingly irrelevant and perhaps boring details assume their

full significance immediately after the Khmer Rouge victory. They represent essential background material to the start of the frontier war.

7. Long before Sihanouk was overthrown, the United States had been violating Cambodia's border and her territorial integrity. For a detailed and most revealing account of U.S. policy toward Cambodia, and especially of the secret U.S. bombings which occurred prior to 1970, see William Shawcross's *Sideshow: Kissinger, Nixon and the Destruction of Cambodia* (New York: Simon and Schuster, 1979).

8. Sihanouk, Norodom, *Chroniques de Guerre et d'Espoir*, pp. 64-65. Paris: Hachette/Stock, 1979.

9. *Ibid.*, pp. 66-67.

10. *Ibid.*

11. A particularly serious attack occurred on 30 April 1977 when two regiments and two independent battalions simultaneously struck thirteen villages in An Giang province and indulged in an orgy of killing and destruction.

12. Less than two years later Nguyen Co Thach became Vietnam's foreign minister.

13. *Statement of the Government of Democratic Kampuchea To Its Friends Far and Near Across the Five Continents and To World Opinion*, Phnom Penh, 31 December 1977.

14. *Ibid.*

15. Sihanouk, *Chroniques de Guerre et d'Espoir*, p. 110.

16. Sihanouk was not the only one to believe that he could easily have negotiated a mutually acceptable agreement with the Vietnamese. During my visit to Hanoi in December 1978 I was informed at the highest level, including by Vice-President Nguyen Huu Tho and Prime Minister Pham Van Dong, that had Kampuchea retained its Government of National Union and the National United Front — with Sihanouk as its founder-leader — in the post-war years, and had Sihanouk remained as Head of State, there would have been no frontier problems, let alone a frontier war.

17. Sihanouk, *Chroniques de Guerre et d'Espoir*, pp. 113-4.

18. Time Magazine, 14 February 1977, p. 11, as quoted in the Thai protest note.

19. An Giang was the province in which American military advisers, in March 1962, launched their first big operation to herd the South Vietnamese people into "strategic hamlets" or glorified concentration camps. The author's first book on the U.S. "special war" intervention in South Vietnam opens with an account of "Operation Sunrise," based on accounts from ethnic Khmer refugees from An Giang, who were interviewed at Phnom Den across the frontier from Ba Thuc. See *The Furtive War*, pp. 11-32 (New York: International Publishers, 1963).

11.
THE CHINA
CONNECTION

When the Vietnamese and Heng Samrin forces overran the main Khmer Rouge base at Ta Sanh — ten miles from the Thai border — at the end of March 1979, they captured the Khmer Rouge archives intact. (They also almost captured Pol Pot and Ieng Sary who, as the troops approached, were seen being transported in sedan chairs at great speed towards the Thai frontier. Ieng Sary departed so precipitately that he left his Chinese passport behind!) Among the archive documents, which were carefully stored away in long bamboo tubes, were fascinating revelations of the Chinese-Khmer Rouge military arrangements.

During the struggle against the Lon Nol forces it was the Vietnamese who were first called in to train and set up military units for the resistance war; who came to the rescue of those forces on innumerable occasions; and who transported down the "Ho Chi Minh Trail" the arms and other supplies essential to the pursuance of the war. But after 17 April 1975 it was the Chinese who took over military affairs and immediately set about expanding what had by then become the Khmer Rouge armed forces (the Sihanoukists and others having been physically eliminated in the meantime) from six divisions at the end of the war to twenty-three by the time the Khmer Rouge were overthrown.

Among the records left behind by Pol Pot and Ieng Sary is a statement by the deputy chief-of-staff of the Chinese People's Liberation Army, General Wang Shang-jung, after discussions with Son Sen, titular head of the Khmer Rouge armed forces, on 2 February 1976. It starts by referring to negotiations which had taken place in June 1975, two months after the Khmer Rouge took over in Phnom Penh, and to military missions sent from Peking to Kampuchea in August and October of that year "to examine the situation." It also refers to the delivery of arms for 1976, "on which the two parties exchanged viewpoints during the visit of Comrade Ieng Sary to Peking in April 1975." A total of 13,300 tons had been agreed on, of which only 3,200 tons had been delivered. There remained 10,000 tons, "including 4,000 tons of arms and ammunitions, and 1,301 automobiles of various categories."

> We think that — except for the motor vehicles, which are too numerous to be delivered completely in the month of March (our ships cannot take more than 200 at a time), the hundred artillery pieces of 120 mm, of which the quality remains to be tested, and the question of the shells for the 120 mm cannon — the rest should be delivered during the month of March. You have agreed to span out the delivery of the petrol and empty drums and we are discussing this question with our responsible branches.

General Wang Shang-jung presented what he described as a "relatively summary draft agreement" in principle for the "organization and reinforcement" of Kampuchea's infantry forces. "As for the other branches, they cannot be dealt with in detail at present in view of the different quality and types and great numbers" of equipment involved. He suggested that the details of these be left to the Chiefs of Staff of both armed forces to work out and then be ratified in a separate agreement. The draft which he proposed would cover deliveries from 1976 to the end of 1978. The agreement dealt more with delivery dates than with quantities. However, some matters were quite specific.

> In 1976, we will deliver first of all necessary arms and equipment to give basic training to cadres on-the-spot. This will include:
>
> (1) Part of the equipment of an anti-aircraft artillery regiment, part of the equipment for a radar regiment and equipment for a military airfield.
>
> Four escort vessels and four fast torpedo boats for the naval forces.
>
> Part of the equipment for a tank regiment, part of the equipment for a liaison regiment, part of the equipment for three artillery regiments and the equipment for a battalion of pontoon bridges for infantry use.

Other equipment and arms to be delivered are the following:

(2) Anti-aircraft guns for the Air Force will be delivered in 1977. Radar equipment will be delivered in 1977-78. Combat planes, including bombers, will be delivered according to the rhythm of the training of plane crews and the building of new airfields. Another part of airfield equipment will be delivered in accordance with the tempo of new airfield construction.

As for the six further naval escort vessels, four will be delivered in 1977 and two in 1978. As for the additional eight fast torpedo boats, four will be delivered each year in 1977-78.

The equipment for three infantry artillery regiments, except for 130 mm cannons, will be delivered from the beginning of 1977, the other equipment will be delivered during the last six months of 1976. Equipment for the tank regiment will be successively delivered in 1977-78. Equipment and arms for the liaison regiment will be delivered in 1977. Three hundred kilometers of overhead communication cables will be delivered in 1976, so there remains another 1,000 kilometers. Please let us have your concrete requests about this and we will make arrangements accordingly....

(3) Regarding the procedure and methods of delivery:

The major part of such equipment can be transported by boat and unloaded at Sihanoukville (Kompong Som) port. The planes will have to be dismantled and crated for the transport and will be reassembled in Kampuchea. Submarines and tankers can proceed directly to Kampuchea, but what has to be done to guarantee the navigation and security of the vessels is a relatively complex question which will require later discussions on the concrete details.

Much of the rest of the document deals with technical details, including the difficulty for the Chinese of preparing the various documents in Kampuchean as well as in Chinese. Even the use of French was difficult. "Perhaps it will suffice to have the text in Chinese. If you find no difficulties in using English instead of Kampuchean or French, we can satisfy you ." The question of technical advisers was also raised by Wang Shang-jung. His estimate of the number of technicians needed for the various branches, including pilots and maintenance personnel for the air transport service, was a relatively modest five hundred — for a start. Another six hundred or so would be needed to train Khmer Rouge air and naval personnel. "Our comrades come to Kampuchea to both help you and learn from you. But we think the number of personnel will gradually be increased. In the long term it will be difficult to avoid problems from that situation.''

Wang Shang-jung suggested that in 1976 471 Kampuchean personnel be sent to China for Air Force training and another 157 for the Navy, "the selection and timing to be discussed later." Regarding five major military projects to be built by the Chinese, he stated:

> Our government agrees to undertake the building of one new naval base, one airport, one arsenal, the expansion of the weapons-repair workshop and also of the port of Kep. Because these are projects which involve the supply of complete sets of equipment from our country, the Ministry of External Trade will be in charge of these undertakings. The precise scale and time schedule for the completion of these projects will be discussed with you after a survey. We would like you to let us know when the personnel for survey and designing should come to Kampuchea.

China also agreed, General Wang said, to send technicians and the necessary spare parts to repair military equipment captured from the Lon Nol forces.

A big problem in the implementation of the military aid program, the general noted, was the lack of Chinese-speaking Kampuchean interpreters:

> In 1976, we need over one hundred interpreters for technicians, surveyors and designers — also for students to be trained in China. However, up till now we have only ten. We hope that you will try to settle part of the problem.

It must have been very embarrassing for Son Sen to explain that Chinese-speaking students had not been exempted from the general massacre of intellectuals, with its high priority on those speaking foreign languages — even Chinese!

An annexed document listed the types and quantities of arms and munitions to be delivered from 1976 through 1978. The tank regiment, for instance, would include seventy-two light tanks (type 62) and thirty-two amphibian tanks (type 63). Weapons for three artillery regiments would include thirty-six each of 130 mm and 85 mm artillery pieces and 122 mm mortars and eighteen double-barrelled 37 mm anti-aircraft guns. Everything was most carefully detailed. For instance, the Chinese were sending 10,058 shells for

85 mm cannons mounted on tanks. Equipment for a telecommunications' regiment included 459 radio transmitters, 2,203 field telephones, 910 kilometers of various kinds of cables, and 1,300 sets of antennas. Supplies for the Air Force included thirty fighter planes (model 6) with six fighter-trainers and seventeen bombers with three bomber-trainers.

All this military field equipment was to be supplied on a nonrefundable basis. The fact that this was specified in the annex dealing with such supplies makes it implicit that the big projects — naval base, airport, arsenal, and others, details of which were to be negotiated with the External Trade Ministry — were to be on a refundable, commercial basis.

That the Khmer Rouge were practicing a "guns before rice" policy is obvious from the harrowing reports from every province of deaths from starvation. The cooperative farmers could never touch the rice they slaved to grow. It was taken off to storehouses and then loaded at night onto trucks and barges which headed for who knew where! According to an extract from a document on the Khmer Rouge four-year economic plan for 1977 through 1980, there was a planned exportation of from 3 to 3.5 million tons of rice. It was to start with 400,000 tons in 1977, increasing to 1.1 to 1.3 million tons in 1980. The total exports for 1976 were given as 150,000 tons. As the average rice production figures usually given for the relatively prosperous pre-war 1960s were about 2.5 million tons per year, the target export figures were enormous and do much to explain the generalized famine conditions from 1975 onwards. Although the area to which the rice was to be exported is not mentioned in this particular report (dated 22 December 1976), it is clear that it must have been China, Kampuchea's only effective trading partner at that time.

Why did the Khmer Rouge implement a "guns before rice" policy? Ieng Sary once explained that: "With revenue from agriculture, we are building industry which is to serve the development of agriculture."[1] This was just another of the Big Lies! No industry was built at all. That projected — arsenals to manufacture weapons and workshops to repair those that had fallen into Khmer Rouge hands — was certainly not to serve agriculture. Why build a naval base and a military airfield when there were such pressing tasks of economic reconstruction?

Part of the rationale is seen in an extract from the minutes of a summit meeting of Chinese and Kampuchean leaders in Peking on 29 September 1977. Taking part on the Chinese side were Chairman Hua Kuo-feng, deputy prime ministers Teng Hsiao-ping, Li Hsien Nien, and Keng Piao, and deputy foreign minister Han Nien-long — the leadership's "heavy artillery" at that time. On the Kampuchean side were their counterparts: Pol Pot, Ieng Sary, and "Volvet" (the code name for Son Sen). An extract from Pol Pot's report, according to the documents seized at the Ta Sanh base, stated:

> If the revolution in Southeast Asia seizes this occasion to intensify the offensive, the situation will improve and we will solve our problems. We have had exchanges of views with the friends in Burma, Malaysia, Indonesia and Thailand,[2] who agree with us. It will be a very great political victory. Although in questions of detail there are still some complications, in the North we have the support of our Chinese friends, in Southeast Asia there is unanimity among our friends. This strategic aspect stimulates us.

Who was there left to arm against? Kampuchea has frontiers with three countries: Thailand, Laos, and Vietnam. Pol Pot was obviously not concerned about Thailand; and he could hardly have been worried about Laos with its population of less than 3 million! The whole thrust of his report was toward the importance of seizing the initiative, and it coincided with a period in which Khmer Rouge forces were striking deep into Vietnam all along the frontier. He made a brief reference to this.

> Regarding Vietnam, we have had numerous negotiations but they have been in vain and one cannot know in what century the problems will be solved.... If before I felt at ease I feel still more at ease today with the Chinese friends at our sides....

The enthusiasm of the Khmer Rouge to be armed and the enthusiasm with which China undertook the task of arming them were based upon their common interest in doing what the French and Americans had been unable to accomplish: to inflict a military-political defeat on Vietnam. If that seems completely absurd as an ambition of the Khmer Rouge alone, it seems less absurd in the light of Pol Pot's remarks about being "still more at ease with the

Chinese friends at our sides."

Both China and Kampuchea knew that they had a "green light" from the United States in this undertaking. In his memoirs Henry Kissinger revealed that at a confidential dinner with Chinese deputy foreign minister Chiao Kuan-hua at the Century Club in New York on 13 November 1971, the two had agreed that they had a common interest in preventing Cambodia "from becoming an appendage of Hanoi."[3] Chiao Kuan-hua was in New York as the head of his country's delegation to the United Nations. In diplomatic language, given the state of United States-China relations at that time, this "common interest" could only mean collusion to disrupt relations between Vietnam and Cambodia. Kissinger, of course, was sounding out the Chinese on the basis for a concrete agreement on strategy to be formalized when Nixon visited China a few months later. The Vietnamese leadership is convinced that the agreements reached during that visit encouraged China to advance southward and "teach as many lessons to Vietnam" as lay within the capability of its armed forces. In the Pol Pot-Ieng Sary clique China found a willing and eager ally for this task.

The refusal of the Khmer Rouge to participate in the negotiations which resulted in the Paris Agreement of 27 January 1973 was certainly due at least in part to the influence of Peking's perverse opposition to a negotiated settlement of the Vietnam war. Since 1967 the Chinese had been on record as rejecting negotiations of any sort, which they equated with "betrayal." On 27 January 1967 I had interviewed North Vietnam's Minister of Foreign Affairs, Nguyen Duy Trinh. He had said that if the American bombing of North Vietnam were halted, negotiations with the United States to end the war in Vietnam could be started. This was the beginning of the process which led to the Paris talks. But I was attacked in Peking and in China's embassy in Paris as a "betrayer" of the Vietnamese revolution for participating in this process!

The "Black Paper" issued by the Ministry of Foreign Affairs of Democratic Kampuchea in September 1978 gives the following account of the Vietnamese attempt to get the Khmer Rouge to seek a negotiated settlement under terms which would ensure them a future political victory.[4]

From mid-1972 up (*sic!*) talks between Kampuchea and Vietnam took place every month. As the Kampuchea's delegation always kept silence about the Paris negotiations, after two or three meetings the Vietnamese asked for its opinion. The Communist Party of Kampuchea's delegation put back this question in return: "Whom to negotiate with? Would we have to negotiate with the Lon Nol clique?" But the latter was already dying.... "Would we have to negotiate with the US?" The Kampuchea's revolution had not to negotiate with the aggressors of Kampuchea.... Besides the Communist Party of Kampuchea had nobody to carry out negotiations.

The Vietnamese replied: In our opinion Kampuchea's comrades must negotiate. If the Kampuchea's comrades have no cadres to carry out negotiations with the US, we can do it in their place.

The Vietnamese impudence is boundless!

In October 1972, Vietnamese pressures became more imperious.

In fact, the US and Vietnamese had already put the broad outline of the draft of Paris Agreements into shape. Pham Hung and Hay So[5] asked to meet once again with the Central Committee of the Communist Party of Kampuchea. The talks lasted four days instead of the initially scheduled two days. During the talks the Vietnamese have shown their rare insolence and were in a towering rage. Both sides expressed once again their points of views and each side kept abiding by its position. The Communist Party of Kampuchea yielded nothing under the Vietnamese pressures.[6]

There were further talks on 24-26 January 1973 at which Pham Hung presented Pol Pot with the text of the Paris Agreement, then already initialled and awaiting formal signature on January 27, together with some explanations about the conditions for elections. According to the Khmer Rouge:

At the moment when he was about to go home, Pham Hung said he had been entrusted by the Vietnamese party to inform the Communist Party of Kampuchea that on the day of their meeting to finish off the text of the Agreements, Kissinger asked Le Duc Tho to inform the Kampuchea's side that if Kampuchea did not cease fire, the US strategic and tactical planes would destroy Kampuchea within 72 hours. This was an open threat uttered to the Communist Party of Kampuchea....

When Comrade Secretary Pol Pot came back home, he received a letter from the Vietnamese party in South Vietnam...(which) only confirmed the Kissinger's threats underlining that if Kampuchea did not cease fire, he would totally destroy the Kampuchea's revolution within 72 hours. The Vietnamese asked the Communist Party of Kampuchea to more carefully consider the problem. Did Kissinger really talk like that? Probably. But anyway, the Vietnamese were involved in this affair....

As it has been mentioned above, the Communist Party of Kampuchea did not know with whom to negotiate, for Lon Nol was already dying. As for the US, they were the aggressors. They had to stop their aggression?.... Besides a cease-fire would spread confusion in the determination of the people and the Revolutionary Army of Kampuchea in waging their struggle.

On the other hand, at the end of 1972, the political situation of the whole of Southeast Asia showed that it was in Kampuchea where the revolutionary situation was the best. South Vietnam was under the Thieu clique's control. It was the same in Laos which, except some regions, was controlled by the administration of Vientiane. As for Kampuchea, the Kampuchea's revolution, on the whole, grasped the situation well in hands and controlled the country. If the map was coloured, black colour would be in every place, except in Kampuchea where red colour would dominate. The objective of the US imperialists was to take this red place and turn it into black colour.... If the Kampuchea's revolution failed, the Vietnam's revolution would also fail. It would be the same for the other revolutions in South East Asian countries....

So, when the Vietnamese informed the US that they had failed in forcing Kampuchea to negotiate and cease-fire, the US were very mad and decided to send their B-52 to bomb Hanoi in December 1972, until the Vietnamese implored them to stop bombing and resume negotiations.[7]

Thus is the gospel according to the Khmer Rouge! Even in their version, however, it is clear that the Vietnamese kept the Kampuchean resistance leadership informed as to the progress of the negotiations in Paris; advised them to negotiate a settlement on their own to end the bloodshed; offered their services if the leaders of the Kampuchean resistance did not want to have direct talks; and relayed Kissinger's threats to bomb them into submission if negotiations were rejected. That this should be interpreted as "betrayal" reflects more the low political level and rabid anti-Vietnamese prejudice of the Pol Pot-Ieng Sary leadership than any realities of the situation.

In his memoirs Kissinger notes that:

> The failure of the Vietnam agreement [of 27 January 1973—W.B.] to include a cease-fire in Cambodia was clearly one of its tragedies. But there should be no doubt where the fault lies. I constantly pressed Le Duc Tho for a cease-fire in Cambodia; he pleaded his lack of influence with the Khmer Rouge.[8]

Kissinger is obviously trying to absolve the United States of responsibility for its monstrous B-52 bombings of Cambodia from the signing of the Paris Agreement on 27 January 1973 until Congressional action stopped them in August of that year. During that time B-52 bombers dropped 240,000 tons of bombs on Cambodia (half as much again as were dropped on Japan — excluding the atomic bombs dropped on Hiroshima and Nagasaki — during World War II). Kissinger expresses regret that Congress took such action, thus interfering with the doctrine of "application of force" — a key element in his concept of diplomacy. He also claims that he was negotiating for a cease-fire in Cambodia that would have brought Sihanouk back into his "pre-1970 balancing role," which the United States had previously done its best to destroy.

> The record shows (as I shall make clear in a second volume) that we were prepared, indeed eager, for Sihanouk's return under such conditions and that a negotiation was beginning. What ended the 1973 negotiation was a Congressionally mandated halt to our bombing in the middle of the year; at that point, certain of victory, the Khmer Rouge lost all interest in negotiations — and Sihanouk's role as balancer was doomed.[9]

The Khmer Rouge account in the "Black Paper" makes it clear that the Vietnamese knew the B-52 bombings would be carried out, just as they had known beforehand and braced themselves for the 1972 "Christmas" bombing of Hanoi. During the Paris negotiations the Vietnamese had advised the Khmer Rouge to do as they were doing and accept a negotiated settlement under terms which would ensure them a future political victory. Comparing the Kissinger and Khmer Rouge accounts, it seems as if those bombings truly could have been avoided had not the Khmer Rouge refused to negotiate a cease-fire and rejected everything but a battlefield solution.

In these circumstances the best the Vietnamese negotiators could do in Paris as far as Kampuchea was concerned was to include in the Paris Agreement confirmation of the Geneva Agreements on Cambodia and Laos.

(a) The parties participating in the Paris Conference on Vietnam shall strictly respect the 1954 Geneva Agreements on Cambodia and the 1962 Agreements on Laos which recognized the Cambodian and the Laotian people's fundamental national rights, i.e. the independence, sovereignty, unity and territorial integrity of these countries. The parties shall respect the neutrality of Cambodia and Laos. . . .

(b) Foreign countries shall put an end to all military activities in Cambodia and Laos, totally withdraw from and refrain from reintroducing into these two countries troops, military advisers and military personnel, armaments, munitions and war material.

(c) The internal affairs of Cambodia and Laos shall be settled by the people of each of these countries without foreign interference.

(d) The problems existing between the Indo-Chinese countries shall be settled by the Indo-Chinese parties on the basis of respect for each other's independence, sovereignty and territorial integrity and non-interference in each other's internal affairs.[10]

The Paris Agreement did put an end to overt U.S. intervention (apart from the seven months of bombings) in the war in Kampuchea and did provide for an additional legal safeguard for the withdrawal of Vietnamese troops from Kampuchea. The troop withdrawal had already been provided for within the terms of the April 1970 Summit Conference of the Peoples of Indochina, which stipulated that troops of one country could enter the territory of another only by express invitation. That the Vietnamese respected this (and Article 20 of the Paris Agreement) is clear even from the Khmer Rouge "Black Paper."

Kampuchea has been totally and definitely liberated on April 17, 1975. South Vietnam has been liberated on April 30, 1975. The Vietnamese had to leave Kampuchea and go back home. The Communist Party of Kampuchea requested the Vietnamese to withdraw before the end of May 1975, and at the latest, at the end of June, 1975. But in fact, only one part of the Vietnamese withdraw from Kampuchea. . . .

It was in Ratanakiri province [in northeast Kampuchea—W.B.]

where they were most numerous to remain in the Kampuchea's territory. There were more than 1,000 scattered here and there in many places by groups of ten to one hundred... The Kampuchea's regional forces requested them to withdraw. The Vietnamese replied that the territories located North of Andaung Meas and Voeunsay were Vietnamese territories.... In Mondulkiri province, the Vietnamese troops also refused to withdraw. They finally withdrew only under the threat of the provincial Secretary to drive them out by force.

At Snuol (Kratie province) the Vietnamese accepted to withdraw for they were aware of the measures taken in Ratanakiri and Mondulkiri provinces.[11]

Following Ieng Sary's discussions in Peking in April 1975, even before Vietnam had completed its victory over the Saigon regime, it was clear that the wartime cooperation between Vietnamese and Khmer Rouge forces was to be transformed into peacetime confrontation. In such situations it is always difficult to discover who fired the first shots. But it is possible to make a well-founded guess by checking out which side persisted in initiatives to get the shooting halted! In this regard the record is clearly in favor of the Vietnamese.

Valuable testimony concerning the Khmer Rouge attitude toward Vietnam and the Pol Pot-Ieng Sary subservience to Peking is provided by Norodom Sihanouk, both in his book[12] and in conversations with myself. Sihanouk had been confident that there would be no territorial problems between Kampuchea and Vietnam. He recalls meetings with Pham Van Dong in Peking in March 1970, at which they agreed on mutual support for the armed struggle against Lon Nol.

Prime Minister Pham Van Dong called on me and, in the presence of Premier Chou En-lai, swore in the name of the Democratic Republic of Vietnam that the latter would always respect the land frontiers as well as all islands belonging to the "Kingdom of Cambodia."...

In the general euphoria at the end of the Summit Conference of the Peoples of Indochina (April 24-25, 1970) Pham Van Dong promised Norodom Sihanouk — again in the presence of Chou En-lai — that after "our common victory over American imperialism" he, Dong, and I, Sihanouk, would go together to some part of the Vietnam-

Kampuchea frontier and plant a "Friendship Boundary-Stone" which would be the symbol of mutual respect between two neighboring and fraternal countries for their territorial integrity and national independence.[13]

In conversations with me in December 1978 various Vietnamese leaders, including Pham Van Dong, Nguyen Huu Tho, and Nguyen Co Thach, revealed that there was no doubt in their minds that had Sihanouk remained as Head of State and the Khmer National United Front (FUNK) as the leading body in Kampuchea there would have been no frontier problems and certainly no armed conflict between the two countries.

It was Sihanouk who revealed that the Khmer Rouge leadership envisaged a "three-part surgical operation on Vietnam." In discussions which had taken place while Sihanouk was under house arrest in Phnom Penh from July 1976 through the end of 1978, Khieu Samphan had explained to him exactly what this entailed. Sihanouk summarizes it as follows:

> *Primo:* To refuse categorically to any Vietnamese whomsoever the right to live in Kampuchea. Measures taken by the Khmer Rouge to implement this included the physical liquidation of a large number of residents "suspected of being agents or spies of the Vietminh or Vietcong" and, on the other hand, the expulsion *manu militari* of all other Vietnamese residents. This was done *in the second half of 1973.* [author's emphasis]

> *Secondo:* To order Kampucheans of both sexes to work twice, even ten times harder than the Vietnamese in order — as Khieu Samphan explained — that Kampuchea should become stronger than Vietnam in all fields (military, economic and ideological)....

> *Tertio:* Accept a large-scale, armed confrontation with Vietnam. With what aim? We had to fight it out over the Viet sanctuaries in Kampuchea, so as to wipe them out. Also we had to demand a more "just" definition of the land and maritime frontiers between Kampuchea and Vietnam. Finally, we had to stand up to the threat of "Soviet-Viet expansionism" which, without Democratic Kampuchea as a barrier, would not fail to sweep over the rest of Southeast Asia — and even further. We saw on January 7, 1979, how this large-scale armed confrontation ended![14]

Sihanouk was certainly in no pro-Vietnamese mood when he wrote this. He was already calling for UN armed forces, or others that he would lead himself, to drive the Vietnamese troops out of Kampuchea. But he was honest enough to recognize the origins of the Khmer Rouge-Vietnam confrontation and courageous enough to write about it as he saw it, even from Peking! And he deserves full credit for putting it all down on paper in Peking at a time when, as he mentions several times, he was dependent on the Chinese government for his "daily bread."

Although he repeatedly referred to China as Kampuchea's "greatest friend," he implicitly held China responsible for every sphere of activity inside the country. Sharply questioning the Khmer Rouge claim that it was they who had "liberated the Kampuchean people, nation and state from all foreign tutelage and foreign dependence," Sihanouk wrote:

> The People's Republic of China, which is sincerely and authentically anti-colonialist and anti-imperialist, has had to take charge in so-called "Democratic Kampuchea" of finance, the pretended "national" economy, industry, national defence, river and maritime ports, diplomacy et cetera. All this could only satisfactorily function thanks to the many-sided and massive aid and extremely important and generous "cooperation" granted by Peking....
>
> Pol Pot and Ieng Sary try to cover themselves with glory by claiming a total independence without precedent for 2,000 years. What a mockery! The reality is that whether China wanted it that way or not...the "foreign" policy of the Pol Pot-Ieng Sary government has always been, in fact, in the tow of the Chinese government.[15]

In his book Sihanouk discreetly omits any comment as to why the Chinese leadership never lifted a finger to secure his release during three years of house arrest, of which he writes: "Each night when I went to bed, I had no guarantee that I would still be alive the next day."[16] When I asked him if the Chinese leadership had given any explanation as to why they had abandoned him to such a plight, he laughed ironically and said:

> Madame Chou En-lai (Teng Ying-chao) explained that as Kampuchea is a sovereign, independent state, to intervene on my behalf would have meant interference in the internal affairs of a sovereign state and was therefore impermissible. (His voice leaped almost a complete octave.) That's absolute rubbish, Monsieur Burchett! China controlled everything in the Kampuchea of the Khmer Rouge.

1. *Keesing's Contemporary Archives*, 3 February 1978, p. 28807.

2. Ieng Sary had visited these countries plus Singapore and Pakistan in March 1977.

3. Kissinger, Henry, *Henry Kissinger: The White House Years*, p. 1414. London: Weidenfeld and Nicolson and Michael Joseph, 1979.

4. *Black Paper: Facts & Evidences of the Acts of Aggression and Annexation of Vietnam Against Kampuchea*. Phnom Penh: Department of Press and Information of the Ministry of Foreign Affairs of Democratic Kampuchea, September 1978 (English as in original).

5. Pham Hung is a veteran member of the Political Bureau of the Vietnamese Workers Party. During the anti-U.S. resistance war he was its senior representative in South Vietnam. Hay So is described in the Khmer Rouge document as a member of the Vietnamese party's Central Committee who had tried to organize an anti-Pol Pot coup in 1975!

6. *Black Paper*, pp. 72-74.

7. *Ibid.*, pp. 74-76.

8. Kissinger, *Henry Kissinger: The White House Years*, p. 1414.

9. *Ibid.*, p. 1415.

10. Chapter VII, Article 20 of the "Agreement on Ending the War and Restoring Peace in Vietnam," signed in Paris on 27 January 1973.

11. *Black Paper*, p. 78.

12. Sihanouk, Norodom, *Chroniques de Guerre et d'Espoir*. Paris: Hachette/Stock, 1979.

13. *Ibid.*

14. *Ibid.*

15. *Ibid.*

16. *Ibid.*

12.
CHINA PREPARES TO ATTACK VIETNAM

Between the end of November and the end of December 1978 I spent a very depressing month in Vietnam, mostly along her southwest border with Kampuchea and her northern border with China. It was a month darkened by the shadows of impending events.

The first evil omen was to learn upon my arrival in Ho Chi Minhville that South Vietnam's most popular and talented actress — and one of its true heroines — Thanh Nga had been assassinated four nights earlier. It was no ordinary killing, and the whole city was in mourning. Thanh Nga had received a telephoned warning that she would be killed if she played the title role of the tenth century heroine, Queen Duong Van Nga. Duong Van Nga's husband, the reigning monarch at the time, had been killed by the Chinese occupiers for resisting their rule. The queen continued the resistance and encouraged a young general, who succeeded in expelling the occupiers. The widowed queen then defied Confucian morality by marrying the general. Thus, she was a symbol of national liberation and women's liberation. Thanh Nga ignored the warning and played the role with great success. She was shot dead, together with her husband, as they returned home after a performance on 16 November 1978.

Over a year previously, she had ignored a similar telephoned warning not to play the role of Trung Tac, the elder of the two famous Trung sisters. In the first century AD the Trung sisters had raised an army and, with themselves at its head, had expelled the Chinese occupiers for three years. During one performance a grenade had been thrown and a fragment from it had lodged in Thanh Nga's right shoulder.

180

In both cases the attackers had escaped. When I asked who was responsible, I invariably received one of two replies: "Ask in the Fifth District" or "Ask in the North"! The Fifth District of Ho Chi Minhville included Cholon, the heavily Chinese former twin city of Saigon, and was the district with the highest proportion of Chinese residents. The Hoa, as the Vietnamese designate the ethnic Chinese, constituted 65 percent of the population of the Fifth District. The "North" had by that time become the synonym used in referring to Peking.

I went to see the Chairman of the People's Committee for the Fifth District, Nghi Doan. He was a big, smiling man, an ethnic Chinese who was a member of the National Assembly and also of the Communist Party Committee for Ho Chi Minhville. I wanted to find out how an atmosphere had been created which could result in the two assassination attempts against Thanh Nga. With Nghi Doan were two other members of the Fifth District People's Committee, one of them also currently a member of the city's Party Committee. Their replies were long, detailed, and depressing. Nghi Doan did most of the talking, constantly referring to his colleagues for confirmation of dates and figures.

> The Fifth was the center for Hoa commerce and service trades, also for the big capitalist traders and bourgeois compradores. If one spoke of Saigon in those days, one had to speak of the Fifth District as the home base of the big compradores. One of the main problems of administering Ho Chi Minhville was that all the trade was in the hands of the big Hoa capitalists and compradores. It was the center of the rice trade, with the "Rice King" May Hy in control. It was the center of banking with over thirty banks and banking services involving U.S., British, French and Hongkong capital but always with participation by Hoa compradores. To be a bank director, you had to be a high functionary in the administration or a high-ranking officer in the armed forces. It was not necessary to have capital — but rank and authority. The Vietnamese were directors et cetera in name only — they got some financial kick-backs for the use of their names — but the finance was put up by the Hoa compradores and all transactions were controlled by them. They manipulated all financial transactions, the entire import-export trade, the internal trade circuit.[1]

> A number of these had relations not only with Taiwan, but also with Peking....

Nghi Doan mentioned a certain Tran Thanh, a Taiwan Chinese who had financed a very lucrative sodium glutamate factory in Saigon with 48 percent Taiwan capital, putting up most of the rest himself. Shortly before the Liberation of Saigon, Tran Thanh transferred his capital to Peking and returned to his native district in Kwantung province (of which Canton is the capital). There he built a modern highway to impress the Chinese leadership with his "patriotism" and with the potential usefulness of himself and his co-fraternity in Vietnam.

Before Liberation, there were forty schools (primary and secondary) and six hospitals, all in the hands of Tran Thanh and other Hoa compradores, in the Fifth District. The director of the Trieu Chau hospital was Tran Thanh — naming it after his native village in Kwantung. In this hospital were secret agents of both Peking and Taiwan. Peking — even under the puppet Nguyen Van Thieu administration — send cadres to "help" Tran Thanh run the hospital. It was the same thing with the schools. They were in the hands of people like Tran Thanh. Most of the directors and teachers were from Taiwan, but Peking also infiltrated its agents. The principle was that there could be no expansion of mainland China's influence abroad, if it were not based on the educational system of the young Chinese. For years prior to the liberation of Saigon, Peking started preparing bases among the compradores and traders — but also among the young people. After Liberation, these secret organizations switched over to counter-revolutionary activities against the new regime, under such names as "Association of Young Chinese for National Salvation" and "Association for Studying the Works of Chairman Mao." They started distributing leaflets in favor of Mao. Of course, we had been following the preparations for such activities from the time Peking started exporting the Cultural Revolution in our direction. So we took some measures to limit the damage.[2] But we found agents were being sent in directly from Secret Service organs in Kwantung and other South China provinces. They had identity papers stamped with counterfeit seals. [Nghi Doan handed me a few and demonstrated that very expert scrutiny was needed to distinguish false from authentic documents—W.B.] Young Hoa were sent out of here, given crash courses as secret agents, then sent back again. Fortunately we got on to this quickly.

In March 1978 there had been a nationalization of wholesale and large retail trading enterprises. Some three thousand big merchants were affected, of whom six hundred were Vietnamese and the rest Hoa. Nghi Doan explained that the policy toward Vietnamese and Hoa was identical but as the latter were far more important numerically and financially "they had to take the consequences." This action unleashed a flood of protests from Peking, in which "oppression, persecution, and discrimination" against Chinese "residents" and "nationals" were charged.

> An "Association for Struggle of Chinese Residents" surfaced. One of its leaflets urged the Hoa "to rise up — unify yourselves — be worthy of the task of defending our Chinese Motherland." Another from the "National Salvation" group went further and urged "struggle against the Vietnamese dominating class — the enemy of our Nation.... Unite for a Radiant Future...."

> With this type of agitation going on it was easy to whip up the sort of atmosphere of chauvinism and racism in which a Thanh Nga could be murdered.

I then asked Nghi Doan and his comrades from the Fifth District People's Committee what was behind the exodus of Chinese "boat people." They replied:

> As for the boat people! We wanted the Hoa people to remain with us. After the socialist transformation of trade, we tried to attract the former merchants to move into productive activities to develop regional — even if capitalist — enterprises. We offered loans, from 10,000 to 20,000 dongs [in terms of what that was worth in state-supplied equipment, it was roughly equivalent to the same amount in dollars—W.B.] to add to their own capital to develop such enterprises. But many of them had the mentality of exploiters — they could not face the prospects of life outside their luxury villas. So they try, by all means, to flee abroad. There is a big network of black marketeers, who formerly lived off the drug traffic but now trade in human beings. It is run by Hoa people who have close connections with Hongkong and elsewhere abroad — including Peking. When we catch people trying to flee, we reason with them and try to persuade them to lead a normal life. But eventually they succeed, even after several failed attempts. The coastline is very long. For those who are prepared to pay big sums to the "leaky boat" racketeers, preventing them is very difficult. And we have more pressing problems on our hands than setting up an organization big enough to stop them.

Shortly after the nationalization of the big trading enterprises there had been an unprecedented incident on the Fifth District's Tan Hang Street. On 20 March 1978 cadres had come — as to all other areas of the city — to try to persuade people to volunteer for civic work on Saturdays, a common and widely followed practice in the first years after Liberation. They ran into an organized demonstration, with banners and slogans around the theme: "We Are Hoa — No Obligation To Do Voluntary Work." The demonstrators waved flags of the People's Republic of China and carried portraits of Chairman Mao. When the cadres tried to explain the need for continuing volunteer labor, they were stoned and bottles rained down on them from upper-story windows. Police had to be called and Chinese photographers were on hand to record the example of Vietnamese "oppression" of ethnic Chinese. Following this — and after a suitable propaganda build-up — Peking announced that it was sending two ships to Haiphong and Ho Chi Minhville to start evacuating those they were by then describing as "persecuted Chinese residents" and "nationals."

To grasp the importance of the use of such terms — and of the refusal of Saturday work by the demonstrators on Tan Hang Street because they were "Hoa" — one needs to know that in 1955 the Chinese and Vietnamese Communist Parties signed an agreement providing for residents in China of Vietnamese origin and residents in Vietnam of Chinese origin to come under the jurisdiction of the Chinese and Vietnamese Communist Parties, respectively, and within two years to become Chinese and Vietnamese citizens. From the time the agreement was signed, they were to have the same rights and obligations as other citizens of China and Vietnam. This had been scrupulously applied in Vietnam and Hoa citizens occupied high positions in the party, the government, and the economy. At a Conference of Overseas Chinese held in Peking at the end of 1977 and beginning of 1978, this concept had been reversed. The delegates from the 20 million overseas Chinese in Southeast Asia were told that if they had Chinese blood in their veins they should remain faithful to the "Motherland" and contribute their wealth and skills to the campaign for the "Four Modernizations."

The Vietnamese government responded to Peking's announcement that it was sending two ships to pick up Chinese who wanted to leave Vietnam by issuing a statement to the effect that it had no objection to the departure of any Hoa who wanted to leave or to the ships coming to ports designated by Vietnam and in compliance with normal international maritime procedures. Hanoi fixed the dates on which the ships could arrive, at Haiphong and at Vungtau (formerly Cap St. Jacques) — 50 miles southeast of Ho Chi Minhville — rather than at Ho Chi Minhville. When the first ship arrived at Haiphong, the captain gave as the reason for entry into Vietnamese waters "to repatriate expelled and persecuted Chinese nationals." This was a formula which the Chinese knew the Vietnamese could not possibly accept.

After weeks of negotiations, the two ships hauled up their anchors and returned to China without any passengers. But Peking made a great deal of propaganda about the "rescue mission" and her prestige among the Hoa people took a nose dive.

I was later told at a high level in Hanoi that the Peking leadership

had planned by clandestine means to create large-scale disorders when the boats arrived at Haiphong — and especially at Ho Chi Minhville. The psychological climate had been created and it was planned to move into top gear. But there was "clandestinity within the clandestinity." We knew about the planned provocations and the chief provocateurs were "invited to take a holiday." The whole affair turned into a fiasco.

This was true. But my impression of the Chinese-dominated sector of Ho Chi Minhville in early December 1978 was that there was an "explosive" situation and that elements there were just awaiting the igniting of a fuse to spring into action. The compradores had connections with a gangster underworld, as in Shanghai in the "old days." They were not likely to take their defeat over the nationalizations lying down. Nor was Peking likely to reconcile itself to the "mercy boats" fiasco!

From Ho Chi Minhville to the provincial capital of Tay Ninh was less than an hour's drive to the north. What shocked me there were the replies from the provincial military authorities as to how they assessed the aims of the Khmer Rouge cross-border attacks. "Prisoners insist that their instructions are to push south and gradually consolidate positions from which to capture Ho Chi

Minhville." It seemed so absurd that I did not even report it.

At the provincial headquarters of the Mekong Delta province of Dong Thap, a few days after my visit to Tay Ninh, I got similar answers from Mai Van Hai, the secretary of the provincial People's Committee. From a point as close to the frontier as he deemed safe, Mai Van Hai described the "mini-war situation" along the frontier. Distant booms and crackling explosions of incoming artillery fire confirmed his description. While he was briefing me on the military situation, a messenger came with a dispatch to the effect that the Khmer Rouge had launched an attack with two regiments into one of the frontier districts the previous night.

> They shelled the district centre of Hong Ngu with 130 mm cannon, but we were tipped off and managed to evacuate the town in time. They already occupy parts of the frontier districts up to a depth of 8 kilometres. They took advantage of the recent floods and the rivers flowing into Vietnam from Cambodia to send in flotillas of Chinese-made river-craft with light artillery, to shell villages deep into the interior. [In the autumn of 1978 the Mekong Delta provinces were struck by one of the greatest floods in Vietnam's history—W.B.] They have also infiltrated commando groups, dressed like our peasants, who attack our fishermen. They have paid dearly for such attacks, but they still keep coming.

I questioned Mai Van Hai about the reasons the Khmer Rouge captives gave for the continuing attacks along the frontier. He replied: "They are convinced that they are taking part in a great national effort to 'liberate' the Mekong Delta and what they refer to as Prey Nokor (Ho Chi Minhville)." Asked if it were possible to silence the Khmer Rouge artillery, Mai Van Hai explained that the floods made it very difficult for the Vietnamese People's Army to get their own guns into position and that in any case the VPA was mainly busy with flood relief work.

If the situation along Vietnam's border with Kampuchea was dangerously tense at the end of 1978, that in the North — along the border with China — was hardly less so. I arrived at the Dong Dang railway station — three kilometers from the Vietnam-China border — on December 24. China had severed Vietnam's only rail link with the outside world forty-eight hours earlier. Road links had already been closed. My first meeting was with Hoang Van Thach, Communist Party Secretary for Langson province. His opening remarks were not reassuring.

> The situation along the border is very tense. For the past two days no trains have been allowed to leave or enter the country. The Chinese have just unilaterally expelled our railway liaison team from the international check-point at P'ing Hsiang (about 15 kilometres inside China). All along the border Chinese fire at our patrols on sight. One of our border posts, 40 kilometres from here, was captured yesterday morning by Chinese troops using hand grenades. The situation is getting tenser all the time and the fault is entirely on the Chinese side. Our troops at no time or place have set foot on Chinese soil — the frontier is clearly delineated with marked boundary stones.

> In the past, Chinese frontier guards used stones and catapults to harass our patrols. Now they use automatic weapons, grenades, and mortars. Whenever there were border incidents in the past we would meet and discuss. For the past month there have been no more discussions. We used to meet at our side, or their side, of Friendship Gate [an arched, stone tower right on the frontier—W.B.]. Now they fire on us even if we are coming to discuss. The only contact now is by telephone. Tension has reached its highest point and anything could happen.

This sobering assessment was amplified by Lieutenant Nguyen Tien Hoa, deputy commander of the Nam Quan border post just one kilometer south of the frontier. He was young but had the nut-brown face of a veteran whose life had been spent at the liberation struggle's hot spots. To get to his command post, our car had to squeeze along ditches to avoid a series of tank traps made of big boulders cemented together. From his position onwards there were barbed wire barricades which could be locked into position within moments. The borders of the road leading to "Friendship" Gate were lined with coiled barbed wire.

> Just up the road [he said] is what we used to call "Friendship" Gate. Now we simply call it the "Northern" Gate. The road back to Langson used to be very good, but we have had to destroy part of it. We also had to set up obstacles north and south of our Nam Quan post. Recently the Chinese set up a big radar antenna atop a peak just on their side of the border and it turns 24 hours a day spying on our positions. There is shooting all along the border and "land-

grabbing" operations almost every day and commando-type forays at night.

When I asked about the aim of these operations, Nguyen Tien Hoa replied that they were "to seize high ground" and to capture military or civilian personnel "whom they drag across to their side of the frontier." He insisted that all the incidents took place inside the Vietnamese side of the frontier as defined on both Chinese and Vietnamese maps. The type of operations he described — the seizure of "jump-off" positions and the capture of "tongues" for intelligence — were classical tactics which precede an offensive.

The Langson Pass area which I was visiting had been the principal route used by China in its innumerable invasions of Vietnam for over two thousand years. It is an area of high peaks and steep slopes. Only an expert map-reader — and the local inhabitants — would know where the exact frontier lay. It looked like a half bearded, half clean-shaven face. The Chinese had planted pine trees very thickly on their side — coming partly down the slopes and cribbing a few hundred meters here and there, according to the Vietnamese. The "clean-shaven" slopes were Vietnamese, cultivated right up to the tree line. Many of the fields were criss-crossed with freshly dug communication trenches, the red gashes showing up clearly against the stubble of rice and maize. Between what was concealed in them and what was concealed in the pine forest, it was obvious that there was an "eyeball-to-eyeball" confrontation taking place, with only a boundary marker between the "eyeballs" in some places.

With Hoang Van Thach, Nguyen Tien Hoa, and some Chinese residents I discussed the extremely complex question of the Hoa exodus. The central question in persuading many Hoa to leave — as I was able to confirm in spot checks with ethnic Chinese in Langson, where one thousand of the city's four thousand Hoa inhabitants had left, and later in Hanoi — was mentioned by Hoang Van Thach.

They mainly left under the illusion (sic!) that China was about to attack, because Vietnam had now taken a pro-Soviet, anti-Chinese position. Many of those who left were very unhappy — they had lived peacefully together with the Vietnamese for generations. But local Chinese agents, primed by others infiltrated from across the border, told them that if they did not leave for China, they would be killed as traitors when the Chinese army took over Langson. Should the Soviet-Vietnamese win, they would be killed as "enemies." The only way out was to leave for the "Motherland"!

We explained the policy of our government. We would prefer them to stay, but if they decided to leave, we would give the necessary facilities and they could take all their belongings with them.

It was becoming clear that the question of the status of ethnic Chinese had been drastically changed by the Peking decision earlier that year that they were henceforth Chinese "residents" or "nationals." These terms appeared for the first time in official Chinese foreign language publications from 1978 onwards (the term "ressortissants" — nationals or subjects — being used in French publications). Thousands of merchants, who would have been content to leave Ho Chi Minhville legally by getting an exit visa, presenting a certificate to show they had paid their taxes, and then going by commercial transport, took to the "leaky boats" because Chinese agents — including consular officials sent from Hanoi — warned them that paying taxes would be considered "disloyal" since it would imply recognition of Vietnamese jurisdiction over Chinese "nationals"! *De facto*, from early 1978 on, China was claiming extra-territorial rights for ethnic Chinese. Thus it could happen that Chinese in Langson could be threatened with execution as "traitors" if they stayed on despite "orders" to leave.

As a consequence of the 1955 agreement between the two Communist Parties, there had been an agreement providing for the Chinese Embassy in Hanoi to issue "tourist visas" for ethnic Chinese wishing to visit relatives in China. On the basis of these visas, the Vietnamese would automatically issue exit and re-entry visas. The repercussions of the changed status of the Hoa on this procedure were explained to me by Hoang Van Thach.

The Chinese agents wanted to reinforce the idea that the Hoa were really "foreigners." After explaining government policy we freely permitted those who wanted to leave to do so. They could get exit visas immediately and we greatly speeded up the formalities. But the agents told the Hoa that they must in no way abide by Vietnamese regulations so they should not apply for exit visas. To reinforce this they said that those who left without papers and visas would be given priority treatment whereas those who complied with the regulations would be regarded as "collaborators." So many to whom we gave proper papers tore them up before they crossed the frontier. This was to reinforce the idea that we were "expelling" them.

To my question as to whether the provincial authorities had the power to expel "undesirables," Hoang Van Thach replied emphatically: "Absolutely not! No one has ever been expelled from Langson province."

Lieutenant Nguyen Tien Hoa had been an eyewitness to the whole drama of the frontier crossings as Langson gradually became a converging point for Hoa leaving from all over Vietnam, including from Ho Chi Minhville. He expanded on Hoang Van Thach's account.

The whole thing started on May 7, 1978, when the first Hoa group arrived and prepared to leave Vietnam. We informed the Chinese at the border post and then let them leave. The Chinese accepted them — those with documents and those without. We completed all the agreed formalities for residents of Chinese origin to visit China. We provided transport for those who wanted it. There were many moving, tearful scenes between family members leaving and those who wanted to stay. Privately we thought it was a crime to see wives separating from husbands, parents from their children. Parents would come chasing after their children and vice-versa, until the last possible moment. There were Chinese photographers and film crews on the other side to portray those with tears as "victims of Vietnamese persecution."

By July 11, 1978, 30,000 Hoa were concentrated between this border post and "Friendship" Gate, because of the slowness of the Chinese in issuing entry documents. By then we were allowing them to leave from our side without exit visas. At 10:30 a.m. on that day, the Chinese border guards informed us that they would not accept any more without the formalities originally agreed on — and which the Chinese authorities had repudiated — being complied with. We started issuing exit visas again at record speed, but the border authorities refused to issue entry visas. A delegation from the Hoa went to talk with the Chinese border authorities and was informed that they should all return to Hanoi and get entry certificates from the Chinese Embassy there. The border authorities knew very well, as we did, that the Chinese Embassy was refusing to issue any documents while stepping up pressures on Hoa residents to leave. We took advantage of this impasse to launch another appeal for people to return to their home towns and villages. A few hundred agreed to do this and we arranged transport for them. But their places were taken by thousands more who kept piling up.

Flashpoint was reached on August 25, when a medical group from the Langson Public Health Department started to check up on the fast deteriorating health situation. The group was attacked by Hoa elements directed, according to Nguyen Tien Hoa, by plainclothes Chinese police with battery-operated megaphones. (He produced photos showing typical crew-cut Chinese, with standard white, short-sleeved shirts, shouting into megaphones.) In the melee which ensued, Chinese border guards attacked and captured the Quoc Khung peak, which dominated road and rail communications in the Dong Dang area and had been the object of several previous attacks. The Vietnamese rushed frontier militia to the area and retook the peak a few hours later. Taking advantage of a weakened Chinese presence at the border post, some Hoa activists dismantled the frontier barricades and poured across the frontier in an unbroken and unstoppable stream. Lieutenant Nguyen Tien Hoa concluded by saying:

> It was from that day on that tensions between our two sides started to build up with their frontier guards firing on ours at sight. It was immediately after August 25 that the Chinese started building the big radar station and massing troops just behind the frontier, building artillery emplacements and roads to service their military positions.

The conviction that I reluctantly acquired during that fateful month was that the assassination of Thanh Nga, the huge radar antenna dominating what used to be called "Friendship" Gate and turning twenty-four hours a day to spy on Vietnamese defenses, the violent Khmer Rouge attacks against Vietnamese frontier areas, and everything else I saw and heard — only the highlights of which are related here — were all part of one terrifying scenario. I had studied Chinese and Vietnamese history sufficiently to know that in Chinese invasions over more than two thousand years the attackers — including the Peking-based Mongol armies of Kublai Khan in their three 13th century invasions — always supported their main thrusts through the Langson Pass with subsidiary attacks: amphibious operations along Vietnam's eastern coast and rivers and invasions by land through what was then the Champha empire in the south or through Laos. Within this historical context the Khmer Rouge attacks against Vietnam's southwest frontier while the Chinese built up massive invasion forces along the traditional invasion routes in the north made military sense. The thousands of Chinese military advisers with the Khmer Rouge forces — the Vietnamese put the figure as high as twenty thousand — were a significant element of the scenario. It seemed clear that the frontier areas from Vietnam's deepest south to its furthest north were about to be the scenes of another combined operation to crush the Vietnamese and sweep away that historic obstacle to China's advance to the south! It was a conclusion to which I came with great sorrow and disillusion.

1. In September 1975 Huynh Tan Phat, prime minister of what then was still the Provisional Revolutionary Government (and now the deputy prime minister of the Socialist Republic of Vietnam), told me that his was the first government ever to try to get its hands on the South Vietnamese economy. "Neither the French, the Japanese, the French in their comeback in 1945, nor the Americans, even tried," he said. "It was so completely in the hands of the *Hoa* that they preferred to work through them." Our discussion took place a few hours before Huynh Tan Phat signed a decree cracking down on the various "Rice," "Tobacco," "Textile," and other "kings"!

2. Within a few hours of the liberation of Saigon, French flags began appearing in the windows of French residents, apparently to make the point that they were not Americans. Flags of the People's Republic of China were flying all over the Fifth District and other predominantly Chinese quarters. Both the French and — even more so — the Chinese were mortified when they were ordered to take them down. It was the flag of revolutionary North and South Vietnam which monopolized the scene. It was *their* victory that was being celebrated.

KAMPUCHEA SURVIVES—
WHAT LIES AHEAD?

13.
FROM RESISTANCE
TO LIBERATION

The full story of the Kampuchean people's resistance to the Khmer Rouge regime will never be known. The extermination of tens of thousands of anonymous heroes and heroines — often to the last man and woman in the uprisings in which they participated — makes it impossible to piece together a complete picture. It *is* possible to affirm that the struggle was extremely widespread and was waged with great heroism by unarmed civilians as well as by units of the armed forces. All the members of the ruling "People's Revolutionary Council" and other leading bodies of the People's Republic of Kampuchea took part in, or led, resistance efforts. Leaders of resistance groups within the Khmer Rouge armed forces included Heng Samrin, who later became president of the People's Republic of Kampuchea, Hun Sen, its foreign minister, and So Phim, who was first vice-president to Khieu Samphan after the latter replaced Sihanouk as Head of State in 1976. So Phim led one of the most extensive insurrections within the armed forces. He was betrayed and executed.

Armed resistance to the Pol Pot-Ieng Sary Khmer Rouge leadership started as early as 1973. That year Sai Phu Thong, now one of the vice-presidents of the Khmer United Front for National Salvation (FUNSK), headed an armed insurrection in Kampuchea's southwest province of Koh Kong, which borders on Thailand. This insurrection was precipitated by the revulsion of local Khmer Rouge cadres to the brutal measures ordered against the civilian population. It was put down with great ferocity and all provincial Communist Party cadres were executed. Sai Phu Thong's resistance group was the earliest and biggest, maintaining five small bases with from twenty to sixty armed forces in each. Altogether they had only two small radio receivers and no transmitters. On seventeen occasions Sai Phu Thong sent emissaries to seek help from the Vietnamese. But Hanoi's loyalty to the Khmer Rouge in those days was such that the emissaries were turned back from the frontier. Three of the groups were intercepted and wiped out by the Pol Pot forces. Sai Phu Thong, a Khmer of Thai origin, finally managed to escape into Thailand and was protected by ethnic Khmers in the frontier areas until he could come back to support the nationwide upsurge to end the Pol Pot regime.

A similar armed insurrection, led by Bu Thuong, started a little later near the Laotian border in northeast Kampuchea. Insurrections within the armed forces gained momentum, especially from 1977 onwards, but most were repressed with customary Khmer Rouge ferocity. The almost total lack of communication between the various resistance groups kept them ignorant of each other's existence and activities and for a long time prevented the organization of a nationwide insurrectionary movement. Nonetheless, the revolts within the Khmer Rouge armed forces and the isolated popular uprisings continued.

An account of spontaneous popular resistance was related to me by Dr. Abdul Coyaume, a vice-president of the National Salvation Front's Phnom Penh committee. He is in charge of ethnic minority affairs and also — as an epidemiologist — of the city's public health service. Dr. Coyaume is a Cham. This Khmer Islamic community, according to Dr. Coyaume, used to number 700,000 but was reduced to 150,000 by the Khmer Rouge.[1] Traditionally fishermen, the Chams lived mainly along the Mekong and Tonle Sap Rivers. Dr. Coyaume lived in the village of Kokor, which together with the villages of Koh Prak and Roang constituted Kompong Sien district of Kompong Cham province. At the time of our meeting in early December 1980 he had just visited the three villages and had found them entirely deserted. Of the former twenty thousand Cham residents of Kompong Sien, none remained. This does not necessarily mean that none had survived; but the stench and memory of death was such that survivors did not want to return. Dr. Coyaume described what has become known as the "Krauchmar Uprising."

It was in October 1975, just after the planting out of the main season rice was completed. We were preparing to celebrate Ramadan, the most sacred Islamic holiday. Angkar cadres arrived and everyone was called to a public meeting. The leading cadre said: "You are now revolutionaries — you must no longer respect religion. You can use the Koran for toilet paper. Bring them out and we will make a bonfire of them." People refused and the Pol Pot troops started going into the houses to confiscate copies of the Koran. Our men fought back and there was a tug-of-war over their possession. The troops started chasing away the women and children and rounding up the men. They were taken off and executed.

Word quickly spread that this was going on in all the Cham villages along the middle reaches of the Mekong. It took the form of resistance to save the Koran. But this was only the pretext for the racist extermination of our Cham people. They said that our women wore their hair long like the Vietnamese and so were "contaminated." Not far from my village was the very fertile island of Koh Phal, "Prosperity Island" in the middle of the Mekong. There was the same struggle over the Koran. The Pol Pot troops started rounding up the men. Many jumped into the river. Some were drowned, some killed by machine-gun fire in the water. The Pol Potists then sent a naval unit from Kompong Cham to wipe out every living being remaining on Koh Phal. The island has been renamed Koh Phès, the "island of ashes."

According to Dr. Coyaume (and confirmed by my own interviews with Cham survivors, beginning with those who escaped into Vietnam in 1977-78), the Chams were placed in the "A" category, together with officers and troops of the Lon Nol armed forces, for priority in extermination.

The killings started immediately after what we considered to be our common victory. The first phase was to call for volunteers to help plant out rice. Those who volunteered were never seen again. The killings went on sporadically in 1975 and 1976. In July 1977, the local Khmer Rouge leaders said that our district was too densely populated and some people must be distributed to other districts. My village was in what was designated as "district 42" and it was ordered that 120 families must be transferred to "district 41" for a start. Half of the families were Chams. They could not take any household effects with them — Angkar "would provide." The first to leave spent a night in a school while a few trucks went back and forth picking up

197

the others. From then on they had to abandon everything except the clothes they were wearing. They were then taken to the Chup rubber plantation where pits, some of them ten metres deep, had been prepared. Men, women and children were killed separately, their bodies thrown into different pits.

Prom Than, who had come along to the discussion with Dr. Coyaume, was also a vice-president of the Front's Phnom Penh Committee and was responsible for religious affairs. I asked him why Pol Pot was particularly against the Chams. He responded that the Pol Pot-Ieng Sary leadership was against all religions.

The Khmer Rouge leaders killed off about three quarters of the Buddhist bonzes but they could not kill all the Buddhist believers as they represented virtually the entire people. But, as for the Chams, they could kill off not only the mullahs but also all the believers because it was a foreign race with a foreign religion. And the Chams fought back with every means at their disposal to defend their religion and special customs.

Before 1975, the Chams lived in very close-knit communities, usually grouped around their mosques, and with very great solidarity between them. Pol Pot immediately set about breaking all this up. There was a deliberate policy of division, dispersal and extermination. To survive, people had to abandon their customs. Mosques were turned into pigsties and depots for human excreta. Women had to crop their hair, men had to eat pork — refusal meant instant execution — prayers had to be abandoned, the Chams had to conceal or deny their identity. But at enormous sacrifice they never ceased to fight back in some form or another.

One example of the kind of desperate and hopeless popular uprisings that occurred was provided by Chau Kong, a former secondary school teacher at Siem Reap (the capital of the province of the same name, in which the Angkor ruins are situated). He now works at the Africa and Middle East Department of the Ministry of Foreign Affairs and was my English-speaking interpreter during my December 1980 visit to Kampuchea.

When the urban centers were emptied after the Khmer Rouge overthrew Lon Nol in April 1975, Chau Kong had been transferred from the provincial capital to Kuok Thiok village in Siem Reap's district of Chikrong. In April 1977 he was sent to work on building a dam at a place called Rohal Truol.

The "old" residents had been working there, but they were to be replaced by "new" residents. When, in the name of "Angkar" the "old" residents were "invited" to return to their villages they were suspicious that they might be taken off to be killed. They stayed at the site. The "new" residents were already conditioned to know that Angkar "requests" were the equivalent of a death sentence. "Old" and "new" got together and appointed two leaders, Chhoeut from the "old" and Siv from the "new," to stage demonstrations against Angkar. These broke out at the worksite but almost simultaneously (also) in each of the twelve villages of Chikrong district. The Angkar cadres tried to prevent them, at first by arguments, then by force. They only fanned the fires of revolt. Many Angkar cadres, troops, and chiefs of work groups and cooperatives were attacked with axes, hoes, iron bars, and clubs — and killed. The uprisings lasted two weeks by which time virtually all Angkar cadres in Chikrong district had been wiped out. "Old" and "new" residents fought side by side.

It started in the first days of April. In Kuok Thiok village some Pol Pot troops arrived to try and stop the demonstrations — they were killed. Big troop reinforcements were then sent and on April 19 the governor of the whole zone, including Siem Reap, Kompong Thom and Oddar Meanchey provinces, came and made a speech about the Revolution having "liberated us from imperialism" and the benefits and privileges Angkar had brought us. He charged us with showing "ingratitude" by the demonstrations and warned that the "revolution is still alive."

People shouted back that we were not against the Revolution, we were against the killings and not having enough to eat. We were carrying out a "revolution within the revolution." The governor replied that some cadres had been killed and that Angkar, pursuing its correct policies, would ensure that "justice would be done." Troops then dragged in Chhoeut and Siv and the governor said that Angkar "requested" their presence for further education." We knew that was their death sentence.

Everybody was then lined up and to each a question was put: "Did you take part in the demonstrations?" Those who answered frankly "yes" were put to one side, those who replied "no" to another side. When all were separated, those who had answered "yes" were told to return to the village and then lie down. Their hands were tied behind them and they were led off in broad daylight and killed in the village outskirts. For those like myself who answered "no" there were Angkar "requests" every night for our presence and no one returned. On the night of April 21-22, I managed to escape to another district. As far as I know, I was the only male from Kuok Thiok, and one of a handful from Chikrong district, to survive.

It is a fair assumption that those in the death pits of Roluos were victims of a popular uprising similar to that in Chikrong district but on the opposite side of the country. The village of Roluos, on the banks of the Bassac River, is about fifteen kilometers from Phnom Penh. At the time of my visit in mid-December 1980 only twelve pits of a total of one hundred and twenty-nine — discovered in August 1980 — had been exhumed. (The work of disinterring the skeletons had been temporarily halted because members of the exhumation teams fell ill from the stench and horror of it all. As I also did.) Each opened pit contained from sixty to one hundred and twenty corpses. Most had their hands bound behind them with pieces of electric cable and their eyes covered with strips of their own clothing. There were men, women, and children. Tufts of hair and dried flesh still adhered to their skulls and bones. It seemed clear that entire families had been wiped out. The state of the remains indicated that the victims must have been killed shortly before the Pol Pot-Ieng Sary regime was overthrown. But nobody could say from where the estimated eleven to twelve thousand victims had been brought to the execution site. Dead people "tell no tales," as an old English saying aptly notes!

The villagers of Roluos, who were hand-harvesting a good crop of early rice at the time of my visit, could contribute nothing to solving the mystery. Forcibly evacuated far from their village in the first days after the Khmer Rouge takeover, they had returned only after the regime was overthrown. Several had fallen seriously ill after the opening of the death pits. It was assumed that the victims were from a community which had risen up against the local Khmer Rouge despots. But nothing at the pits provided any clues as to who the victims were or from where they had come.

Vandy Kaonn, referred to earlier as a Sorbonne-trained sociologist, had survived by pretending to be an illiterate peddler of cigarettes. Deported to Prek Kak village in the Stung Trang district of Kompong Cham province, he had witnessed individual gestures of defiance and had himself tried to take poison by making a brew from a certain plant known for its lethal qualities. He told me:

and had himself tried to take poison by making a brew from a certain plant known for its lethal qualities. He told me:

> Everyone was ready to rise up against Pol Pot. If I had had a gun, I would certainly have taken part. But it seemed hopeless. Many people committed suicide. They felt they were going to die anyway — why prolong the agony?

He cited the case of a young student "expansive and generous" in his work group, who decided to end his days but at least to do so in a gesture of defiance to encourage resistance. In Prek Kak, as elsewhere, child spies hid under the dwelling places at night to identify anyone uttering a word of a foreign language. Those denounced were led off the following day and were never seen again. One day, to everyone's fear and astonishment, the young man got up at the work site and sang a song — some popular hit of the 1970's — in French. When he had finished he was led off shouting: "I know death awaits me. Now I'm ready to die." His parents went into a decline, his mother dying a month later and his father hanging himself shortly after her death. Vandy Kaonn added:

> At the Stung Trang work site, many intellectuals were killed for having inadvertently uttered a word in French or English after returning from work. The student's father left a note saying: "May my soul never be reborn on this thousand times cursed land!" Poor man! The only reproach one could make was that he was mistaken in the object of his malediction. It was not Kampuchea but the Khmer Rouge on whom he should have laid his dying curse.

Can it be imagined that father and son would not have taken to arms had there been the slightest possibility of helping to overthrow the regime? Such cases must be multiplied by scores of thousands. Wherever I have travelled — and this includes all the most populated provinces of Kampuchea — I have heard of similar desperate gestures of individual resistance. Had they been able to coordinate and concentrate their forces, the regime would have been overthrown much earlier.

Pin Yathay writes eloquently of the hopes aroused by rumors of uprisings in different parts of the country and of the impossibility of verifying them and the even greater impossibility of joining up with such groups.[2] One of the most important uprisings — and one which helps to explain the later mass defections of Pol Pot's troops and the whirlwind victory of the Vietnamese-backed anti-Khmer Rouge forces in January 1979 — was that headed by Chakray, the deputy head of the Chiefs of Staff and the Phnom Penh garrison commander. It took place in February 1977 but Pol Pot's espionage system within the armed forces was too well organized. The insurrection had hardly begun when Chakray was killed and his chief aides were captured. They were later burned alive at the Phnom Penh stadium.

The resistance to the Khmer Rouge regime of Pol Pot, Ieng Sary, and Khieu Samphan is too complicated, and the known elements too incomplete, to be dealt with in a few pages. It will doubtless later be the subject of a full-sized book. FUNSK vice-president Ba Thong is in charge of collecting documents on the subject. But only if the anonymous skeletons in the thousands of mass graves could give evidence, or the chief culprits were brought to trial in person, could even an approximate account be pieced together. From my own necessarily limited investigations, it has become clear that the idea that more than three million Kampucheans went passively to their deaths is false. They resisted individually and collectively, as unarmed civilians and as units within the armed forces, mainly sporadically and spontaneously, as best they could. But they were in a hopelessly impossible position as long as the guns, firepower, organization, communications, transportation and — above all — leadership were in the hands of Pol Pot and his clique, who were increasingly the willing instruments of their army of Chinese advisers!

In December 1980 I discussed the overthrow of the Khmer Rouge regime with Yos Por, a member of the Central Committee of FUNSK who was then acting as a senior adviser to the Ministry of Culture, Press, and Information. A rare survivor of the Khmer section of the former Indochina Communist Party, who interestingly enough had studied political philosophy in Chungking during the Chinese Cultural Revolution, Yos Por had taken part in the anti-French and anti-U.S. liberation struggles and had played a leading role in the formation of FUNSK and in drafting its constitution. He had saved his life from Pol Pot's extermination squads by fleeing across the frontier into Vietnam. Yos Por's extensive experience in the revolutionary struggle enabled him to explain what had happened clearly and concisely.

It was the people's struggle which liberated our country in April 1975. But the Pol Pot-Ieng Sary group transformed Kampuchea into a concentration camp. They treated our people like *things* instead of human beings. Pol Pot, Ieng Sary and their wives established a family dictatorship. All true revolutionaries who contributed to the victory over Lon Nol were killed — old revolutionaries who fought for independence against the French also. They not only killed revolutionaries but set the rural people against the town people and then set the rural people against each other.

There were revolts within the Khmer Rouge armed forces from 1973 onwards because true revolutionaries could not support the repression against our own people. But these uprisings gathered strength from 1976 onwards because Pol Pot was also killing the families of his own armed forces. The wives and children and relatives of loyal Khmer Rouge officers and troops were also being killed. They wanted to destroy the regime responsible for such atrocities — they all yearned for a normal life and security for their families and friends.

All militants knew of the contradictions within the leadership and that the true revolutionaries were being liquidated. Many of the most respected militants had to seek refuge in Vietnam as the sole means of survival. They regrouped there as elements of a consolidated revolutionary force dedicated to overthrowing what had become an intolerable, anti-national fascist dictatorship. Towards the end of 1978 the time was ripe for the birth of a national united front to liberate the country. Various resistance groups were finally able to establish contact and liberated areas were able to join up. This made possible the holding of the inaugural congress of the National Salvation Front at Chhlong in Kratié province on December 2, 1978, to unite all classes and forces for the overthrow of the Pol Pot-Ieng Sary clique. Taking part were many old cadres and revolutionaries and other new elements like Heng Samrin, Hun Sen and others who had originally supported Pol Pot but had long rejected his anti-national, genocidal policies.

Within 33 days of the formation of the Front, the Pol Pot-Ieng Sary forces were thrown out of the country; a People's Revolutionary Council was set up to lead the people, to run the country and defend it.

I asked Yos Por how, as a veteran Communist and one who had worked with the Khmer Rouge leadership, he explained their genocidal policies towards their fellow revolutionaries, which led to revolts and uprisings and to the collapse of their armed forces.

> Fear. The Pol Pot-Ieng Sary clique was afraid. Afraid of true revolutionaries, afraid of the people. They had a guilt complex for having usurped the leadership of the Khmer People's Revolutionary Party (Pracheachon) born from the Khmer section of the Indochina Communist Party. The so-called Kampuchean Communist Party which they later founded is at the origin of the blood-stained tragedy which engulfed Kampuchea between 1975-79. They had a guilt complex also for having turned against the closest friends and allies of the Kampuchean people who made great sacrifices to help us in our anti-French and anti-American resistance struggles. They succeeded in turning our best friends and the entire people against them and thus dug their own graves.

When the Vietnam People's Army moved in to smash the nineteen Khmer Rouge divisions massed along the Vietnamese frontier, including three divisions which had actually penetrated Vietnam's Tay Ninh province, they crushed the backbone of the Khmer Rouge forces and thus created the conditions for popular uprisings and the speedy dismantling of the Pol Pot regime. The latter melted away like snow on a hot stove once the VPA had struck the initial blows. I asked Vandy Kaonn to describe the atmosphere in his area when it was understood that an offensive had started against the Khmer Rouge regime.

> I and many others always nourished the illusion that there would eventually be an intervention by the United Nations to end the nightmare. It was inconceivable to us that we would all be left to perish. Every time I heard heavy artillery I thought: "The UN is coming at last."

> At the beginning of January 1979, when we heard the sound of heavy artillery advancing in our direction, the people of Prek Kak village rose up and seized Chim, the local Angkar chief and most barbarous executioner. Formerly his very appearance made everyone tremble. But he started to shake like a leaf when the sound of artillery was heard. His guards started mumbling: "We can't fight against that," as they heard the explosions of big calibre shells. "They have enormous tanks." From that moment the people started to act.

What, I asked Vandy Kaonn, was his own immediate reaction and that of those with him at the time. He smiled and said: "It was mealtime and like everyone else I had the right to one ladle of rice gruel. I helped myself to two extra ladles. Normally the Pol Pot cookhouse guards would have arrested and killed me. I said to them: "You're finished." They replied: "Yes! We're finished." He continued:

What happened next caused me to change my opinion about the decisive elements of warfare. I had expected to see an enormous army, corresponding to the noise of the exploding shells and the terror on the faces of the Khmer Rouge. Nothing of the sort. Quite a few Pol Pot troops started pointing their guns at their officers, who started throwing their weapons on the ground.

Until then I had thought only military strength was decisive. But then I understood that political strength was the decisive factor. Suddenly there were rumours of FUNSK troops all over the village. They turned out to be Pol Pot troops who had changed sides. They were the spearhead of the liberation forces, having been prepared for the role they were now playing well before the arrival of Vietnamese tanks and artillery.

Careful political work had been done for months before. The whole population was with FUNSK from the first moment. It was the true liberating force. FUNSK cadres launched the slogan "No Vengeance" and when the armed forces arrived they intervened many times to save Pol Potists from being lynched. Those who were still loyal to Pol Pot started throwing down their arms and it was impossible to avoid some cases of personal vengeance, but in general the FUNSK line was respected.

As a sociologist, I was enormously interested in learning how a regime is changed — and there I was, suddenly in the front seat of change. In fact it was very simple. The Pol Potists tried to contact the people: "Remember me! I never really was for Pol Pot!" Suddenly they saw the future and threw away their arms.

We had been indoctrinated by the Khmer Rouge that it was only military force that counted, in the Maoist line that "power comes out of the barrel of a gun." It was not true. It was the force of a people united in suffering which counted in the overthrow of Pol Pot. My main task towards the end was mixing human manure with my hands, under the surveillance of a group of ferocious Khmer Rouge guards. Suddenly, at the sound of the advancing artillery they became like little lambs and started to pretend that they were always for the people and detested Pol Pot's policies. What could they do to prove this now? We told them to use their arms to round up Khmer Rouge stragglers, which they did very enthusiastically!

Vandy Kaonn explained that numerous attempts had been made to get him to admit that he was an intellectual and that it was clear that among the Khmer Rouge cadres, at least by 1977, there were those who genuinely sought the opinions of suspected intellectuals as to how they saw the future. "But the Khmer Rouge groups were all scared stiff. They knew that in each group of five there was at least one Pol Pot spy and that his denunciation was inevitably a death sentence." Asked how far he thought the regime had intended to go with the exterminations, Vandy Kaonn replied:

We were sometimes subjected to harangues giving the "diehard" leadership's "diehard" line. One aspect of this was the "one in ten" thesis to justify the constant killings. If there was one suspected enemy in a group of ten, it is better to kill the ten rather than let one escape. It was in this sense that I heard Khmer Rouge cadres discussing a directive circulated in 1977 to the effect that to guard the "purity" of the revolution it would be enough if from four to eight families survived in each village. The new system could be built on that. Thus, in Prey Kak seven families survived.

In 1978, the line changed somewhat in the sense that children must be the basis of the new society and cadres were ordered to provide "special care for young children." At the same time they were ordered to step up the extermination of "enemies." In practice this meant that every Angkar village head had to kill or be killed. Merit in Pol Pot's eyes by that time was judged by how many "enemies" a cadre had liquidated.

Vandy Kaonn said that he often heard local Khmer Rouge cadres boasting among themselves about how many "enemies" they had killed and exchanging ideas as to the most economic and effective methods of killing. When I asked what he thought had been the decisive factor in the collapse of the regime once the military blows were struck, he replied:

People in the rural areas saw that Pol Pot had lied to them. People from Phnom Penh and other urban centres were not brutal enemies as they had been depicted, but decent people who had obviously enjoyed a better life than those in the rural areas under Pol Pot.

People everywhere, including those within the Khmer Rouge armed forces and administration, became increasingly concerned over the fate of their own families when they saw what was happening to obviously innocent families from Phnom Penh and other urban centres.

Long before the end of 1978, people fundamentally rejected what there was of Pol Pot's ideology. It was seen that the Pol Pot-Ieng Sary leadership was clearly stupid. "How can we work and build up the country under such conditions?" was a universal query.

People just needed the certainty that there was powerful military backing to deal with the Khmer Rouge main force units and they rose up everywhere.

The analyses of Yos Por and Vandy Kaonn were accurate and explain the astonishing rapidity with which the Pol Pot forces collapsed. Vietnamese armor and artillery certainly played the decisive role in dealing with the Khmer Rouge main force units and their Chinese advisers. But careful political preparation led to thousands and perhaps tens of thousands of Khmer Rouge troops turning their guns against their officers and accelerating the disintegration of entire divisions. The Vietnamese attack started on 25 December 1978. Its targets were every one of the nineteen divisions which Pol Pot had massed along the entire frontier from Kampot province in the extreme south to Ratanakiri in the extreme north. Within fourteen days Khmer Rouge power had collapsed throughout the entire country, except for a few bases in the Elephant and Cardamom Mountains and along the frontier with Thailand.

The self-proclaimed great military "genius" Pol Pot, who was in effective charge of Khmer Rouge military affairs, made a monumental error in stationing almost half of his main force units in the areas known as the "Parrot's Beak" in Svay Rieng province and the "Fish Hook" in Kompong Cham. Both areas adjoin Vietnam and are known for the revolutionary ardor of their inhabitants. The Pol Pot divisions were encircled in massive outflanking movements, their tanks and artillery were destroyed by superior Vietnamese fire-power and accuracy, and their cadres were liquidated largely by their own troops revolting against the intolerable repression within the armed forces. Fugitives — including Chinese advisers — were killed or rounded up by the local population, which had armed itself with discarded weapons and was seething with hatred against any vestige of the Khmer Rouge regime.

By 1 January 1979 FUNSK was able to announce that its policies were already being introduced into the liberated areas. There was nothing very "revolutionary" about them. Essentially, they halted the abominable practices of the regime which was being overthrown. They included freedom of movement,[3] election of management committees at factories and cooperative farms, freedom of religion, and the reintroduction of education and public health services. In effect, an amnesty was pronounced for officials and troops of the Khmer Rouge regime who gave themselves up. They were free to return to their home villages or, pending the complete liberation of the country from Khmer Rouge rule, they would be given jobs in the areas where they had surrendered.

Western intelligence sources estimated that Vietnam had used some 100,000 troops of their own plus an initial 20,000 troops of the National Salvation Front. The latter were speedily reinforced as entire units broke away from the Pol Pot forces and joined those of the Front.

When one compares the performance of the Vietnamese People's Army and the Front forces in shattering Pol Pot's twenty-three divisions in fourteen days and in occupying all nineteen provincial capitals within twenty days with that of the 600,000-strong Chinese army in its invasion of Vietnam (which began on 17 February 1979), one sees the difference between an action supported by the people and one that is not. On the main invasion front — the Langson Pass — Chinese regular army units succeeded in advancing sixteen kilometers in sixteen days against border guards and local people's militia. It was by far the slowest advance — despite tanks and trucks instead of horses and foot soldiery — in the entire two thousand-year history of Chinese invasions of Vietnam. Overwhelming Chinese numerical and material superiority could not overcome the military reality that the Vietnamese people were against them and were determined to defend their homes and villages and their socialist system. In Kampuchea the overwhelming desire of the people was to help the Vietnamese and their own Front troops to destroy the regime which had inflicted such unprecedented sufferings on them. Military strategists and social scientists will undoubtedly ponder this in the years to come and perhaps will arrive at conclusions similar to those of Vandy Kaonn concerning the "decisive elements of warfare."

By mid-1981, despite massive Chinese aid routed through Thailand, Khmer Rouge troops based in sanctuaries in Thailand and in camps straddling the Thai-Kampuchea border had to carry their rations, arms, and munitions on their backs on their forays into Kampuchea. There was no possibility of getting food from the Kampuchean people, of establishing caches of arms and munitions in the villages, or of obtaining help with transport or even information from the people. The local people had become their deadly enemies because the Khmer Rouge represented everything contrary to their deepest aspirations. This denial of popular support translated into military terms meant that the Khmer Rouge forces were reduced to terrorist activities. These forays could last no more than four or five days before the Khmer Rouge had to return to their bases on the Thai border to pick up whatever Chinese military supplies had become available and whatever food from the international agencies could be diverted from that which was supposed to relieve the distress of Kampuchea's civilian population. Were it not for these supplies, the danger posed by the Khmer Rouge remnants would already have been eliminated!

1. Figures vary widely as to the total Cham population in Kampuchea. However, there is general agreement that an attempt was made by the Khmer Rouge to completely exterminate the Chams and that those who survived did so by concealing their ethnic origin.

2. Yathay, Pin, *L'Utopie Meutrière*. Paris: Robert Laffont, 1980.

3. Freedom of movement included the right of all people to return to their original homes and villages. Tens of thousands took advantage of this to flee the horrors of the previous regime by the shortest and speediest routes, which meant that they ended up in Thailand. The interpretation that they were fleeing "Vietnamese invaders" seems to have been greatly exaggerated.

14.
THE SURVIVAL
MIRACLE

My first visit to Kampuchea after the overthrow of the Pol Pot regime was in May 1979. Driving by car from Ho Chi Minhville to Phnom Penh, one's first impression after crossing the Vietnam-Kampuchea frontier on Highway 1 at Ba Vet was that of the great abandonment of cultivable land. We drove for almost twenty-five miles through formerly rich rice fields and flourishing villages along a road normally lined with bustling markets. It had become a ghostland. No villages, no markets, no cultivation, none of the graceful sugar palms so typical of that landscape. Only their stumps remained. This was a portion of the "no-man's land" created by the Khmer Rouge in depth between Kampuchea and Vietnam to avoid social and political contamination of the new "pure" society to be built under their leadership. The wasteland continued almost to the outskirts of Svay Rieng, the capital of the province of the same name in what is known as the "Parrot's Beak," where the tip of a triangle of Kampuchean territory pushes to within forty miles of Ho Chi Minhville.

A few miles before Svay Rieng City, we came upon rectangular cultivation units up to a thousand yards in length and five hundred yards in width. They were enclosed by six-foot-high earth walls in various stages of disintegration. On the external side of one of the thousand-yard-long earth walls was a wide irrigation canal; inside the four walls were fields, each about a hundred yards square, separated by traditional foot-high terraces. Theoretically, the canal would feed water into the higher fields and this would flow by natural gravitation to those at the lower levels. The paddy fields would thus be nourished by the controlled level of water essential for normal harvests. But on the flat lands between Svay Rieng and Phnom Penh, there was no reservoir or catchment area to supply water to the canals. The levels within the surrounding dike walls obviously had not been well calculated; nor had the dike walls or even the terraces been well compacted. Contempt for science and machinery, and probably also the physical weakness of those engaged in the digging and dike-building work, had left their mark in crumbling walls and uneven puddles of water which were obviously obeying the objective laws of gravitation and not the subjective laws devised by the local Khmer Rouge cooperative manager!

The most typical sight on the road between Svay Rieng and Phnom Penh was the small groups of people, almost exclusively women and children, pulling and pushing homemade carts with a pitiable few belongings inside — a few sleeping mats, some manioc roots, and a cooking pot. They were on their way back to where they hoped to find their native villages and traces of their relatives. Tragic faces and emaciated bodies. To talk to them was to uncover tiny elements of a mosaic of suffering unprecedented in our times.

The great Khmer Rouge madness required not only the creation of a huge no-man's land between Kampuchea and Vietnam but also a transfer of population from the eastern provinces bordering Vietnam to the western ones bordering Thailand and vice-versa. After Pol Pot was overthrown, the first decree of the Heng Samrin government was that all were free to leave their concentration camp barracks, to reunite with their families and return to their home villages. For the lucky ones who could find family members quickly, there was some motor transport. For the great majority it meant weeks of painful research to gather news of family members from whom they had been separated even at the places to which they had been evacuated. It also meant taking time to make primitive carts — mainly coffin-shaped boxes on roughly shaped wooden disc wheels — and to find a cooking pot per family or group of families. In imposing their notion of "collective society," the Khmer Rouge had demanded that such symbols of individual living as cooking pots be destroyed.

Interviews with those small family groups were necessarily brief, occurring while they snatched a few minutes rest under the shade of roadside trees. They were always painful, often tearful, and involved explanations as to why there were no men-folk ("killed by Pol Pot"), why there were only girl children ("our boys were taken by Pol Pot into the army"), and what they hoped to find at their destination ("perhaps some relatives or friends"). The only smiles came from those who, after weeks of pulling and pushing their carts, had only another day or two's trek to arrive where their village used to be. It was not for me to wipe the smiles off their faces by describing the wasteland between Svay Rieng and the Vietnamese frontier where there was no longer any trace of villages.

These brief snatches of conversations with the "road people," as I came to call them, made real those which I had had with Kampuchean refugees on the Vietnamese side of the frontier five months earlier. There is always an element of doubt in refugees' tales. The very fact of being a refugee means that one has an "axe to grind" against the regime from which one has fled. But with the "road people" it was very different. Here I was in an area which I knew well, on a road on which I had travelled very often.[1] The evidence of destroyed villages, schools, and pagodas; the traces of old ricelands, terraces still mainly intact but from which no harvests had been taken for years; the crumbling dikes and dried-up canals of huge new rectangular units which had obviously failed; the tears and stammering descriptions of wholesale slaughters and an unbelievably oppressive and odious life system imposed by the Khmer Rouge; the lack of anything which was normal to life in Kampuchea as I had known it — all provided overwhelming confirmation of the accuracy, even the understatement, of the worst of the refugee accounts.

Along the Svay Rieng-Phnom Penh road, I came to understand why Khmer Rouge leaders with whom I had been on friendly terms — Thiounn Prasith, for instance, who was their representative at the United Nations — had refused to meet me during my UN visits and why Ieng Sary could not look me in the eyes at the Belgrade meeting of Non-Aligned Foreign Ministers in July 1978. Along the Svay Rieng-Phnom Penh road there was still the stench of murder in the air and too much tragedy in the faces of the people.

The third of my visits to Kampuchea after the overthrow of the Khmer Rouge occurred one year later, in May 1980. I was accompanied by my wife Vessa and daughter Anna. It was an ambitious project: by road from Ho Chi Minhville to Phnom Penh, as I had done the previous May, then continuing on by road to Siem Reap to view the nearby Angkor temples which we knew well but which Vessa and Anna had not seen since the Khmer Rouge holocaust. Part of the reason for the long road trip was that a film on my forty years of journalistic activity — a mixture of retrospective and topical work — was being made by an Australian producer. Due to U.S. B-52 bombings and to the Khmer Rouge policy of concentrating on road destruction rather than maintenance, the trip was an arduous one.

At Kompong Kdek, about twenty miles from Siem Reap, one of our two vehicles blew a tire. We had just crossed the first of the Angkor period bridges when we halted to change the wheel. As we were about to continue on to Siem Reap, a Vietnamese officer appeared — almost at a run. He took me and my Australian-trained Vietnamese interpreter, Nhu, aside and said: "You must not continue. We have just intercepted a radio message from some local Khmer Rouge agent to one of their advanced bases in the Siem Reap area that you are here, giving the details of your minibus. Spend the night here (it was half-an-hour before sunset) where there is no security problem." I objected because we had a full day of work at Angkor planned for the next day and a tight schedule of future activities. But I also knew that part of the Kompong Kdek-Siem Reap road was lined by dense jungle. "We will send a patrol early tomorrow morning," said the officer, "and if all is well, you can continue at dawn. But you must not risk continuing in the dusk to Siem Reap." And thus it was decided.

We filmed at Angkor the following day. One of the sequences was an interview with Vessa against the background of the five towers of Angkor Wat. Among other things she said, "When I say good-bye to my husband on his frequent travels, I never know whether I will see him again. But it's a privilege." Early the following morning we said good-bye. Vessa and Anna were returning to Phnom Penh, travelling along the same terrible road from Phnom Penh to Ho Chi Minhville and on by air to Hanoi and Bangkok to pick up a pre-scheduled charter flight to Paris. With the film crew I was to continue on another road along the southern side of the Tonle Sap (Great Lake) via Battambang, Pursat, and Kompong

Chhnang back to Phnom Penh for some further filming there.

In the pre-dusk hours of May 7, at a point about forty miles from Phnom Penh, there was a sudden sound of firecrackers. Shouting "Down!", I set the example by crouching as close to the floor of our Chevrolet minibus as possible. Almost instantly I felt blood dripping onto my arm. It was coming from our Vietnamese driver, Pham Van Muon, who was directly in front of me. Everybody — film producer David Bradbury, cameraman Peter Levy, soundman Jim Gerrand, Vietnamese interpreter Nhu, and Kampuchean conducting officer Sary — hugged the floor as bullets tore into the minibus. Bradbury, the last to go down, glanced at where the sound of the firing came from and saw men with scarves around their heads firing from behind some huge boulders. There was a big explosion and the minibus jumped slightly. That's the end, I thought. A direct hit from a heavy weapon!

To my amazement, the minibus was still advancing although the warm blood was dripping faster than ever. I could see driver Muon's hands steadily clasped on the steering wheel. A bullet from the first burst had gone clear through his cheek, subsequent ones wounding him in the neck and shoulders; but he never faltered until he had driven us out of the field of fire. Because the firing was coming from the right, he was the one person who could have certainly saved himself. The only door on the left was that of his driver's cabin. There was a sharp slope on the left into which he could have leaped to safety. But he didn't. Instead he saved all our lives, halting the car only when we came to a roadside Vietnamese military post. There we got him out of the driver's seat to receive some first aid.

By the time the minibus came to a stop, a mixed Vietnamese-Kampuchean patrol was already setting off for the site of the ambush.[2] In the action which followed, two Khmer Rouge were killed and seventeen were captured. It was presumed that only one of a group of twenty had escaped. Among those captured was their chief, who affirmed that the aim of the operation was to "get Burchett." I accepted this as an official acknowledgement that I was effectively denouncing the Pol Pot-Ieng Sary regime and its backers.

Thanks to the excellent driving of filmmaker Bradbury, who

214

took over at the wheel, driver Muon received emergency surgery in a Phnom Penh hospital within a few hours of the attack. Despite the blood heavily leaking out of his mouth and nose, driver Muon had not ceased complaining about Bradbury's fast driving until we unloaded him at the hospital. The doctors there later explained that even a half-hour's delay probably would have cost him his life!

At the hospital the following day, Pham Van Muon explained that the big bang which I thought meant the end was from a bazooka missile, the last of six which gradually approached the minibus and which he observed through the rear-vision mirror. Just before it exploded, he had accelerated in a final burst of speed after the fifth had come dangerously close.

Seven months later I interviewed a perfectly cured Pham Van Muon, by then a national hero for his devotion to duty. I remembered that he had complained that Bradbury drove too fast in getting him to the hospital, and asked him why. "Because the tires on the Chevrolet were Russian," he said, "and did not fit too well. I was responsible for the good care of the Tourist Company's vehicle. I had already risked the tires in accelerating to avoid the sixth bazooka shot."

During my December 1980 visit I learned that the "survival miracle" of the film crew and myself was of more than trivial significance. The failure to "get Burchett" symbolized a setback of strategic importance. The shots at our vehicle were quickly followed by the ambush of a train from almost the identical spot. One hundred eighty Kampucheans were killed. Both ambushes were intended to be the opening shots in a 1980 rainy season offensive, during which the Khmer Rouge hoped to prove that they could not only retake — and hold — territory along the Thai border but also maintain guerrilla bases deep inside Kampuchean territory. The knocking-off of Burchett only forty miles from Phnom Penh would have been a powerful supporting argument! The attackers failed by only a few millimeters. Had the bullet which went through Muon's cheek been a trifle higher, it would have blown his head apart and then nothing could have saved us from the bazooka attacks. As it was, local villagers indicated from where the ambushers had come and to where they had retreated and they were wiped out. Those who ambushed the train a few weeks later suffered the same fate. The 1980 rainy season offensive never got underway because the local people's armed security forces had been developed at village and district levels to the extent that they could deal with Khmer Rouge infiltrators or at least denounce their whereabouts to the Vietnamese.

To relate my own survival to that of the Kampuchean people is obviously only a bit of symbolic imagery based on the Khmer Rouge's repeated failures to hit their targets. But the "survival miracle" of the Kampuchean people was very evident during my November-December 1980 visit and could not be attributed to a few badly aimed shots by the Pol Pot-Ieng Sary remnants. It was due, first of all, to the very pronounced "will to survive" of the Kampuchean people, backed by a massive effort of international aid. The changes in the situation during my first four visits were dramatic. A summary of the progress toward survival that I observed during those visits would have to include the following.

May 1979 — My main impression is of the "road people." Small groups of almost exclusively women and children, they are pushing and pulling primitive carts across the face of Kampuchea, heading for their native villages and hoping to find family members who have survived. When I interview the new president Heng Samrin, he defines the priority tasks of his government as getting families reunited, people back into their villages, schools and pagodas reopened, and life normalized.

August 1979 — The documented horrors of what had gone on are presented to the trial *in absentia* of Pol Pot and Ieng Sary on charges of genocide. Western doctors and the handful of surviving Kampuchean doctors are discussing whether or not the sterility of the women, caused by psychological and physical stresses, is irreversible. Two British filmmakers, John Pilger and David Munro, make a film depicting the horrors of what had happened and sharply criticizing the indifference of the international aid organizations.

May 1980 — International aid is arriving and being distributed in substantial quantities where it is needed, despite a campaign in certain sections of the Western press to the contrary. CIA predictions of a catastrophic famine and charges that seed rice is either being siphoned off to the Vietnamese or eaten by starving Kampucheans are proven false by my on-the-spot inquiries and interviews with the international aid agencies. The David Bradbury film crew, in our thousand-or-so kilometer tour of the country, considers the sight of a baby to be a major filmable event. If babies are being born and rice is being sown, the nation might survive. This point is hammered home by the second Pilger-Munro film, shot in June 1980. It very credibly demonstrates the effectiveness of international aid inside Kampuchea but strongly denounces the high proportion of humanitarian aid being siphoned off to beef up the Khmer Rouge remnant forces in the Thai-Kampuchea border area.

November-December 1980 — The will to survive has triumphed. By the end of the year, 1.3 million hectares of rice should be reaped. The international aid agencies believe that the prospects for ending the food crisis are so bright that the unprecedented emergency action — which had brought thirty-two aid organizations together under the leadership of UNICEF and OXFAM — can be discontinued, with the agencies then reverting to more specialized forms of aid — child welfare, public health, village welfare, and the other social services which they traditionally undertake. The population of Phnom Penh has increased from 7,000 (in May 1979) to about 350,000. Markets are flourishing there and elsewhere, and the currency introduced a few months earlier has been widely accepted. The fishing industry in the world's most fish-rich waters has been revived. Most important of all, there are mothers suckling babies all over the place. There are more smiles per square kilometer in Kampuchea than in any other place I have visited in my forty years of journalism. The contrast with May 1979 is dramatic!

My visual impressions in the urban and rural markets and in the ricefields and fishing grounds along the Tonle Sap River were confirmed in interviews with Kampuchean officials, international aid personnel, and others. The recovery so far was of astonishing dimensions. This did not mean that there would not be immense problems for years to come. But these problems would be in fields other than those concerned with the physical survival of the Khmer nation. The most pessimistic estimate was that Kampuchea might still need some 200,000 tons of rice from outside sources in 1981, but that from 1982 on the country would be exporting substantial quantities of rice. The international effort had been considerable and decisive but it would have been useless without the strongly expressed "will to survive" of the Kampuchean people.

The general impression towards the end of 1980 was that Kampuchea had made impressive gains in several fields, beginning with security. The policy of total amnesty, except for a handful of Khmer Rouge leaders — starting obviously with Pol Pot and Ieng Sary, who were condemned to death *in absentia* at the August 1979 genocide trial — had a decisive effect on security. Khmer Rouge troops, I was assured, give themselves up more and more frequently and are re-integrated into their home villages. I was told of many cases in which groups from the Thailand frontier bases, approaching villages on aggressive missions, are so impressed by the normality and increasing prosperity of village life that they send in emissaries to negotiate surrender. Sometimes this is done on the spot; sometimes they return to their bases and persuade their comrades to join them in giving themselves up in large groups. This is obviously a result of Vietnamese experience with a policy of clemency for all except the "big fry." It is clearly difficult to eliminate the remaining Khmer Rouge bases which straddle the Kampuchean-Thai border without violating Thai territory in large-scale encircling offensives. This the Vietnamese-Kampuchean forces are loath to do. Eliminating pockets of Khmer Rouge remnants — such as those which staged the ambush near Kompong Chhnang — is mainly accomplished by political rather than military means.

Internal security is increasingly being handled by local Kampuchean militia groups. The Vietnamese move out of an area as soon as they are satisfied that these groups can handle any threat from hostile forces. In a country with as much jungle and mountainous territory as Kampuchea, guerrilla groups can find hideouts for years. But with no popular support, it is increasingly difficult for them to operate, to replenish their supplies, or to get intelligence information. In many cases, I was told, relatives went out with militia groups to the jungle hideouts and appealed to their brothers, sons, or husbands to come back home (another technique in which Vietnamese expertise is great). This was beginning to have a snowball effect and will undoubtedly become increasingly effective as the economic situation is stabilized.

Another success has been in the field of political consolidation.

The National Salvation Front is functioning at the provincial and district levels, with affiliated women's and youth organizations being formed at the village level. Within the Front and the mass organizations, members of a new Communist Party are undoubtedly being recruited from among the most outstanding activists. At the end of May 1981, what was in effect the founding congress of a new party was held in Phnom Penh. To maintain continuity and distinguish it from the Khmer Rouge usurpers, it was designated as the Fourth Congress of the Pracheachon (People's Revolutionary) Party.

Based on the incredibly bitter experiences of the past, the structure of a new progressive Kampuchean society is taking shape. It is an irreversible process which cannot be affected by U.S.-Chinese threats or by dollar-paid votes for Pol Pot at the United Nations. It will be a socialist society because there is no alternative and even the horrendous crimes committed by the Khmer Rouge in the name of "revolution" and "socialism" have not turned the people against a socialist-type organization of their lives. "Collective in production, individual in living" is a slogan one hears ever more frequently. The destruction of the boundaries between fields has made it impossible for the peasantry to find the confines of their former properties. And the killing of such a high proportion of the male labor force makes collective working of the land by what are called "solidarity groups" both logical and acceptable. Similarly, the extermination of capitalists and factory owners leaves no alternative — even if one were desired — to some form of collective ownership and operation of these enterprises. Even in the days of Sihanouk a high proportion of what industry existed, as well as the banking and import-export sectors, were state-run. The weakness in those days was that the state-owned enterprises were mostly staffed by corrupt officials for whom managerial posts were prizes of privilege and who siphoned off the profits into their own bank accounts. One can take it for granted that guarantees will be worked out for control "from below" as well as "from the top" to limit the possibilities for future corruption and sabotage of public wealth.

The Pol Potist extermination of anyone who was even literate makes it enormously difficult to find managerial staffs and skilled workers. This means, among other things, that the burden borne by the Vietnamese will continue for many years. The essential Vietnamese military role in preventing a Khmer Rouge comeback is now fairly well recognized in the outside world — at least by those who follow affairs in the region — but the extent of Vietnamese aid in the economic, public health, and other fields is less well known. It was Vietnamese engineers and workers who restored the essential roads over which international aid travelled and who rebuilt hundreds of bridges and got the Phnom Penh-Kompong Som and Phnom Penh-Battambang railways working again. It was the Vietnamese who got the first sixty factories in Phnom Penh and some of the provincial centers back into production and who rebuilt and re-equipped provincial and district hospitals (totalling 3,600 beds up to June 1980), providing four hundred medical cadres, including two hundred doctors, and thousands of nurses and dispensary personnel. All this plus 140,000 tons of food and seed rice — supplied up to the end of June 1980 — represents part of the Vietnamese relief effort.

During my May 1979 visit Ngo Dien (who then headed the Vietnamese advisory group and subsequently became Vietnam's prestigious ambassador to Phnom Penh) briefed me on the terrible human and material destruction wrought by the Pol Pot regime and the long-term effects it would have on the Kampuchean people. He concluded:

> We will have to make big sacrifices to help them and we will do this. But a major, long-term problem because of the almost total lack of cadres is the risk that we will rebuild the country in a Vietnamese way and not in a Kampuchean way. That would pile up problems for the future. So we have to be terribly careful of the manner in which our aid is handled and above all of the relationships between our experts and technicians and the Kampucheans whom we will train eventually to do the jobs themselves.

The general opinion of the representatives of the international aid agencies with whom I spoke was that not only had Vietnam played a vital role in the "survival miracle" of the Kampuchean people but also that it had done so in a manner corresponding to the concerns expressed by Ngo Dien.

The Kampuchean nation is struggling back onto its feet again. And the quality of the international cooperation which has made this possible — Western aid agencies of the most different backgrounds working with each other and with those of the Soviet Union, Vietnam, and other socialist countries in a spirit of co-operation that transcended ideological and national barriers — contains a message of hope for the future of the entire world.

1. The ambush scene — as much as was filmable — forms the final part of David Bradbury's documentary film about the author, "Public Enemy Number One." It was first presented at the Australian Arts Festival in Sydney, Australia on 8 January 1981 and later that year was shown at the Cannes International Film Festival in France. It won a Second Prize at a documentary film festival in Baltimore (U.S.A.) in April 1981, a First Prize at an American documentary film festival in New York in June 1981, and in the same month a First Prize at the Australian Documentary Film Festival in Sydney.

15.
POSTSCRIPT

Brigadier-General Nguyen Huu Hanh was Chief-of-Staff of the Saigon Army for just two days. He was appointed by General Duong Van (Big) Minh when the latter assumed the presidency on the afternoon of 28 April 1975. Early on the following morning Nguyen Huu Hanh reported to his president that the military situation was hopeless and that it was useless to try to oppose the entry of the revolutionary Vietnam People's Army forces into what had just been re-named Ho Chi Minhville. Nguyen Huu Hanh recommended that a declaration to this effect be broadcast to the ARVN (Army of the Republic of Vietnam) troops. This was done and much useless bloodshed was avoided.

Nearly six years later Nguyen Huu Hanh — who on 30 April 1975 had actually issued the order for the Saigon troops to lay down their arms — revealed an extraordinary incident which took place at the last moment before the surrender.

While the president was recording his "end the fighting" speech in the prime minister's office, for immediate broadcast over Saigon radio, a French "journalist" turned up demanding that I arrange an interview with the president on a matter of extreme urgency. "Immediately"! He turned out to be the former General François Vanuxem.[1] It was 9:00 a.m. on the morning of April 30 and I told him that he would have to wait until the president had finished recording his message to the nation.

The president received him after he had finished his recording and Vanuxem's first words were: "I have just come from Paris where I saw important personalities, including those from the Chinese embassy. The consensus is that it is good for you to continue denouncing the United States, but to follow the Chinese position. If you do that the Chinese will bring pressure to bear on Hanoi for a negotiated settlement. But you must fight on for at least 24 hours.'' He then explained the technical means by which contact could be established with Peking. ''Big'' Minh refused, saying that the bloodshed had to be stopped immediately. It must be understood that people like ''Big'' Minh and myself and many others of our social and professional status in South Vietnam were frightened of China and frightened of North Vietnam because we thought Hanoi was totally under Peking's influence. I had expected to be shot by the first soldier who burst into the presidential palace. Instead, he asked me the quickest way to reach the flagpole. Then I was very moved by my first contact with General Tran Van Tra, commander of the VPA forces. His first words were: ''Between us there are no victors or vanquished. The Vietnamese nation is the victor.'' On the other hand I was shocked that the Chinese would use such a go-between as General Vanuxem to try to persuade us to continue the slaughter of Vietnamese by Vietnamese. And for whose benefit?[2]

Another on-the-spot observer of at least some of the events Nguyen Huu Hanh was relating was the Italian journalist Tiziano Terzani. After describing the atmosphere in Saigon's Caravelle Hotel when Duong Van Minh made his surrender broadcast, he wrote:

The surrender broadcast had been delayed for five minutes because at 9.50, just as Minh was about to send one of his officers [Nguyen Huu Hanh–W.B.] to the radio station with the recording, General Vanuxem, that relic of colonial France, had arrived. Once again he tried to persuade the president not to surrender, but to launch an appeal to the Chinese and Russians to intervene. Minh listened to him, then saying: ''All right, all right,'' had ordered the officer to leave.[3]

All this is very reminiscent of the attempts — twenty-one years earlier — by U.S. Secretary of State John Foster Dulles to persuade the French not to surrender at Dien Bien Phu and not to negotiate an end to the war at Geneva in 1954. (Dulles even offered an atom bomb or two to help the French at Dien Bien Phu.) Dulles was unable to prevent the French defeat. When the French were forced to pull out of Indochina, the United States decided it had to ''fill the vacuum'' by moving in to replace them.

The Vanuxem mission and subsequent Chinese intervention in all three states of what had been known as Indochina in colonial days served notice that imperialist states were not the only ones that disliked "power vacuums." If the United States failed in its attempt to replace France, China would replace the United States. This is the reluctant conclusion to which I have had to come in investigating the China-Vietnam-Kampuchea situation. It is a melancholy reality of the background to the tragedy of what happened in Kampuchea.

The thesis that China was prepared to fight the United States "to the last Vietnamese" was originally launched by the Yugoslav embassy in Peking and reaffirmed by Jean Sainteny, France's onetime Proconsul in Indochina. At the time it was indignantly refuted by myself and other pro-Chinese "Vietnam watchers." But it has been subsequently proven to be only too correct. And when pressures on Vietnam to desist from inflicting total defeat on the U.S.-backed Saigon regime failed, Peking switched its strategy to that of trying to fight Vietnam "to the last Kampuchean." That is the essence of what has been taking place since April 1975 in the triangular struggle between China, the Khmer Rouge, and Vietnam.

There is abundant evidence that China had originally hoped to make a direct north-south push into Vietnam, using political, economic, diplomatic, and other "destabilizing" measures to bring that war-weakened nation into its geopolitical orbit. The Vanuxem mission was a reflection of that. China also had "its man," Hoang Van Hoan, in the Politburo in Hanoi and probably had exaggerated ideas as to the extent of his influence.[4]

After twenty years of socialist rule with a remarkably united and experienced leadership, North Vietnam remained an insuperable obstacle for any direct push to the South by diplomatic or any other means. So the indirect means of outflanking the North by gobbling up Laos and Kampuchea was attempted.

In early 1979 the Laotian government discovered that a road which the Chinese had contracted to build as an "aid project" for Laos had changed its course. Instead of heading almost due south from the Chinese border through Phong Saly province, it was swinging east towards the Vietnamese frontier at a point near the highly strategic Dien Bien Phu valley. This fact was revealed to *The New York Times* by the former prime minister, Prince Souvanna Phouma. He also revealed that, in the guise of railway construction workers, two battalions of Chinese troops had occupied a town in the northern Laotian province of Nam Tha. The Laotian government ordered a suspension of the road-building work and asked that all Chinese personnel be withdrawn. As the battle-hardened Pathet Lao troops had been reinforced by that time by Vietnamese troops, the orders and "request" were complied with. But, according to Laotian government sources, five divisions of Chinese troops remained massed on the Laotian border and the Chinese had taken over the remnants of the Meo mercenaries of "General" Vang Pao, who fought against the Pathet Lao national liberation fighters in the service of both the French and Americans. Attempts to form a "Lao Rouge" movement inside the country failed dismally, as have efforts to turn any important section of the population against the Vietnamese.

The obvious shortcut to South Vietnam was through Kampuchea. Underpopulated, highly fertile, and fish-rich Kampuchea was a substantial prize in itself. Furthermore, if South Vietnam proved as tough a nut to crack as the North was, Kampuchea could be an alternative gateway to Southeast Asia and the contact point with the twenty million ethnic Chinese who inhabit the region and hold key economic positions there. Peking believed it held ace cards in the 1.2 million ethnic Chinese in the South, more than half of them in Ho Chi Minhville, and in the more than half-a-million ethnic Khmers in the Mekong Delta. With the Khmer Rouge in control in Kampuchea and Chinese military advisers in charge of the Khmer Rouge, it seems to have looked very easy!

Mao Tse-tung has been quoted as stating at a meeting of the Political Bureau of the Chinese Communist Party in August 1965:

> We are bound to recover Southeast Asia which includes South Vietnam, Thailand, Burma, Malaysia and Singapore. Southeast Asia is very rich in minerals and to recover it is worth all the efforts we make. This region will be advantageous to China's future industrial development, and will make up for all the losses. The east wind will prevail over the west wind when we have recovered Southeast Asia.[5]

It is curious that Indonesia was not included in this statement. Less than a month after it was made, China backed a Communist-led coup there. The coup failed and the leadership of the numerically strongest Communist party in Asia — outside China — and the well-structured mass organizations, trade unions, peasants' movement, and others under its influence were totally destroyed.

Vietnam had refused Peking pressures to get involved in the China-backed abortive coup of September 1965.[6] This refusal marked a low point in Chinese-Vietnamese relations at that time. But it also marked a low point in China's attempts to direct the policies and strategies of Asian Communist parties. With its on-again, off-again support for armed struggle, China had not only backed a coup attempt which had led to the virtual destruction of the Indonesian Communist Party but also had misled the Communist parties in Malaya and Burma into the most abysmal defeats. Had not the Vietnamese insisted on keeping decision-making in their own hands and on protecting and giving political and military aid to the fraternal movements in Kampuchea and Laos in a principled and disinterested way, the revolutionary movement in those states would have suffered the same fate as that of Indonesia.

A similar fate is awaiting the revolutionary movement in Thailand. At a press conference in Bangkok on 8 November 1978 Chinese vice-premier Teng Hsiao-ping proclaimed that while China's right hand would seek good state-to-state relations with Thailand, its left hand would help local guerrillas to overthrow the Thai government. This was a demagogic gesture aimed at serving notice that China was the champion of revolutionary armed struggle in Southeast Asia. It was also interpreted in Maoist circles as an ideological rebuff to Vietnam. In a visit to Thailand some months earlier, Vietnam's premier Pham Van Dong had declared that, with the fighting ended in Vietnam, there could be peace and friendship between the two countries.[7]

With the overthrow of the Khmer Rouge regime and the consolidation of the socialist regime in Laos, China has made great efforts to mobilize both the Thai government and the various guerrilla groups for counter-revolutionary activities against the socialist governments in Kampuchea and Laos while carrying out its own direct aggression against Vietnam. The failure of Chinese attempts to attack Vietnam through its proxy, the Khmer Rouge, has exposed Chinese support for the internal aims of the Thai Communist Party for what it really is: support for an instrument of Chinese expansionist aims in the area. As such, it is an instrument which will be discarded when it is no longer useful.

If the United States could consider itself as playing — in a historical context — a short-term role as an international gendarme to "contain communism," China was content to let the United States play that role while it schemed for the larger stakes of long-term, permanent control of the area, the resources of which would then be used against both the United States and Japan. If the United States thinks in terms of years and the duration of a presidency, China thinks in terms of centuries and the duration of a dynasty! The U.S. love match with China will be discarded when it is no longer useful![8]

And if China thinks in terms of centuries and the duration of a dynasty, Vietnam thinks in terms of her more than two thousand years of resistance to Chinese domination and her role as an involuntary barrier to China's southward expansion. Today, however, that role is no longer involuntary. Socialist Vietnam is highly conscious of the fact that there is no contradiction between her national and international responsibilities.

Without having some grasp of the facts summarized in this final chapter — and they are far from complete — it is impossible to understand from afar what has been happening, and why, in the China-Kampuchea-Vietnam geopolitical triangle. It is a sad, sad story not only in terms of the immeasurable human sufferings in the countries involved but also in terms of the blasted hopes of hundreds of millions of people throughout the world who believed in a new order of international, socialist solidarity in which peace would reign supreme.

On the brighter side, the Kampuchean people have given the entire world an extraordinary example of humanity's will and capacity to survive under seemingly hopeless conditions. On 22 March 1981 I was in Phnom Penh to observe the decisive stage of the municipal elections in the Kampuchean capital. These elections were a full-dress rehearsal for the nationwide elections which took place on 1 May 1981. Having witnessed elections in Kampuchea from time to time over the past quarter of a century, I consider those that took place in Phnom Penh to be the first truly democratic elections ever held in Kampuchea.

Obviously there were never any democratic elections while the country was a French colony. In the early days of Sihanouk's rule, opposition candidates were arrested. After he formed his own party, Sangkum, it was Sihanouk who personally selected which of the Sangkum members could stand for office. He chose from the left, center, and right tendencies to establish some sort of "balance."

The system used in the Phnom Penh elections was the same as that later used in the nationwide elections to a Constituent Assembly. Candidates were nominated in each of the city's eighteen electoral districts by the local committees of the United Front for National Salvation. A very high proportion of the city's residents are enrolled in these committees, but the candidates were not necessarily United Front members. Candidates were pre-selected based, according to my investigations, on the contributions they had made to normalizing life and on their service to the community.

Members to be elected for each district ranged from five to seven, according to the population. During pre-selection up to a hundred or more were nominated in some districts. The ten with the highest number of nominations were then endorsed by the electoral commission set up by the Front. Their names, photos, and brief biographies were posted up outside the polling booths, and these were carefully studied by the voters before they went in to cast their ballots. By this process candidates were reduced from several hundred to 148 standing for election to the 117 seats of the Constituent Assembly. These 117 deputies were chosen in the nationwide elections held on May 1. Their tasks are to amend and adopt the present draft constitution and to elect a cabinet and a State Council.

With no experience in democratic electoral procedures, the National Front leadership proceeded with great caution during the municipal elections which took place throughout the country during the month of March. Elections were held in two Phnom Penh districts on March 1. Voter turnout was 83 percent. On March 15 voters were called to the polls in six more districts. Participation was 97 percent, apparently because explanations and propaganda for a maximum turnout had been better organized. On March 22 the balloting in the ten most heavily populated districts was even heavier. In several of the polling stations which I visited, it was 100 percent by mid-day. Among the innovations to ensure maximum participation were mobile teams which took small ballot boxes to the homes of the sick and handicapped and to hospitals and areas remote from polling booths.

The elections took place in a gala atmosphere. The city was decorated with red bunting and the polling stations competed with each other in decorating their premises with palm fronds and flowers. The Kampuchean equivalent of Western pop groups performed outside the polling stations.

Of the city's 350,000 population, 140,000 were registered voters. Among residents and voters were plenty who had supported the Khmer Rouge, including some activists who had beeen infiltrated to cause trouble. That elections could be held in an atmosphere of total security was a reflection of the astonishing degree of normality attained in the spheres of security, production, public health, education, religious affairs, and democratic rights. Although there must have been some special security precautions taken, one was not aware of them. The National Salvation Front's president Heng Samrin, its vice-president Pen Sovan, foreign minister Hun Sen, and other Front leaders mingled freely with the crowds without any apparent armed escorts. There were no Vietnamese troops around. Journalists from France, England, West Germany, Australia, and other countries — including William Shawcross, whose book "Sideshow: Kissinger, Nixon and the Destruction of Cambodia" is a world best-seller — were able to circulate freely and observe all stages of the electoral process.

It was during the municipal elections that a census could be made, with reasonable accuracy, of the population actually living inside the country. The total population was found to be approximately 5,746,000, of whom 3,417,339 voted.

Kampuchea's ASEAN neighbors were quick to denounce the elections as "fraudulent" and designed only to "legitimize the Vietnam-imposed Heng Samrin regime." On the face of it, one can object to the apparent narrowness of the electors' choice at the national level. In actuality, a great deal of choice was exercised at the grass-roots' level during the pre-selection and elimination process. Which of the ASEAN countries can teach a lesson in democratic procedures to Kampuchea? That nationwide elections were held in Kampuchea with over 95 percent voter participation is obviously a defeat for those — including the majority of the UN member states — who continue to recognize the Khmer Rouge remnants as the government of Kampuchea.

If the internal security situation has improved enough to permit nationwide elections without interference, why haven't the Vietnamese started pulling out? This is a legitimate question which worries many political observers of all shades of opinion. The reply is that they have started pulling out. I was told in Hanoi at the end of 1980 that if the security situation continued to improve at the same tempo as it had during the second half of that year, most Vietnamese advisers could soon withdraw. This clearly referred mainly to advisers on military and security affairs in the interior of the country, who could be progressively withdrawn as security and military forces at village, district, and provincial levels were trained and armed by Vietnam. But it was also true of advisers in the various ministries of the new government.

In May 1979 Ngo Dien told me how difficult it was to help the Kampucheans set up a foreign ministry. "We have found a lot of typists," he said, "but the number of higher cadres who have survived could be counted on the fingers of one hand." As a result, almost the entire staff of the Ministry of Foreign Affairs had to be trained for their jobs. In August 1979 there were twelve Vietnamese advisers at the embryo Ministry of Foreign Affairs. By December 1980 there were only two. This is typical of all ministries.

This withdrawal process was confirmed by the Khmer-speaking Australian scholar Ben Kiernan in the June 1981 issue of *World Affairs*, organ of the Queensland Institute of International Affairs. He is the best-informed Western specialist on today's Kampuchea, having spent four months travelling through most of the country's nineteen provinces in the second half of 1980.

> The forty advisers in Takeo province have all left; in Kompong Cham they've been reduced from twenty to eight; Kandal province [in which Phnom Penh is situated–W.B.] had twenty in 1979; there are now twelve and only five are attached to the administration... All Vietnamese have apparently gone from the Ministry of Education....

> Vietnam's ambassador in Phnom Penh, Ngo Dien, told me that the number of Vietnamese advisers in Kampuchea had been reduced by 50 percent, but increased again by 30 percent with the arrival of

technical and "more qualified" personnel....

> An important prerequisite for Kampuchean independence after Pol Pot's destruction is the building up of a state infrastructure—administration, a co-ordinated economy, a currency, communications network, education system, hospitals and a national army. Vietnamese advisers have contributed a lot to the building of the new infrastructure....

Kiernan, a shrewd and experienced observer, remarks that the Vietnamese withdrawal "must continue steadily if the political aspirations of a large number of Kampucheans are ever to be fulfilled." But he also correctly presents the contradiction between the desire for a rapid Vietnamese departure and the fears of a rapid Khmer Rouge return!

> Large numbers of Khmers are now prepared to accept the Salvation Front's close links with Vietnam, while not accepting an obviously subordinate Kampuchean role. The alternatives — a Pol Pot comeback or renewed civil war and destruction — force many to see consolidation of the PRK [People's Republic of Kampuchea–W.B.] as the only hope for a stable, independent state.

> Steady withdrawal of Vietnam's administrative advisers would be a clear signal of Vietnamese intentions. And it is up to the West and its allies to cease support for Democratic [Khmer Rouge–W.B.] Kampuchea. Until that happens, withdrawal of the Vietnamese troops is a gamble on the lives of Kampucheans which, in the light of recent Kampuchean history, few should be prepared to take.

This is a realistic and correct assessment. It bears out everything which I was able to learn during my five visits since the overthrow of the Pol Pot-Ieng Sary regime.

Ben Kiernan's article also contains an interview with Foreign Minister Hun Sen, an essential element of which was the latter's answer to the question of when the Vietnamese troops will leave Kampuchea.

> When the Pol Pot problem and the problem of other groups trying to overthrow our government is solved. That is, when Thailand stops allowing China, and the U.S. and France, to support Pol Pot, Khieu Samphan, and Son Sann, and when we have negotiated with Thailand a proper solution to the border problem and the refugee problem. Then there will be no external threat to Kampuchea and the Vietnamese will leave.

Yet another question has surfaced because of intensive propaganda from Peking and the Khmer Rouge to the effect that Vietnam wants to revive the concept of an "Indochinese Federation." This implies a fusion of quite distinct and different cultures under a single leadership. Because of the differences in population size and the relatively advanced degree of economic and social development in Vietnam, this leadership could come only from Vietnam. But the formation of such a federation under Vietnam's domination was rejected long ago by Ho Chi Minh himself.

Between Vietnam, Kampuchea, and Laos, however, there are bound to be special relationships just as there are between Sweden, Norway, and Denmark and between those Scandinavian countries and Finland. The three former components of Indochina won their independence by fighting shoulder-to-shoulder against French colonialism, Japanese occupation, and American aggression. They have defended that independence by opposing Chinese takeover attempts. They clearly have a common history of cooperation in resisting foreign domination.

They also have complementary economies. Kampuchea and Laos will soon have thriving agricultures sheltered from natural catastrophes such as the typhoons and floods which regularly strike Vietnam's exposed coastal regions, where most of her food crops are grown. Vietnam is developing a modern industry and can already help her two neighbors to develop industry suitable to their modest needs. Within two to three years Vietnam will be self-sufficient in oil production and after that will be in a position to satisfy the needs of Kampuchea and Laos. It is logical that these states will form an economic unit, the partners of which will have at least the same common political interests as those existing between the members of the ASEAN bloc!

China under its present confused leadership can do little to prevent this process but can be counted upon to do its utmost to sabotage it and also to prevent a normalization of relations between the former states of Indochina and those of the ASEAN countries.

In following this course, China knows it can rely upon the unreserved support of the Reagan-Haig administration in the United States. That administration's policy was defined by Secretary of State Alexander M. Haig Jr. during an Asian trip in the second half of June 1981, which included a stop in Peking. By the end of that trip Haig had clearly established that the United States would thwart all Vietnamese moves to improve relations with any country on which Reagan and Haig could exert pressure in the contrary direction. In reporting on New Zealand's reluctance to go along with Haig's "punish Vietnam" policy Bernard Gwertzman of *The New York Times*, who accompanied Haig during his trip, commented:

> Throughout his Asian trip, Mr. Haig has been attacking Vietnam at every opportunity and declared in Manila last Saturday that the United States would never normalize relations with Vietnam so long as its troops remained in Cambodia and it was "a source of trouble to the entire region."[9]

Haig's inflammatory views were applauded in Peking. But they were received coolly by members of the ASEAN bloc, some of whom recognize that the former states of Indochina and the ASEAN countries have more interests in common than they have individually or collectively with a China bent on its historical obsession of expanding into Southeast Asia.

Following Haig's Peking visit, China and the United States did score what appeared to be a victory in their anti-Vietnamese campaign. In early September 1981 they succeeded in sponsoring a "National Front" allying Sihanouk, Son Sann, and Khieu Samphan.[10] But it will prove to be a Pyrrhic victory.

Sihanouk informed me of this scheme in November of 1979. He swore he would never join a "troika" (as he then described it) with two whom he regarded as his inveterate enemies, including one of those responsible for the death of a number of his children and grandchildren. At that time he had just been invited to visit Singapore but had refused to go. "At least for the time being," he had told me. "It is a trap concocted between Peking and Washington to force me into an arranged marriage with Khieu Samphan and Son Sann." He explained that prior to leaving Peking a few weeks before our conversation he had been subjected to a long harangue by U.S. Ambassador Leonard Woodcock on his duty to work with the Khmer Rouge "and drive the Vietnamese out." One of Woodcock's arguments had been that only the Khmer Rouge had the capability of doing this.

As a device to get a few million dollars into the pockets of its leaders, the "National Front" will undoubtedly be a success. And the CIA, with its rich experience in "destabilizing" governments thought to be acting contrary to U.S. interests, will certainly ensure that the "National Front" is endowed with enough arms and funds to have some nuisance value. However, as an instrument to divert the people of Kampuchea from building a new life, under a truly patriotic leadership and under conditions of democracy such as they have never known in their entire history, the "National Front" is doomed at birth to shameful and abysmal failure since none of its component elements has any base or backing among the people.

The people of Kampuchea have taken their destiny firmly in their own hands and they will never willingly relinquish it. In this undertaking, they will have the support of the most progressive forces of our time.

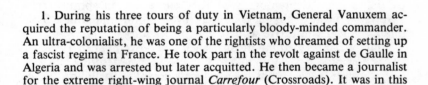

1. During his three tours of duty in Vietnam, General Vanuxem acquired the reputation of being a particularly bloody-minded commander. An ultra-colonialist, he was one of the rightists who dreamed of setting up a fascist regime in France. He took part in the revolt against de Gaulle in Algeria and was arrested but later acquitted. He then became a journalist for the extreme right-wing journal *Carrefour* (Crossroads). It was in this capacity that he demanded the meeting with General Duong Van Minh.

2. Frank Snepp, who has been described as the CIA's "Chief Strategy Analyst in Vietnam," was there until the "bitter end." He refers to Vanuxem's futile mission as follows: "General François Vanuxem, an old French army officer who had known (Nguyen Van) Thieu in the early fifties...had arrived in Saigon to 'advise' him in his final hour. Despite Thieu's resignation, Vanuxem stayed on to urge a strategy of counterattack on the South Vietnamese command...." (Snepp, Frank, *Decent Interval*, p. 401. New York: Random House, 1977) That the Chinese endorsed this and selected a Vanuxem as their policy purveyor is a measure of the depths to which their foreign policy had sunk by that time.

3. Terzani, Tiziano, *Giai Phong: The Fall and Liberation of Saigon,*

p. 86. New York: St. Martin's Press, 1976.

4. Hoang Van Hoan was dropped from the Politburo at the Fourth Congress of the Vietnam Workers Party in December 1976, partly because Politburo decisions were being leaked to Peking. He subsequently fled to China.

5. "Chinese Aggression Against Vietnam." Hanoi: Vietnam Courier, 1979.

6. When China's ambassador to Indonesia returned to Peking, he led a campaign against Premier Chou En-lai and Foreign Minister Chen Yi for having insufficiently supported the coup. Part of the accusation was that they had failed to enlist Vietnam's support. Chou En-lai stoutly supported Chen Yi, and Mao eventually supported Chou En-lai. The ambassador, who temporarily took over from Chou En-lai, had to appear before a public trial in the Peking stadium. He was sentenced to death and executed. In the brief period during which he ran the country's foreign affairs, he caused enormous havoc.

7. As long as Thailand was a base for U.S. air and other hostile activities against Vietnam and Laos, Thai revolutionary forces received support for their armed struggle from those two countries. After the neutralist-minded government of General Kriangsak Chamanan sought friendly relations with both Laos and Vietnam, Pham Van Dong made it clear that the revolutionary forces would have to stand on their own feet and carry on their struggle without Vietnamese aid.

8. In April 1980 I asked General Vo Nguyen Giap what he thought of the love match between Peking and Washington. He gave me one of his gently ironical smiles and said: "We have a saying about arranged marriages. The couple share the same bed but they have different dreams."

9. *International Herald Tribune*, Paris, 23 June 1981.

10. It is not surprising that Singapore hosted this shameful and futile exercise. Singapore has been the foremost champion of the Khmer Rouge murderers and the "hit man" of Washington and Peking at every international conference at which Kampuchea has been discussed.